QUEBEC
ONTARIO

RELATIONS

Membre de L'ASSOCIATION NATIONALE DES ÉDITEURS DE LIVRES

Presses de l'Université du Québec
Le Delta I, 2875, boulevard Laurier, office 450, Québec (Québec) G1V 2M2
Telephone: 418 657-4399   *Fax:* 418 657-2096
Email: puq@puq.ca   *Website:* www.puq.ca

Diffusion / Distribution:

CANADA   Prologue inc., 1650, boulevard Lionel-Bertrand, Boisbriand (Québec) J7H 1N7
         Tel.: 450 434-0306 / 1 800 363-2864

FRANCE   AFPU-D – Association française des Presses d'université
         Sodis, 128, avenue du Maréchal de Lattre de Tassigny, 77 403 Lagny, France – Tel.: 01 60 07 82 99

BELGIQUE Patrimoine SPRL, avenue Milcamps 119, 1030 Bruxelles, Belgique – Tel.: 02 7366847

SUISSE   Servidis SA, Chemin des Chalets 7, 1279 Chavannes-de-Bogis, Suisse – Tel.: 022 960.95.32

QUEBEC ONTARIO

RELATIONS

A Shared Destiny?

Edited by
Jean-François Savard
Alexandre Brassard
Louis Côté

Presses de l'Université du Québec

Bibliothèque et Archives nationales du Québec
and Library and Archives Canada cataloguing in publication

Vedette principale au titre:

Quebec-Ontario relations: a shared destiny?

Translation of: Les relations Québec Ontario.

Includes bibliographical references.

ISBN 978-2-7605-3141-3

1. Québec (Province) – Relations – Ontario. 2. Ontario – Relations – Québec
(Province). 3. Québec (Province) – Politics and government – 2003-   .
4. Ontario – Politics and government – 2003-   . 5. Interprovincial relations
– Canada. I. Savard, Jean-François, 1973-   . II. Brassard, Alexandre, 1972-   .
III. Côté, Louis, 1949-   .

FC2926.9.R43R4413 2013   303.48'27140713   C2013-940619-0

The editors would like to thank the Secrétariat aux affaires intergouvernementales canadiennes (SAIC) of Québec's gouvernment for its financial
support through the "Programme de soutien à la recherche en matière
d'affaires intergouvernementales et d'identité québécoise," which was crucial
for the production of both a French and an English version of this book.
They would also like to thank the Intitute of Public Administration of Canada
(IPAC) for its financial aid in support of the publication of the English version.

Les Presses de l'Université du Québec acknowledges the financial support
of the Government of Canada fot its publishing activities through the Canada
Book Fund and the Council of the Arts.

It also thanks Société de développement des entreprises culturelles (SODEC)
for its financial support.

Cover design
Michèle Blondeau
Page layout
Alphatek

Legal deposit: 2nd quarter 2013
› Bibliothèque et Archives nationales du Québec
› Library and Archives Canada

TABLE OF CONTENTS

INTRODUCTION

JEAN-FRANÇOIS SAVARD, LOUIS CÔTÉ,
and ALEXANDRE BRASSARD

Ontario–Quebec relations have flourished in recent years. Environmental and economic agreements (on infrastructure, trade, investment, labour mobility) have proliferated and joint provincial cabinet meetings were held twice yearly for three years running—2008, 2009, and 2010. Are these closer Ontario–Quebec relations a reaction to the rise of the West, a strategy to work through the economic crisis together, or perhaps an outgrowth of the Charest and McGuinty governments' shared Liberal affinities? Whatever the cause, they are a good opportunity to reflect on the provinces' shared destiny.

This reflection was the genesis of this book. Our exploration of Ontario–Quebec relations led us to review the literature in the field. To our great surprise, we found that very little had been published. While several studies did compare the Canadian provinces in various social, political, and economic spheres, very few focused specifically on Ontario and Quebec or analyzed relations between the two provinces. This paucity of scholarly works led us to seek out specialists in multiple disciplines—history, sociology, politics, economics—to better understand the major issues facing both provinces. The idea for this book was born.

Our objective is twofold. First, we wish to contribute to the body of knowledge on Ontario–Quebec relations; this book can thus serve not only in undergraduate and graduate classrooms, but also as a primer for new hires in intergovernmental bodies. Second, we hope our work may spark renewed interest among researchers, leading to new studies and publications on Ontario–Quebec relations.

Our methodology combines historical and comparative approaches. The first series of chapters focuses specifically on Ontario–Quebec relations from political, economic, social, and public policy perspectives and employs a historical perspective that sheds light on the origins of both past and present relations between the two provinces. The second part compares key public policy issues in the provinces in a wide range of fields. Comparative analyses illustrate the similarities and differences between Ontario and Quebec and provide a better understanding of the issues and policies that drive Ontario–Quebec relations. Despite the historical emphasis in the Part One and the comparative in Part Two, both approaches are intertwined to varying extents throughout the book.

The first part's five chapters look closely at Ontario–Quebec relations, offering a "big picture" view of interprovincial relations from a number of perspectives. The second part's seven chapters focus on public policy and how approaches in Ontario and Quebec are sometimes, but not always, similar and how this impacts Ontario–Quebec relations. The book as a whole offers a broad look at the current state of Ontario–Quebec relations.

In Chapter 1 François Rocher and Marie-Christine Gilbert draw on examples from Germany, Australia, Belgium, the United States, and Canada to identify key concepts for understanding relations between federated entities within a federation and between federated entities and central governments. They also discuss two fundamental points to consider when comparing intergovernmental relations between federal regimes—the institutions of intergovernmental relations and the principles that shape these institutions. The authors make three general observations based on their study. First, distribution of powers between the central government and federated states plays a decisive role in the form intergovernmental relations take. Second, the strength of formal institutional arrangements varies from one federation to the next and influences the role federated entities play in representing regional interests. Third, while all federations have both vertical and horizontal intergovernmental relations mechanisms, the degree of institutionalization of these mechanisms varies from one federation to the next.

In Chapter 2 Jean-François Savard builds on Rocher and Gilbert's analysis by examining intergovernmental relations between civil servants. This shifts the focus from political to administrative intergovernmental relations in Canada. Savard offers two theoretical models to account for administrative intergovernmental relations in Canada: administrative federalism and coherent federalism. After defining these two models, the author reviews the types of institutions and mechanisms present in each one. He finds that in administrative federalism central government institutions predominate to the detriment of federated entities, whereas in coherent federalism institutions and mechanisms make it possible to pursue a balance between federated states and the central power. The author concludes that intergovernmental relations as encountered in Ontario and Quebec are more typical of administrative federalism than coherent federalism. He adds that despite the predominance of the central government in intergovernmental relations in Canada, Ontario–Quebec relations remain dynamic and vital.

In Chapter 3 Alain-G. Gagnon and François Laplante-Lévesque show that such vitality is nothing new: Ontario–Quebec relations "have often been defined by ties of solidarity" (p. 63). Using a historical approach, the authors show how Maurice Duplessis and George Drew established a Quebec–Ontario axis on constitutional matters in the 1940s. This solidarity between the two provinces declined in the 1950s, only to return in the 1960s, with Ontario and Quebec each defending the other's positions against the increasingly centralizing reflexes of the federal government. Using the example of the 1970s and 80s constitutional talks, Gagnon and Laplante-Lévesque point to the ties of solidarity that gradually developed between successive provincial governments—ties that have often gone unrecognized. In the mid-1990s, Ontario–Quebec relations cooled, and although they have since become much friendlier the authors note that the current premiers "have yet to revive the Quebec–Ontario cooperation that characterized the era when Maurice Duplessis and Mitchell Hepburn, and later Daniel Johnson and John Robarts fought as allies to defend provincial rights" (p. 74).

While Ontario–Quebec political relations have fluctuated in intensity over the decades, the same cannot be said of identity. In Chapter 4 Michel Bock examines Canada's francophone communities through the specific lens of identity building. While this process did not necessarily pit Québecois against Franco-Ontarians, it nevertheless slowly drove them apart. Bock reminds us that the 1837–1838 rebellions engendered a French Canadian identity shaped by a socially powerful clergy. The Church's structure carried this enterprise of national identity beyond the borders of Lower Canada through French Canadian migration to Upper Canada and the West. French Canadian identity remained strong enough into the early 20th century for Quebec intellectuals and politicians to join with French Canadian communities in Ontario in the fight against Regulation 17, which forbade the use of French in Ontario schools. But during the second half of the 20th century, the rise of the nationalist movement in Quebec and the decline of the Church chipped away at this shared French Canadian identity, which was replaced by two new identities—Québécois and Franco-Ontarian. This is not to suggest that French-speaking communities in Ontario and Quebec no longer maintain relations, but rather that they no longer share a single identity.

While Ontario and Quebec have always maintained relations—often on cordial or very close terms—it would be wrong to say both provinces always get along. One example is labour mobility, which poisoned Ontario–Quebec relations in the late 1990s and early 2000s. In Chapter 5 Ian Roberge examines the "battle" over the creation of a national securities commission. He finds that in this case relations were far from cooperative and were in fact characterized by strong opposition. The possible creation of the securities commission resulted in two camps, one led by Ontario in favour of the commission, the other led by Quebec opposed to it. What explains this schism between these two federated states? For Roberge there are many reasons for the radically divergent approaches in Ontario and Quebec—political leanings, legislative framework, how different the dominant economic institutions and players in the two provinces are. These differences have created real tension between Ontario and Quebec. The author concludes by noting that while we cannot deny the cooperative nature of Ontario–Quebec relations, neither can we ignore that when it comes to economic matters the two provinces will always be in competition.

Part Two opens with Linda Cardinal and Martin Normand's chapter on Ontario and Quebec's language regimes. In Chapter 6, the authors first define what they mean by a language regime and its constituent parts. Then they describe and analyze the two provinces' respective language regimes and examine each one's specific components. Their study not only allows us to distinguish between the two provinces' approaches to language but also to understand the historical and cultural factors behind these differences. The reader can thus better grasp why, despite their common history, the two provinces gradually adopted highly distinct language regimes. The authors consider the central government's influence on the structure of these language regimes and demonstrate that the differences can be explained by both internal and external factors. Finally, while they stress that there are several symbolic and institutional points of commonality between the two language regimes, they show that, paradoxically, these points of commonality serve mainly to defend opposing viewpoints.

In Chapter 7, Peter Graefe and Angela Orasch ponder whether the two provinces are as different as they first appear on matters of family policy. As Cardinal and Normand do with language policy, they begin by defining both what they mean by family policy and their comparative theoretical framework. They then make a surprising point: Ontario has never had a family policy per se, although the province has often been a leader in the area, including on daycare, for which it has developed a wide range of programs. Quebec, on the other hand, moved swiftly to adopt clear family policies back in the 1960s. Over the following decades, it developed a number of programs in support of families, but not an integrated (and, some would say, imperfect) family policy until 1997. Graefe and Orasch conclude that while the differences between family policy in Ontario and Quebec are clear, the many similarities are undeniable.

In Chapter 8, Louis M. Imbeau turns to Ontario and Quebec budgetary policy, and specifically to deficit-cutting measures, to see whether the two provinces walk their political talk. He also looks at how different the two provinces are, if at all, in their approach to fighting deficits. Imbeau begins with an economic snapshot of the two provinces that reveals a number of similarities and differences. He then analyzes the content of speeches from the throne (called *discours inaugural* in Quebec) to identify the ideological and political components that feed deficit-fighting discourse in the two provinces. With his analysis, Imbeau shows that the political discourse in the provinces is remarkably similar despite the many differences in their economic profiles. He also demonstrates that the two provinces do in fact mostly "walk the talk."

Still in the realm of economic policy, Moktar Lamari and Louis Côté analyze in Chapter 9 the Ontario and Quebec governments' response to the recent economic crisis. The authors first sketch out what led to the crisis, then compare the two provinces' monetary, financial, economic, and social responses. This allows them to isolate seven common characteristics of the various measures employed by the two provinces, both of which seem to have rediscovered the virtues of economic interventionism in the process. Lamari and Côté then examine the challenges faced by the governments as they emerge from the crisis. How can expenditures be cut? How can government revenues be increased? How can economic growth be rekindled? The authors conclude that while measures adopted by the two provinces in response to the crisis are similar, strategies embraced to meet the post-crisis challenge differ substantially. More favourable structural conditions may have allowed Ontario to be in less of a hurry to return to a balanced budget. What is certain is that Ontario's path has been much less controversial than Quebec's.

In Chapter 10, Guy Chiasson, Édith Leclerc, and Catalina Gonzalez Hilarion compare Ontario and Quebec from a policy standpoint on forestry, a key industry in both provinces. The three authors discuss the phenomenon of forestry policy parallelism in the two provinces. Starting with an analysis of the multilateral forestry management mechanisms and the major reforms that have left their mark on Ontario and Quebec's forestry industries in recent years, they find compelling evidence that forestry policy has followed a "shared storyline." But, the authors explain, policy has not "spilled over" from one province to the next, but aligned under the impetus of an international dynamic that has led both governments to adjust their policies. These international developments do not account for everything, however—the authors still observe a number of differences in forestry reforms in Ontario and Quebec.

The greatest difference between the two provinces is unquestionably in international relations. In Chapter 11, Stéphane Paquin finds that the Ontario government practises low-intensity paradiplomacy whereas Quebec puts a great deal of energy into what Paquin calls identity paradiplomacy, whose aim is "to galvanize Quebec's development as a nation and to achieve international recognition as a nation" (p. 230). That being said, while Quebec appears to be more active on the international scene, Ontario also acts internationally. Paquin isolates several variables that explain both provinces' need to pursue international activities and the major structural differences that characterize these actions: internationalization, the type of state (encompassing trade, transborder, environmental, and security interests), the question of identity and minority nationalism, and the personality of decision makers. Paquin examines each of these variables in turn to account for the differences observed in Ontario and Quebec international relations; he concludes that Quebec has developed far more active paradiplomacy thanks to the combined influence of identity claims and the personality of decision makers, who play a significant role as identity builders.

In Chapter 12, Alexandre Brassard brings the work to a close with an analysis on the friendly ties between the Charest and McGuinty governments. Recent interprovincial rapprochement culminated in the first joint provincial cabinet meeting on June 2, 2008. It served to ratify the Ontario–Quebec Trade and Cooperation Agreement as well as a series of sectorial agreements on French-language issues, labour mobility, culture, public security, tourism, transportation, and the environment. What caused this rapprochement between the two provinces of central Canada? The author applies the model of game theory to interprovincial negotiations and describes the major players, their respective positions, their level of support for given issues, and their relative influence. Given the players' positions, were the 2006 agreements predictable? This replay exercise reaffirms the value of formal models to shed light on the dynamic of intergovernmental negotiations in Canada.

PART ONE

QUEBEC–ONTARIO RELATIONS
From Their Origins Up to Today

1. A COMPARATIVE LOOK AT FEDERALISM AND INTERGOVERNMENTAL RELATIONS
Germany, Australia, Belgium, the United States, and Canada

FRANÇOIS ROCHER
and MARIE-CHRISTINE GILBERT

To understand intergovernmental relations, we must first seek to comprehend the mechanisms by which the different levels of government interact within a federation. It is thus the federation's organizational principles that are of interest. Such principles are set against a historical background made up of institutional choices, power relationships, the various actors involved, and, more globally, the different visions of what *objectives* the political system should achieve. In comparing federations from an organizational standpoint, federalism should be seen as a set of normative principles (autonomy, nonsubordination, interdependence, cooperation, and solidarity) based on ideas and values (Vile 1977: 13–14; Rocher 2006). The latter dimension, although important for grasping the nature of federations, will occupy a secondary place in our analysis.

The Latin root of the word federation is *feodus*, which means an alliance or treaty by which two or more political groups form a single political entity (De Witte 2000: 435). By its classical definition, any federal system involves at least two levels of government— a central government and a number of regional governments—each coordinated and independent within its own sphere of jurisdiction (Wheare 1963: 10). Thus, members of a federation possess their own legal system and powers they can exercise without interference from the central government, at least theoretically. That being said, the autonomy and multiplicity of powers of both the federated entities and the central government require them to establish information exchange mechanisms and sometimes joint-action and cooperation mechanisms in order to achieve common objectives, which are defined more or less jointly, depending on the circumstances. What makes a federation distinct as a type of political organization is that it also requires federated entities to interact. Thus autonomy goes hand in hand with interdependence. Since the sharing of powers between the national government and the federated entities is not always explicitly elaborated in the constitution, debates and conflicts regarding the interpretation of these powers are inevitable. The existence of competing powers, the processes of centralization and deconcentration (and more rarely decentralization) of federal powers, and the interpretation of these powers require governments to be in regular contact. "Federal" societies use a myriad of cooperation mechanisms that play a role in how the federation operates.

In this chapter, we will discuss the various cooperation mechanisms that have developed in the German, Australian, Belgian, American, and Canadian federations.[1] By cooperation, we mean relations between the collective entities, i.e., between the federal government and the federated entities and among the various federated entities themselves (Wheare 1963: 112). Rather than discussing how powers are shared (although this aspect is important), we will look at how the various levels of government come into contact and interact with each other. We will first identify the key concepts for understanding intergovernmental relations. We will then look at the type of intergovernmental relations that have developed in the various federations we have selected, highlight the similarities and differences between the various cases, and identify the factors that explain them.

I.   FEDERALISM AND INTERGOVERNMENTALISM: FROM PRINCIPLES TO INSTITUTIONS

To speak of federalism *and* intergovernmentalism in the same breath is redundant, as the first term implies the second. The fact that a federated whole is made up of various levels of government makes intergovernmental relations inevitable. Discussions of this phenomenon

---

1. We chose these five federations because they are quite stable and similar, yet they differ in how the mechanisms governing their intergovernmental relations have developed. See Bolleyer and Bytzek (2009: 375).

in the literature regularly refer to the notion of cooperation, a form of dialogue among federated entities.[2] The expression generally used to refer to cooperation between federated entities is "intergovernmental relations," although "interprovincialism" is widely used in Canada (Leach 1976; Bergeron 1980; Banting 1998; Prince 2001; Pelletier 2008). Intergovernmental relations are most commonly described in light of the mechanisms that link the various governments making up a federation (Opeskin 2001: 137). They are also presented according to the type of interactions that characterize the relationship, whether between the members of a federation and the central government (vertical relations) or among the federation's infranational components (horizontal relations) (Cameron 2001: 131). According to Krane and Wright, intergovernmental relations should be understood as "the patterns of interactions among and between officials representing various jurisdictions and governmental units" (1998: 1169–1170). This interactive dynamic may or may not arise within institutions. For example the political concerns and interests of the federated entities are sometimes incorporated into central government institutions to the extent that "*les fédérations ont prévu des dispositions constitutionnelles qui ont pour effet de 'fédéraliser le centre,' en introduisant les régions dans les institutions du gouvernement central*" (Cameron 2001: 135). The term "intrastate federalism" is used to express this concept. According to Donald Smiley and Ronald Watts, this type of federalism refers to the "arrangements by which the interests of regional units—the interests either of the government or of the residents of these units—are channelled through and protected by the structures and operations of the central government" (1985: 4). It is the role of the upper house to bring together the federal and regional executive governments so that each can participate in decision making within the federation. In Germany for example, "*le* Bundesrat, *composé des délégués des* Länder, *joue un rôle intergouvernemental explicite en encourageant la collaboration entre le gouvernement national et les exécutifs régionaux*" (Cameron 2001: 135). The Canadian Senate, which historically was intended as a Chamber of the Regions, has never really fulfilled that role (Pelletier 2002: 4–6).

---

2. This term is not simply descriptive; it also carries a significant normative burden as it implies a certain form of participation in the development of common objectives. Obviously this refers explicitly to the principle of solidarity that should normally be at the heart of a federal system. However, political reality, the interests at stake, and the nature of power relationships mean that relations between governments are not always based on solidarity, and that political actors may have legitimate reasons for wanting to achieve different goals, to enter into conflict, or to oppose a direction taken by the most powerful protagonists. In other words there may be situations where an absence of cooperation is justified in a particular political situation.

On another hand, the term "interstate federalism" usually refers to the many forms of consultations, cooperation, and coordination that have developed over time but were not explicitly provided for in the Constitution. This type of federalism is a result of administrative or institutional practices that become established procedure over time. They include meetings between government leaders, between ministers responsible for particular sectors, or between civil servants who discuss policy at their respective levels (Cameron 2001: 136). In British—or Westminsterian—parliamentary systems, these relations are often described as "executive federalism" (Smiley 1976, 1987), notably because they involve members of the executive governments, and decisions in federal–provincial conferences are made without the members of the lower house. On rare occasions, decisions are debated in the House, but just for the sake of form (Pelletier and Tremblay 2000: 447).

In interstate federalism another distinction can be made based on the players involved: there are intergovernmental relations that involve all or some of the regional actors and the central government and those that occur between all or some of the regional actors without the central government (Cameron 2001: 135). In both cases the meetings can be formal or informal, depending on their degree of institutionalization. Some intergovernmental relations are informal in that discussions take place "*en dehors de tout cadre officiel, par téléphone, télécopieur et messagerie électronique, ainsi qu'à l'occasion de rencontres informelles entre hommes politiques et représentants des exécutifs*" (ibid.: 134). There is also an informal aspect to intergovernmental relations that was not provided for in the Constitution, but has become standard practice over time. As David Cameron points out, "[p]*arfois des réunions informelles convoquées en raison des circonstances, se transforment en institutions bien établies et commencent à être dotées de ressources en personnel, à arrêter des normes ayant valeur de décisions*" (ibid.).

We will analyze each of the five countries we selected using the above characteristics. We will first discuss the constitutional division of powers and resulting negotiations, because the distribution and separation of powers, the scope of each level of government's prerogative powers, and the extent to which they are questioned by social and political actors all have a significant impact in each case that we would be remiss not to examine. We will then briefly discuss the vertical and horizontal aspects of intergovernmental relations in order to determine the type of federalism (intrastate or interstate) and its specific characteristics for each country. Beyond their purely institutional attributes, intergovernmental relations take place in political arenas steeped in history and have evolved according to their own particular circumstances.

In other words, the constitutional system in which they operate and the government institutions that they partially reflect play a defining role in each case (*ibid.*: 131). We will also take them into consideration.

2. GERMANY

The current German federation resulted from the transition from the German Confederation (1815–1866)—with its federated, monarchical type of government—to the *Reich*, another form of federal system (1871–1918).[3] From an institutional standpoint, the difference between the two involves the elimination of the federal Diet that once concentrated power in a single body (Beaud 2007: 354). The Reich "*réunit trois autorités politiques fédérales: l'empereur, auquel on pourrait adjoindre l'institution particulière du chancelier et deux chambres: la chambre populaire (le Reichstag) et la chambre des États (le Bundesrat)*" (Beaud 2007: 402). In this second type of federation, introduced by Otto von Bismarck in 1871, the *Bundesrat* was the dominant component of the federal system, as it held substantial powers and represented the federation's member states at the national level.[4] The basic law for the Federal Republic of Germany (*Grundgesetz für die Bundesrepublik Deutschland*), enacted in 1949, maintained the *Bundesrat* in this role. It continued to represent the member states—the 16 *Länder* (*Bundesländer*)—in line with the tradition introduced by Bismarck of a second house designed mainly as a council rather than a parliamentary assembly (Beaud 2007: 419). The constitution of 1949 gave rise to a federal system based on the principle of "strict separation" of powers between the federation (the *Bund*) and its members (the *Länder*). H.-P. Schneider specifies that

---

3. R. L. Watts explains that "[t]he German federation owes a great deal to the earlier experience of the German Empire (1871-1918), the Weimar Republic (1913-34) and the failure of the totalitarian centralization of the Third Reich (1934-45)" (2002: 28).

4. O. Beaud mentions that "*l'examen des compétences du* Bundesrat *révèle une impressionnante variété de compétences dans le domaine législatif et administratif, ce qui contraste avec la Diète de Francfort. En ce qui concerne l'activité législative, son consentement est nécessaire à l'édiction des lois de l'Empire (art. 7 RV), ce qui indique que la chambre populaire (Reichstag) n'a pas le pouvoir du dernier mot et peut toujours se voir opposer un veto de la chambre des États. Plus important encore, il détient un droit d'initiative législative, dont la particularité est d'être confié aux États membres en tant que tels (art. 7, al. 2 RV); les motions de ceux-ci doivent être obligatoirement présentées à l'organe collégial pour délibération. Au surplus, le rôle du* Bundesrat *s'étend aux fonctions exécutives. Il est associé étroitement à la conduite des affaires étrangères et de la guerre, les deux domaines de prédilection des fédérations. Il détient en outre d'importants pouvoirs de nature politique puisqu'il décide conjointement, avec le chancelier fédéral, de la dissolution de la chambre populaire [...] il est doté, comme la Diète de Francfort, d'une certaine compétence juridictionnelle puisqu'il est l'instance chargée de vider les litiges constitutionnels entre les États membres de la Fédération allemande (art. 76 RV)*" (2007: 405).

[e]ach order is accountable for its own decisions, even when a federal law delegates power to *Land* parliaments. To enforce this principle, the Federal Constitutional Court (FCC) has prohibited mixed administration and mixed financing. However, the German federation is not based on two completely distinct and separate columns of federal and *Land* powers with no connections. Instead there is a concentration of legislative functions in the federal government and of administrative powers in the *Lander*. The *Lander* actually implement a large part of federal legislation, as well as their own laws (2005: 15).

The constitution nevertheless forced the development of close ties between the central government and the federated entities because the central legislative authorities possess a wide range of powers and many federal laws are implemented by the *Länder* (framework laws) (Watts 2008: 35).[5] It is in this sense that the German federation is interesting for comparative studies, "because of the manner in which the relationships between the federal and state governments interlock and because of the way in which the unique *Bundesrat* serves as key institution in these interdependent processes" (*ibid.*: 36). As Arthur Benz underlines, the structure of intergovernmental relations, or *Politikverflechtung*:

> emerged in a constitutional framework, where the division of competence does not relate to distinguishable policies, but interdependent state functions. Most legislative powers are centralized, whereas powers to implement federal law are mostly allocated to the *Land* government. Consequently, federal government requires expertise from the *Land* administration when designing a law, and *Land* governments affected in their administrative competences by federal legislation have a stake in this process. In this federal system, vertical intergovernmental relations predominate, and horizontal relations between the *Länder* are embedded in them (n.d., 1).[6]

Vertical intergovernmental relations in Germany include horizontal intergovernmental relations to a certain extent due to the necessary cooperation between the *Länder* regarding the adoption of federal laws in the Bundesrat:[7] "[l]and governments have a say in all matters

---

5. A. Benz says that after 1949, "[t]*he* Bundesrat *turned into an arena in which the influential* Land *premiers could encroach upon the politics of the federal government, and which facilitated the emergence of intergovernmental networks of bureaucracies involved in drafting of bills*" (n.d.: 3).

6. The author defines *Politikverflechtung* as a form of joint decision making between the federal government and the *Länder*.

7. As Schneider mentions, "[o]ne of the most surprising aspects of the German administrative system is that most federal laws are carried out by the *Länder*. The basic principle is that the *Länder* shall implement federal legislation as matters of their own concern, as long as the Basic Law does not provide otherwise. The opposite is strictly forbidden; the federation is not allowed to carry out any state law" (2005: 4).

of federal legislation, but with the absolute majority of their votes they can veto those laws which affect competences of the *Länder* and therefore require explicit assent" (Benz n.d.: 5). It is thus essential that the *Länder* first negotiate among themselves to avoid surprises during the vote in the house. These negotiations are initially conducted at the executive level by ministerial officials. The decisions are made "both in the ministries and cabinets of the *Länder* and in the committees of the *Bundesrat*" (*ibid.*: 6). If governments of the *Länder* disagree, the premiers can meet or communicate informally (fireside chats; *ibid.*). The constitution provides for a special mechanism for settling disputes concerning constitutional amendments, namely the Mediation Committee (*Vermittlungsausschuß*), made up of an equal number of members of the *Bundesrat* and the *Bundestag* (Hrbek 2002: 152). R. Hrbek specifies, however, that "[c]onstitutional disputes, amongst them those related to the federal system, are resolved by the Federal Constitutional Court (*Bundesverfassungsgericht*) upon appeal by one of the disputing parties" (*ibid.*: 153). Apart from the *Länder's* participation in legislative decision making, which is the main characteristic of German intergovernmental relations (*ibid.*: 154), there are other horizontal cooperation mechanisms that involve the *Länder's* executive powers. A. Benz stresses that

> [a]lthough the constitution does not contain anything about horizontal cooperation in the federal system, *Land* premiers and ministers convene in conferences. Most of these conferences now work according to formal rules, formulated in standing orders or resolutions. Nearly all of them meet on a regular basis, many, in particular the conference of the prime ministers and ministers of finance, additionally convene in extraordinary meetings if necessary (n.d., 8).

The increase in federal transfer payments and the devolution of powers in the fields of agriculture, education, and fisheries have led to a redistribution of economic resources between the *Länder* and have thus helped heighten conflicts between representatives of the *Länder* about how federal funding should be shared (*ibid.*: 6). Regional economic issues and budget policies are discussed within a "joint task force" and at the meetings of the Council for Fiscal Planning (*Finanzplanungsrat*) and the Council for Economic Development (*Konjunkturrat*). As cooperative structures, the "joint task forces" only generate guidelines, which are nonbinding. As A. Benz stresses, "[s]o far, coordination has proved as not very effective, although it has been mentioned that a considerable share of tax revenues in Germany is determined by joint decision-making" (*ibid.*: 7). Apart from these joint meetings, the representatives of the German *Länder* discuss together at the first ministers' conference, the *Ministerpräsidentenkonferenz*, or, in a more targeted manner, at sectoral such as that of the *Länder*'s education ministers (KMK), which assembles the *Länder* ministers and senators responsible for education.[8] The first ministers' conference involves the federal chancellor and the premiers of the various states and is generally held about twice a year.[9] As is the case with the Council of the Federation in Canada, a different *Land* hosts the conference each year. Intergovernmental departments are responsible for the discussions and for coordinating the meetings. There is also "a broad variety of extra-constitutional bodies and procedures for intergovernmental consultation and co-ordination at the bureaucratic level" (Bolleyer and Bytzek 2009: 386). Again, discussions take place between specialists and technocrats in the various departments concerned, which causes some to consider that the process lacks legitimacy (Benz n.d.: 8). Furthermore, "[a]s in other federal systems, the executive predominates in intergovernmental relations" (*ibid.*: 10). Finally, another "regional" level of cooperation exists, where meetings are held between representatives of various regions such as Baden-Württemberg and Bavaria, for example. Municipal questions related to environmental and urban issues are discussed at these meetings (*ibid.*).

To summarize, when properly implemented, intrastate cooperation (within the *Bundesrat*) leads to the adoption of framework laws that give the *Länder* sufficient freedom of action in implementing their provisions (Schneider 2005: 16). Although interstate cooperation (through ministers' conferences and so forth) is less significant, it nevertheless enables the *Länder* to establish common public policy directions. However, in Germany like in other federations, competition among the *Länder* does not always make cooperation easy (*ibid.*: 14). In the case of regional cooperation, meeting outcomes are ambiguous. On the one hand they facilitate sharing of information and help guide public policy; on the other, "inter-regional networks can work as coalitions against the central government and as a cartel in competition" (Benz 2007: 433). In other words, this regional cooperative dynamic leads to competition between the federal (central) government and the governments of the federated entities (*Länder*) but also among the *Länder* themselves. Because of the sometimes substantial economic

---

8. According to A. Benz: "Only the Conference of the Ministers for Cultural and Educational Affairs has its own bureaucracy, established on the basis of an administrative agreement in 1959. In 2004, the staff of this secretariat amounted to 216 civil servants. Moreover, the conference set up no less than 36 commissions, sub-commissions and working groups" (n.d.: 8). For an example of the type of meetings held by European ministers see: <http://media.education.gouv.fr/file/11_ novembre/76/7/Dossier_participants_4e_reunion_franco_allemande_124767.pdf> (retrieved on June 16, 2010).

9. See the *Bundesrat* website: <http://www.bundesrat.de/nn_6904/DE/gremien-konf/ fachministerkonf/mpk/mpk-node.html?__nnn=true> (retrieved on June 16, 2010).

disparities among the *Länder*—due to their particular social, economic, and political contexts—not all the *Länder* have the same negotiating power (Benz n.d.: 2, 15). In this sense, a collaborative network can lead to a competitive type of federalism (*Wettbewerbsföderalismus*) rather than participative federalism (*Beteiligungsföderalismus*) (Hrbek 2002: 155).

3.   AUSTRALIA

In 1900 the British parliament enacted the *Commonwealth of Australia Act*.[10] However, Australia did not officially become an independent federal state until 1901. C. Macintyre and J. Williams pointed out that

> Australia is simultaneously one of the youngest democracies and one of the oldest federations. In 1901, the six Australian colonies united in "one indissoluble Federal Commonwealth under the Crown of the United Kingdom." That decision was the result of deliberation, compromise, and debate over the needs and aspirations of the community although notably it excluded any consultation with the indigenous people (2005: 3–4).

Not surprisingly, Australia's federal model is based on Great Britain's bicameral parliamentary system, where legislative power is divided between a lower house—representing the population—and an upper house (the Senate), which equally represent the states and whose members are elected by universal suffrage (Vergniolle de Chantal 2008: 52). Initially the two houses had an equivalent status, but the Senate took on a different role due to the powers it was granted. The Senate can *"rejeter n'importe quel projet de loi—y compris le budget—et sa position est définitive: en cas de blocage, la seule option qui demeure est la dissolution"* (Vergniolle de Chantal 2008). Like in Canada, however, the Senate, which was originally designed as a chamber of states, never fulfilled that role due to the partisan divisions that reflect those of the lower house (Watts 2008: 34). As a parliamentary federation, Australia developed institutions and processes typical of "executive federalism" rather than a more formal structure integrating intergovernmental relations at the federal level (Watts 2008). Intergovernmental meetings take place vertically between the Commonwealth, the states, and the territories via the Council of Australian Governments (COAG). This body was set up to replace the annual Special Premiers Conferences, which it is said "had no formal

---

10.   R. L. Watts specifies that the modern Australian federation "consists of six states (of wich the two most populous, New South Wales and Victoria, comprise 59 percent of the federal population) plus one capital territory, the Northern Territory, and seven administered territories" (2002: 27). The text of the constitution is available online at <http://www.aph.gov.au/senate/general/Constitution/index.htm> (retrieved June 17, 2010).

bureaucratic support, and eventually became restricted to relatively brief tactical meetings between leaders prior to COAG meetings" (Wanna *et al.* 2009: 13; concerning COAG, see Warhurst 1983, 2008; Tiernan 2008). According to J. Wanna *et al.*:

> The Australian federation was designed on the assumption that the levels of government would operate with a high degree of independence (called "coordinate federalism") and thus made little provision for integration of policy making and implementation between the Commonwealth and the States. Adaptations have been made over time, with the emergence of COAG being the most salient example; however, further improvements could be pursed to enhance and ensure enduring engagement and cooperation (2009: 11).

As an institution that promotes cooperation between the central government and the states, COAG carries out the following functions: "initiating, developing, endorsing and monitoring the implementation of policy reforms of national significance which require cooperative action by Australian governments."[11] However, it is criticized for being an instrument under the control of the Commonwealth (the central government), as the latter has the power to convene, change, or cancel COAG meetings as well as define the agenda and determine the priorities to be discussed (Wanna *et al.* 2009: 15). Some say that in order for COAG to more closely reflect multilateral cooperation among the Commonwealth, states, and territories, mechanisms would have to be developed to allow the states and territories to put topics that concern them on the agenda (Wanna *et al.* 2009). Similarly, COAG's secretariat would have to become independent, because it is now part of the Department of the Prime Minister and Cabinet, which itself is attached to the institutions of the Commonwealth.

Discussions between regional governments (states or territories) take place mainly within the Council for the Australian Federation (CAF). CAF incorporates the concept of the Leaders' Forum, a government meeting of leaders created in 1995 at the same time as COAG. CAF, established in 2006, generates horizontal intergovernmental relations in that it assembles the state and territorial premiers and chief ministers. It is comparable to Canada's Council of the Federation and the National Governors Association in the United States (Bannon 1992). CAF is the forum where intergovernmental agreements and public policy are discussed. Apart from developing common positions and a few recommendations on environmental, educational, and tax issues, no reform

---

11. See the following document: <http://www.coag.gov.au/intergov_agreements/ federal_financial_relations/docs/IGA_FFR_ScheduleA_Institutional_Arrangements. pdf> (retrieved on June 24, 2010).

has ever been adopted.[12] Some of the criticisms levelled at CAF stress that "[t]he Council for the Australian Federation should develop a strategic forward agenda to facilitate horizontal cooperation" (Wanna *et al.* 2009: 15). There are other mechanisms for cooperation among federal bodies in the form of specialized councils made up of ministers from various jurisdictions responsible for a common sphere of activity (Saunders and Leroy 2006: 59).[13] There are also joint regional government administrators' meetings specially designed "for the purposes of an intergovernmental scheme for which uniform administration is also deemed necessary" (*ibid.*: 60).

Finally, as the Australian constitution grants certain powers to the Commonwealth, most of which are competing, the administration of the Australian federation depends to a large extent on a vast interstate network of ministerial councils and informal cooperative meetings to ensure the uniformity and coordination of laws and policies (Saunders 2002: 35–36). Globalization and internationalization have greatly affected vertical intergovernmental relations in Australia because the Commonwealth, due to its responsibility for external affairs, intervenes in spheres under state jurisdiction (the environment and human rights) (*ibid.*: 38). The Commonwealth has also succeeded in dominating the Australian federation through interpretation of the constitution and skillful political manoeuvering (Macintyre and Williams 2005: 6). It is partly through its grip on direct and indirect taxation that it has been able to leverage its financial strength to force the states to adopt certain policies (Macintyre and Williams 2005).

---

12. The Council for the Australian Federation posts the results of its intergovernmental meetings online. In its 2009 report it mentions that CAF succeeded in imposing several amendments to the Independent Review of the *Environment Protection and Biodiversity Conservation Act 1999* and that it has set itself the task of promoting cooperative federalism. The document is available online at <http://www.caf. gov.au/Documents/CAF Report Card Oct 2009.pdf> (retrieved on June 17, 2010). It also says that "CAF's policy recommendations detailed in its paper *The Future of Australian Schooling* (2007) helped to shape the Melbourne Declaration on Educational Goals for Young Australians. Made by all Australian education Ministers, the Declaration sets the direction for Australian schooling for the next ten years ... The outcomes framework articulated by the report is also reflected in the new National Education Agreement agreed by the COAG in 2008" (Wanna *et al.* 2009: 14).

13. More specifically, "each ministerial council is supported by a standing committee of officers, usually comprising heads of the relevant departments; other working groups may be associated with particular council as well. Each council has a secretariat, usually but not always based in a Commonwealth department and rarely dedicated to the work of the ministerial council alone. Ministerial council carry out a range of functions pursuant to formal intergovernmental agreement as well as in accordance with their own, often self-crafted, terms of reference" (Saunders and Leroy 2006: 59).

4. BELGIUM

The Kingdom of Belgium (*Koninkrijk België*), created in 1830, was converted to a federal state in a 1993 after a long process of federalization that started in the 1960s (Watts 2008: 43–44; Reuchamps and Onclin 2009: 21). Belgium is a parliamentary constitutional monarchy like Canada—though a different type—with six federated entities. The federation is composed of three regions—Flemish, Walloon, and Brussels-Capital—which reflect the country's territorial federalism and three cultural and linguistic communities (Dutch-, French-, and German-speaking). The communities and regions have parliaments (councils) that exercise legislative power and governments, which are the executive bodies (Polet 1995: 8). As entities in their own right, the communities and regions stand on an equal footing and relations between them are not hierarchical (Massart-Piérard 2005: 192). Belgium's federal institutions include the king and a bicameral parliament comprising a Chamber of Representatives and the Senate, considered as a "chamber of reflection," that guarantees "*de la qualité de la législation et lieu de rencontre entre l'autorité fédérale et les entités fédérées que sont Communautés et Régions*" (Polet 1995: 6; see also Reuchamps and Onclin 2009). The Senate is composed of senators elected by direct universal suffrage, others elected by Dutch-speaking and French-speaking electoral colleges, and yet others appointed by the community parliaments (Reuchamps and Onclin 2009: 35). Substantial changes have been made to the Belgian Senate since 1993. The Senate can now examine bills and propose amendments, which the Chamber of Representatives can accept or reject (Lecours 2002: 63). Similarly, the Senate has the power to initiate legislation, but as A. Lecours (2002) stresses, the Chamber of Representatives has the last word. Furthermore, only a few areas—international relations and anything concerning the structure of government (bicameral laws)—require the approval of both houses. In these cases, the Senate and the Chamber of Representatives have equal weight (Lecours 2002). We could see this as a form of intrastate federalism, because the communities are represented and cooperate via the country's central institutions.

Unlike most federations, the Belgian federation did not arise from an association of sovereign political entities, but from the decentralization of a unitary state (Dumont *et al.* 2005: 10). Belgian federalism is distinctive in that it is built on the concept of the *equipollence* of norms, an organizational principle by which each federated entity is sovereign within the scope of its exclusive jurisdiction, so that the federal government takes no precedence over the federated entities, nor are they subordinate (Lagasse 2003: 119; Massart-Piérard 2005: 199). Powers are distributed based on the principle of exclusivity, both at the federal and regional/community levels. As Swenden and Jans explain,

> Federal and regional laws stand on equal footing and are subject to the constitution (or Special Majority Laws) only. Competencies attributed to either level of government are in general rule of an exclusive nature, in which one level of government is solely responsible for legislation and administrating policy. Belgian federalism was construed to require as little intergovernmental cooperation as possible (2006: 886).

We must qualify this last statement, however, as "*malgré une répartition exclusive des compétences, il s'avère que les chevauchements de compétences entre les différentes entités sont inéluctables*" (Reuchamps and Onclin 2009: 32). Since the distribution of powers among the communities, regions, and the federal government is called on to change, and since Belgium is a particularly complex state where relationships among the various levels of government and among the federated entities themselves are constantly multiplying (Massart-Piérard 2005: 191–192), the federation has had to develop consultative mechanisms for resolving conflicts between federation members and the federal government. According to Min Reuchamps and François Onclin, "*la coopération au sein de la fédération belge est principalement institutionnalisée; et pour cause, dans un fédéralisme de dissociation, on peut craindre que la coopération ne soit pas spontanée*" (2009: 32). To settle disputes among the various levels of government, the federation set up the Court of Arbitration (*Arbitragehof*) in which the federated entities and the federal government could draft cooperation agreements (Dumont *et al.* 2005: 10). The Court of Arbitration, renamed the Constitutional Court in 2007, is mainly responsible for resolving disputes between the federal government, the communities, and the regions with regard to legislative norms affecting certain constitutional provisions (Reuchamps and Onclin 2009: 33). Thus intergovernmental relations in Belgium are characterized by various political entities that try to collectively resolve disputes that territorial, jurisdictional, or economic divisions prevent them from settling (Massart-Piérard 2005: 194). Each new situation or transfer of powers generates new intergovernmental relations between the federal government and the federated entities and among the federated entities themselves (*ibid.*: 205). For example, the central government and the federated entities must cooperate on social issues, which come under both federal jurisdiction (medical and unemployment insurance) and community jurisdiction (preventive health care). Similarly, the federated entities have to cooperate among themselves, especially with regard to competencies related to the labour market, since the communities are responsible for coordinating vocational training and the regions for handling job placement for unemployed workers (Swenden and Jans 2006: 886; Polet 1995: 3).

The mechanisms by which the governments of the Belgian federation interact with one another take various forms. Horizontal relations involve cooperation between two or more regions (or two or more communities). Given the equipollence of federal and regional/community norms, federal–regional (or federal–community) cooperation in certain areas could be considered as a form of horizontal cooperation (Swenden and Jans 2006: 887). Vertical intergovernmental relations in general, like in other federations, reflect the cooperation between the federal government and the federated entities. The most important and most formal mechanism for vertical intergovernmental cooperation is the Deliberation Committee, which is similar to first ministers' meetings in Canada except that its composition and operation are defined by legislation (Poirier 2005: 465). The committee is composed of the federal prime minister, six federal ministers, and six ministers representing the regions and communities. Since 1995 however, only a third of the disputes it was supposed to handle have been resolved (Swenden and Jans 2006: 29). In the event of an impasse, the Council of State, which has jurisdictional and consultative powers, can be called on to intervene (Reuchamps and Onclin 2009: 33).

Collaborative federalism in Belgium takes the form of bilateral (community/region) meetings that sometimes result in institutionalized cooperation. For example, the French Community (Brussels-Wallonia), the German Community, the College of the French Community Commission (COCOF) of the Brussels-Capital Region, and the Walloon Region created the Wallonia-Brussels Council of International Cooperation (CWBCI) in 2002 (Massart-Piérard 2005: 200).[14] Other horizontal cooperative mechanisms were developed at the same time as the Deliberation Committee, such as interministerial meetings where common issues are discussed. For example, there is an interministerial meeting on external affairs because in Belgium, foreign policy is developed by the federal government together with the federated enti-

14. As its Web portal indicates, "[l]e CWBCI fut officiellement installé le 15 mars 2004, par le Ministre-Président de la Communauté française de Belgique, le Ministre-Président du Gouvernement de la Communauté germanophone, le Ministre-Président de la Région wallonne et le Ministre-Président du Collège de la Commission communautaire française de la Région de Bruxelles-Capitale. La création du Conseil Wallonie-Bruxelles de la Coopération Internationale (CWBCI) est une réponse originale et jusque-là inédite en Belgique, des pouvoirs publics à une revendication des acteurs de la coopération bilatérale indirecte née dès le début des années 1990" <http://www.wbi.be/cgi/bin3/render.cgi?id=0023115_article&ln=ln1&userid=&rubr=gen> (retrieved on July 6, 2010).

ties (Massart-Piérard 2005: 193). Issues concerning international treaties are also discussed since preliminary cooperation agreements are required for treaties on issues that are not under the exclusive jurisdiction of the federated entities (*ibid.*). The various federal and regional/community parliaments must share information and present their respective points of view before decisions are made. If not, the decisions could be declared illegal (Swenden and Jans 2006: 887).

In short, although Belgian federalism is made up of exclusive jurisdictions (Massart-Piérard 2005: 192), intergovernmental cooperation does still exist. The structure of internal jurisdictions and the necessary cooperation between political entities and the federal government give rise to a wide range of interactions among the various levels of government (*ibid.*: 204). Similarly, "community conflicts" between Flemish and French-speaking political forces require federated entities to negotiate. (Leton 2009: 101). In conclusion, although the expression "intergovernmental relations" is not often used—the word "cooperation" being the preferred term (Poirier 2002: 24)—such relations may be the reason why the Belgian federation has been able to weather such a high level of disagreement and ambivalence (Deschouwer 2005: 22).

5. UNITED STATES

At the Constitutional Convention held in Philadelphia in 1787, the main federalist—and to some extent, antifederalist—concepts were set out in the Constitution, thus creating what was to become a federal state.[15] Under the Constitution of 1787, "each state was represented equally in a unicameral legislature, and retained its sovereignty and every power that was not expressly delegated to the Congress" (Allen and Lloyd 2002: 75). The U.S. federal system established under the Constitution of 1787, which was subsequently ratified, features a limited delegation of powers and responsibilities (Watts 2008: 29). The Constitution grants certain exclusive jurisdictions to the central government, defines a number of shared jurisdictions, and attributes all other powers—including residual powers—to the states. Consequently the strict separation of powers prevents the subordination of one body

---

15. Guillaume Massin explains that the government represents what is now called the federal state. At the time of the Articles of Confederation, "*federal government*" was synonymous with "confederation." The term "confederation," defended by antifederalists, was often contrasted with the expression "national government," preferred by the federalists. The term "federal state" was used as of the War of Secession, when the government started to concentrate power to combat the rebellion (Massin 2002: 8).

by another. However, despite the separation of powers, "[o]ne effect of the expansion of federal activity in domestic policy has been the creation of a complex web of intergovernmental relationships in which local, state, and federal authorities bargain with each other in both the making and implementation of public policy" (Katz 2005: 34). In contrast to the Australian and Canadian federal systems, where horizontal intergovernmental relations are characterized by meetings between executive governments, in the United States they occur between the executive branches via the National Governors Association (NGA) and between the legislatures through the National Conference of State Legislatures (NCSL). Both are overseen by the Council of State Governments (CSG) which protects states' prerogatives when new policies are put on the table.[16]

The National Governors Association (NGA) was founded in 1908 and brings together the fifty state governors to discuss public policy.[17] It is a national, bipartisan organization that "promotes visionary state leadership, shares best practices, and speaks with a unified voice on national policy."[18] The organization has four standing committees (Economic Development and Commerce; Education, Early Childhood and Workforce; Health and Human Services; and Natural Resources), which are chaired by a different governor each year. NGA is composed of the Office of Federal Relations, largely responsible for representing regional interests at the federal level; the Center for Best Practices (or NGA Center), which serves as a training and information-sharing body

---

16. This is one of the missions of the Intergovernemetal Affairs Committee. One of the committee's mandates is to "interpret changing national conditions and to prepare states for the future, and to promote the sovereignty of the states and their role in the American federal system." See the CSG website at <http://www.csg.org/about/ committeesandtaskforces/intergovermentalaffairscommittee.aspx> (retrieved on June 28, 2010).

17. "Founded in 1908, the National Governors Association is the collective voice of the nation's governors and one of Washington, D.C.'s most respected public policy organizations. Its members are the governors of the 50 states, three territories, and two commonwealths. NGA provides governors and their senior staff members with services that range from representing states on Capitol Hill and before the Administration on key federal issues to developing and implementing innovative solutions to public policy challenges through the NGA Center for Best Practices. NGA also provides management and technical assistance to both new and incumbent governors." The document is available on the National Governors Association website: <http://www.nga.org/portal/site/nga/menuitem.cdd492ad-d7dd9cf9e8ebb856a11010a0/> (retrieved on June 27, 2010).

18. Concerning its organizational mode, "[b]ipartisanship is ensured by NGA's Articles of Organization. The party affiliation of each committee chair rotates annually, the chair and vice chair represent different parties and the vice chair succeeds the chair. The Executive Committee is composed of four members of the chair's party and five members of the other party" <http://www.nga.org/portal/site/nga/ menuitem.cdd492add7dd9cf9e8ebb856a11010a0/> (retrieved on June 27, 2010).

for the state governors; the Office of Communications, which coordinates information; and the Office of Management Consulting & Training (OMCT), which provides management services and training to governors and their staff. As expressed in the NGA preamble, NGA's role is to ensure "that the duality of our federal system remain intact and that elected officials strive to preserve and promote a balanced relationship between the state and the federal government."[19]

The National Conference of State Legislatures (NCSL) is also a bipartisan body, but in contrast to NGA, it offers services only to the legislative assemblies of its members. It was created in 1975 to provide research, technical assistance, and opportunities for policy makers of the fifty states to exchange ideas with a view to defending the interests of regional governments before Congress and federal agencies.[20] The executive branch sets the terms and conditions of laws, but they can also be elaborated by this type of independent body composed of representatives from each region (Opeskin 2001: 144). NCSL also has internal committees, including the NCSL Executive Committee, which coordinates meetings, and the Legislative Staff Coordinating Committee (LSCC), which acts as a permanent secretariat.[21] There are twelve standing committees that meet four times a year to determine common positions on federal/state policy and support lobbying activities in Washington.

Thus one of the key roles of NCSL and NGA is to lobby members of Congress, the White House, and federal agencies. In this sense, the two organizations act as interest groups because of the pressure they apply. This dynamic is in line with a vertical power relationship since the states must negotiate with the federal government. According to N. Bolleyer (2006: 487), the interests defended by the two groups (NGA

---

19. <http://www.nga.org/portal/site/nga/menuitem.cdd492add7dd9cf9e8ebb856a11010a0/> (retrieved on June 27, 2010).

20. See NCSL at <http://www.ncsl.org/> (retrieved on June 28, 2010).

21. According to the NCSL website, "The National Conference of State Legislatures' Executive Committee is the governing body of the Conference. The executive committee and Conference officers have supervision, control and direction of the affairs of the Conference, its committees, and publications. It also implements the policies and supervises the disbursement of its funds. The executive committee, an elected body, is composed of 60 members: seven officers; 27 at-large legislator members; three annual meeting representatives; four regional legislators from the Council of State Government; three *ex officio* members; and 16 legislative staff members. Officers include a president, president elect, vice president, immediate past president, staff chair, staff vice chair, and immediate past staff chair. Each member is entitled to vote on any matter coming before the committee. Legislative staff are entitled to vote only on organizational matters—not on matters of public policy. The Executive Committee meets three to four times a year at such time and place as the committee decides. The president may call special meetings as necessary" <http://www.ncsl.org/> (retrieved on June 28, 2010).

and NCSL) do not always coincide with those of all the member states. Legislators in NCSL try to prevent encroachments on their legislative powers, while the executive branches in NGA "are interested in gaining as much leeway as possible in the implementation phase—meaning large amounts of federal money without any strings attached" (*ibid.*). Bolleyer also points out that "the fact that in the United States the legislatures participate directly in the intergovernmental game indicates the weakness of legislative autonomy protection" (*ibid.*). The meetings held by these two organizations and the resulting lobbying are described as "collaborative federalism," although, as E. Katz remarks (2005: 34), the fact that collaborative federalism is transformed into a type of coercive federalism enables the federal government to gradually encroach on state legislation.

The last consultative mechanism that generates horizontal and, to some extent, vertical intergovernmental relations is the Council of State Governments (CSG). It is the only one to serve all three branches— executive, legislative, and judicial—of state government.[22] Under the authority of the Governing Board and the Executive Committee, some fifteen subcommittees and affiliated groups meet to develop common positions with regard to federal policies.[23] A distinguishing feature of CSG is its Intergovernmental Affairs Committee, which is responsible for issues related to federalism and safeguarding states' interests. As its website indicates, "[t]he committee strives to interpret changing national conditions and to prepare states for the future, and to promote the sovereignty of the states and their role in the American federal system."[24] Another of CSG's distinctive features is the National

---

22. "The Council of State Governments is our nation's only organization serving all three branches of state government. CSG is a region-based forum that fosters the exchange of insights and ideas to help state officials shape public policy. This offers unparalleled regional, national, and international opportunities to network, develop leaders, collaborate, and create problem-solving partnerships" <http://www.csg.org/about/default.aspx> (retrieved on June 28, 2010).

23. "The Governing Board and Executive Committee oversee the business affairs, policy, and program development of CSG. Together, the Governing Board and Executive Committee are the main decision-making body to which all other CSG committees, task forces, regions, affiliates, and staff report, and also give final authority to CSG's policy positions and resolutions. The Governing Board includes 55 governors and two legislators, one from each chamber, from each of the 50 states and five territories."

24. <http://www.csg.org/about/committeesandtaskforces/intergovermentalaffairscommittee.aspx> (retrieved on June 28, 2010). Among other duties, it "monitors and acts on critical intergovernmental matters pertaining to all three federal branches of government; seeks intergovernmental partnerships, particularly with former CSG members now serving in the federal government or Congress; coordinates with other state and local government associations on intergovernmental issues where states have a vested interest. The committee also oversees the filing of amicus briefs on behalf of state and local governments in the U.S."

Center for Interstate Compacts, through which two or more states can sign formal agreements, called interstate compacts, without necessarily requesting the consent of Congress. In principle, this is contrary to Article 1 of the Constitution,[25] which specifies that "no state shall, without the consent of the Congress, enter into any agreement or compact with another state." Only agreements concerning powers delegated to the federal government or modifying the balance of power with the latter require the consent of Congress. In this case, horizontal relations between CSG's member states give rise to another type of vertical relation between the CSG executive and the Congress. Again, according to N. Bolleyer, "for the states to act as one order of government against the central government and to successfully defend their own authorities, successful interstate coordination is a precondition. If it is not feasible, state resistance is of limited use" (2006: 488).

In short, intergovernmental relations in the United States are characterized by two phenomena, the institutionalization of cooperative mechanisms according to the division of legislative and executive powers in the states (through NGA and NCSL) and the fact that this cooperation is not always in the interests of the state, but rather in those of the various political actors. In addition, "the internal constitutional power-sharing structures have been impressively projected outside state boundaries and have strengthened the pressure on state local actors to compete for national funding" (*ibid.*). This competition has affected the balance of power between the states and the central government in that "disunity among the states serves Congress to legitimize its own action as it can point to the failure of the states to do the job on their own" (*ibid.*). With regard to the results of intergovernmental relations,

---

25. These compacts are defined as follows: "Compacts are agreements between two or more states that bind them to the compacts' provisions, just as a contract binds two or more parties in a business deal. As such, compacts are subject to the substantive principles of contract law and are protected by the constitutional prohibition against laws that impair the obligations of contracts (U.S. Constitution, Article I, Section 10). That means that compacting states are bound to observe the terms of their agreements, even if those terms are inconsistent with other state laws. In short, compacts between states are somewhat like treaties between nations. Compacts have the force and effect of statutory law (whether enacted by statute or not) and they take precedence over conflicting state laws, regardless of when those laws are enacted. However, unlike treaties, compacts are not dependent solely upon the good will of the parties. Once enacted, compacts may not be unilaterally renounced by a member state, except as provided by the compacts themselves. Moreover, Congress and the courts can compel compliance with the terms of interstate compacts. That's why compacts are considered the most effective means of ensuring interstate cooperation" <http://ssl.csg.org/compactlaws/Introoverview.doc>.

Despite their strong organizational makeup, with the exception of the CSG supporting interstate compacts, the IGAs [*Intergovernmental Affairs*] do not provide a basis for codecision process and cross-jurisdictional policy harmonization. State IGAs do not represent the state interest but only their particular members, simply because "the state is not a homogenous entity" and this has repercussions for intergovernmental process and structures, most strikingly by fostering centralizing tendencies (*ibid.*: 488–489).

6. CANADA

In 1867 the *British North America Act* created a federal union made up of four provinces: Ontario, Quebec, New Brunswick, and Nova Scotia. Other provinces and territories were gradually added, and Canada now has ten provinces and three territories. Like Australia, Canada is a constitutional monarchy with a British-type parliamentary system. The original 1867 constitution, which resulted from negotiations between members of the political and economic elite, granted substantial powers to the central government. Some of these powers enabled the central government to override provincial decisions under certain circumstances (Watts 2008: 32). Affairs of national importance or public interest, such as military and economic issues (regulation of trade and commerce, transportation, and communications) were attributed to the central government, whereas issues of purely local interest, such as municipal affairs and culture, social programs, and linguistic issues, as well as civil law were relegated to the provinces. These principles were endorsed by sections 91 to 95 of the *Constitution Act, 1867* (Pelletier 2002).

In the Canadian federation, the form and distribution of powers are similar to those in the United States and Australia in the sense that administrative duties are conferred on the level of government granted legislative responsibility (except for criminal law). However, Watts (2008: 194–198) points out that Canada is different from the United States, Germany, and Australia in that the range of shared powers is much narrower. Most powers are attributed explicitly to a specific level of government. In this regard, Canada is closer to the Belgian model (Watts 2008).

Intergovernmental discussions take place mainly when these powers are not specified or their boundaries are contested (Cameron 2001: 131). We should mention that in the Canadian federation, the permeability of powers means that the various levels of government must act jointly in almost all areas of public policy (except foreign policy or defense issues). This phenomenon is reinforced by the fact that the Supreme Court of Canada now tends to interpret the division of powers more broadly, in the name of efficiency and effectiveness, and simply looks at which level of government has the greatest capacity to act in the sector under dispute. The principle of effectiveness justifies the federal government's active involvement in fields traditionally considered to be under exclusive provincial jurisdiction (Brouillet 2005: 320; Leclair 2005: 385).

In Canada, as in the other federations we have presented, the principle of interdependence refers to the means by which the provincial or territorial governments cooperate with each other or with the central government. In contrast to Germany, intergovernmental forums do not allow federated entities to take part in decision making at the federal level. D. Cameron highlights that the way in which regional interests are expressed at the national level (intrastate federalism) depends on the way their representatives are chosen, i.e., by direct suffrage like in Australia and the United States, direct election of delegates by regional governments as in Germany, or through a combination of these methods as in Belgium. The Canadian system of appointing senators has meant that the Senate's original mission of representing regional interests has not been fulfilled because its members are appointed by the executive branch of the federal government (Cameron 2001: 135). Since the Senate only partially fulfills its role as a second chamber and the constitution does not recognize a specific framework or process for ensuring cooperation between the two levels of government, "more than any other federation, Canada relies on intergovernmental negotiation to help resolve political differences" (Jenkin 1983: 101). The Canadian federal system has thus had to develop parallel mechanisms governing intergovernmental relations on an *ad hoc* basis (Knopff and Sayers 2005: 123). As H. Bakvis and G. Skogstad remind us,

> With limited opportunity for formal representation of provincial interests in federal policy-making institutions, provincial governments acquire greater authority to speak on behalf of the people within their borders. One consequence is that in Canada the task of securing the federal balance falls mainly to interstate federalism, since most governmental activity takes place between governments rather than within an intrastate body such as a senate (2008: 5).

The weaknesses of interstate federalism have gradually reduced it to relations between the executive branches of the two levels of government, particularly since the Second World War (McRoberts 1985; Smiley 1987; Watts 2008; Pelletier 2005).

According to the Privy Council Office, in Canada "[t]he instruments/ mechanisms of intergovernmental relations are informal. They are not part of the Constitution and thus have no constitutional status. Nor do they have any basis in law or statute. They have developed on an ad hoc basis, in response to the requirements of the time" (Canada 2010). Intergovernmental relations mainly allow for "the exchange of information, for bargaining, negotiation, and consensus-building" (*ibid.*). Governments have access to various forums for developing common strategies, coordinating activities between ministries, conveying ideas for the purposes of negotiation and persuasion, and even establishing bilateral and multilateral agreements (*ibid.*). Forums for vertical intergovernmental relations include (federal, provincial, and territorial) first ministers' meetings, ministerial meetings (by portfolio, such as health, the environment, agriculture, education, and so forth), and meetings attended by senior civil servants. Horizontal relations include interprovincial meetings that do not involve the federal government (such as the Council of the Federation, discussed below) (Bakvis and Skogstad 2008: 9).

However, the management of intergovernmental relations (whether vertical or horizontal) is not a new phenomenon. It dates back to the early days of the federation and the first interprovincial meeting convened by Honoré Mercier in 1887 (Pelletier 2005: 4). A series of federal/provincial/territorial meetings (FPTM) was held immediately after the war, but it was up to Jean Lesage to convene the first "annual" provincial premiers meeting in 1960. In its modern version, this meeting remains a mechanism for cooperation between the provincial and territorial executive branches (*ibid.*: 4). Like Australia's COAG, the annual premiers' meetings are criticized for being too informal and for the fact that their decisions are not enforceable (*ibid.*: 5). In addition, the meetings are not convened on a regular schedule, and their frequency varies over time and according to the political agendas of the moment (Canada 2010). Apart from these meetings, much of the intergovernmental work is done in the federal/provincial/territorial cabinets. According to the Privy Council, "[s]ome have become institutionalized, with regular meetings, often co-chaired by federal and provincial ministers, and with strong bureaucratic support " (*ibid.*).

Although numerous FPTMs are held every year (Quebec's Secrétariat aux affaires intergouvernementales canadiennes [SAIC] website reported about a hundred meetings in 2009), bilateral and multilateral relations between the provinces and territories (i.e., horizontal relations) have grown significantly over the last decade. In 2001 the Quebec Liberal Party advocated the creation of the Council of the Federation (CF), one of whose main roles would be to permit greater cooperation between governments with regard to economic union and the strengthening of the Agreement on Internal Trade signed in 1994. As originally proposed, the CF was also supposed to examine standards and objectives with respect to Canada's social union, interpret the principles of the *Canada Health Act*, develop pan-Canadian objectives within provincial jurisdictions, limit federal spending powers, and prepare international agreements affecting provincial and federal jurisdictions (Parti libéral du Québec 2001: 16). The CF was officially created in December 2003 with a view to restoring to the provinces and territories *"l'influence ainsi que la force nécessaires pour qu'ils deviennent de véritables partenaires dans le Canada de demain"* (Quebec 2004: 14). For its founders it represented a forum for dialogue and idea sharing, which could eventually lead to formal cooperation agreements. The CF is seen as an instrument for facilitating intergovernmental cooperation and developing a common vision on major issues faced by the provinces and territories, particularly in health, education, fiscal imbalance, the environment, energy, transportation, internal trade, and international representation. Made up of the provincial and territorial premiers, the CF must hold at least two meetings a year. Apart from a permanent secretariat, the December 5, 2003 agreement also set up two bodies: the Premiers' Council on Canadian Health Awareness and the Secretariat for Information and Cooperation on Fiscal Imbalance.[26] The CF's record in first few years was mixed. On the one hand, it is recognized for its commitment to transparency in that its follow-up and progress reports on various issues (internal trade and health, for example) are made public, which demonstrates a concern for premier accountability. On the other hand, the CF forms part of executive federalism, with very little—or no—involvement on the part of the legislative branch, thus contributing to the democratic deficit that characterizes intergovernmental relations in Canada (Pelletier 2008: 219–221).

Horizontal bilateral interprovincial relations have grown in recent years. Numerous agreements have been signed between two or more provinces. For example, Ontario and Quebec signed a general protocol in 2006 aimed at

> improving the quality of health services; improving the movement of people and goods between the two provinces; addressing environmental issues facing both provinces; working to promote the sustainable development of crown land and natural resources; developing cooperative

---

26. See the Council of the Fedeation website at <http://www.conseildelafederation.ca/index.html> (retrieved on June 30, 2010).

tourism activities; promoting understanding and mutual appreciation of both provinces' culture, including heritage; and exploring opportunities to improve public security (Ontario 2006: 2).

This initiative gave rise to specific agreements on labour mobility, procurement, interprovincial trade, and Francophone affairs (Quebec 2008: 9). British Columbia and Alberta also signed the Trade, Investment and Labour Mobility Agreement (TILMA) in 2006. Other provinces strengthened their bilateral or multilateral relations in their respective economic zones: the Atlantic Procurement Agreement, a temporary agreement on agriculture between the four western provinces, Prince Edward Island, and the Yukon, and cooperation agreements between Quebec and New Brunswick. And the list goes on.

In short, since the division of powers dating back 150 years has never been revised, and the various levels of government encroach on each other, the opportunities for conflict have multiplied, leading to the need for forums where governments can negotiate. These forums are concentrated within the executive branch. The expansion of intergovernmental relations has diminished parliamentary and judicial control and undermines the transparency of the executive powers (Cameron and Simeon 2002: 66; Poirier 2009: 120).

CONCLUSION

Intergovernmental relations vary among the federations according to the nature and evolution of the division of powers, the federated entities' ability to assert their interests within central government institutions, and the importance of the issues facing states. Three general observations emerge from our comparison of the five federations (see Table 1).

Not surprisingly the division of powers specific to each federation plays a defining role in how intergovernmental relations play out. Germany's system, for example, features a form of deconcentration of powers under which the *Länder* are responsible for implementing decisions made by the central government. In the United States, with its separation of executive and legislative powers at each level of government, intergovernmental relations are more diffuse and have given rise to numerous organizations made up of senior civil servants and legislators in the various states. The nature of political power in the United States has resulted in federal legislators being the target of lobbying efforts (Watts 2008). In Australia and Canada, powers overlap more (even though this is not always specifically set out in the constitution), which has led the various levels of government to develop consultation/

coordination/cooperation mechanisms that reflect this reality. Belgium, on the other hand, is characterized by a twofold system consisting of a rather strict separation of powers and the nonsubordination of the federated entities vis-à-vis the central government. Nevertheless, as in other federations, a certain amount of overlap exists, which makes it necessary to develop mechanisms for cooperating or managing the inevitable disputes. In all federations the varying permeability of powers (whether *de jure* or *de facto*) is a compelling force driving the establishment of mechanisms for overseeing relations between the member entities.

As for formal institutional arrangements, some federations are distinctive for the ability of their federated entities to exercise their influence within central government institutions (intrafederalism). This is specially the case in Germany and Belgium. In Germany, the *Bundesrat* has a veto over federal laws that affect the federated entities. In Belgium, 21 of the 71 senators are chosen by the community parliaments, which tends to bring the central government and the federated entities closer together. Although the United States, Australia, and Canada also have senates, they have never truly represented the interests of infrastate entities. This has helped bolster the status of subnational governments as representatives of regional interests and has spurred competition between different levels of government as to who can speak on behalf of the entire "nation." Can the central government alone speak on behalf of everyone or must it do so in association with the political actors of each state? The true federal nature of the last court of appeal is clearer in some federations than others. In Germany, half of the sixteen judges that sit on the *Bundesverfassungsgericht* (federal constitutional court) are elected by the *Bundestag* and the other half by the *Bundesrat*. In Belgium, half of the twelve judges that make up the Constitutional Court represent the French and Dutch linguistic groups. This court must include six judges with at least five years of parliamentary experience (three judges per linguistic group). In the United States and Canada, judges are appointed by the central government without the consent of the states or provinces.

Finally, all the federations feature vertical and horizontal intergovernmental relations. Consultation, participation, information-sharing, and cooperation mechanisms with no constitutional basis are found in all the federations. The degree of institutionalization varies from one country to another. It is generally quite high in the United States and moderate in Australia, Belgium, and Canada. These relations are relatively flexible, more or less permanent mechanisms. For example, in the United States, Australia, and Canada, the Council of State Governments, the Council for the Australian Federation, and the Council of the Federation enable the federated entities to discuss common problems and jointly establish their priorities vis-à-vis the central government. Leaders of the various orders of government also meet, at annual first ministers' meetings for example, where meeting agendas reflect the political situation at the time. These meetings make it possible (sometimes) to set governmental priorities. In addition to these institutions, ministers and civil servants also meet more or less informally to discuss common issues. Clearly, managing interdependence is a key concern for all the federations.

All in all, necessity is the mother of invention. Discussions between different levels of government are profoundly affected by the nature of power relationships within each federation. Whether the federation is multinational and multilinguistic like Belgium or Canada, or characterized by the presence of powerful regional economic interests as in Germany, Australia, and the United States, intergovernmental relations are inevitably determined by how the interests of the various actors, social groups, and communities are defined and expressed in the political arena through partisan life, the ideologies involved, and the objectives of the federal association. The institutions of intergovernmentalism merely embody political relationships, which are by nature changeable, contradictory, antagonistic, and competitive.

Table I

Characteristics of Intergovernmental Relations

Country	Distinctive Constitutional Feature	Cooperation Mechanism	Type of Intergovernmental Relations	Type of Arrangement
Germany	Broad powers exclusive to the central government—shared powers/administrative deconcentration (framework laws)	Bundesrat	Vertical/horizontal	
		Constitutional Court	Vertical	Intrastate
		First Ministers' Meetings	Horizontal/vertical	Interstate
	Residual powers granted to states	Joint Task Force	Horizontal	
Australia	Limited number of exclusive federal powers/large number of shared powers	Council of Australian Government (COAG)	Vertical	Interstate
		Council for the Australian Federation (CAF)	Horizontal	
	Residual powers granted to states	Leaders' Forum	Horizontal	
		Specialized councils	Horizontal	
Belgium	Principle of equipollence—principle of exclusvity (nonsubordination) devolution	Senate	Vertical	
		Constitutional Court	Horizontal/vertical	Intrastate
		Deliberation Committee	Vertical	Interstate
	Residual powers granted to the central government (de facto)/to federated entities (de jure)	Interministerial meetings	Horizontal/vertical	
		Community or regional councils	Horizontal	

Table I
Characteristics of Intergovernmental Relations (cont'd)

Country	Distinctive Constitutional Feature	Cooperation Mechanism	Type of Intergovernmental Relations	Type of Arrangement
United States	Limited delegation of federal powers	National Governors Association (NGA)	Horizontal (executive)	Interstate
	Residual powers granted to the states	National Council of State Legislature (NCSL)	Horizontal (legislative)	
		Council of State Governments (CSG)	Horizontal/vertical (executive, legislative, judicial)	
Canada	Exclusive and shared powers (de jure)/overlapping of most powers (de facto)	First Ministers' Meeting	Vertical	Interstate
	Residual powers granted to central government	Council of the Federation	Horizontal	

BIBLIOGRAPHY

Allen, W. B. and G. Lloyd (2002). *The Essential Antifederalist*. Lanham: Rowman and Littlefield.

Bakvis, H. and G. Skogstad (2008). "Canadian Federalism: Performance, Effectiveness, and Legitimacy." In H. Bakvis and G. Skogstad (eds.), *Canadian Federalism: Performance, Effectiveness, and Legitimacy*. Don Mills: Oxford University Press: 3–22.

Bannon, J. (1992). *Cooperative Federalism: Good Policy and Good Government*. Canberra: Federalism Research Center.

Banting, K. (1998). "Social Citizenship and the Social Union in Canada." *Policy Options*, November: 33–36.

Beaud, O. (2007). *Théorie de la fédération*. Paris: Presses universitaires de France.

Benz, A. (2007). "Inter-regional Competition in Co-operative Federalism." *Regional and Federal Studies*, vol. 17, no. 4, December: 421–436.

Benz, A. (n.d.). "Intergovernmental Relations in German Federalism – Joint Decision-Making and the Dynamics of Horizontal Cooperation." Online at <http://www.forumfed.org/libdocs/2009/2009-03-27-Zaragoza-Benz.pdf>, retrieved on June 17, 2010.

Bergeron, G. (1980). "L'État du Québec sous le fédéralisme canadien." In G. Bergeron and V. Lemieux (eds.), *L'État du Québec en devenir*. Montreal: Boréal Express: 331–350.

Bolleyer, N. (2006). "Federal dynamics in Canada, the United States, and Switzerland: How Substates' Internal Organization Affects Intergovernmental Relations." *Publius*, vol. 36, no. 4: 471–501.

Bolleyer, N. and E. Bytzek (2009). "Government Congruence and Intergovernmental Relations in Federal Systems." *Regional and Federal Studies*, vol. 19, no. 3, July: 371–397.

Brouillet, E. (2005). *La négation de la nation. L'identité culturelle québécoise et le fédéralisme canadien*. Quebec City: Septentrion.

Cameron, D. (2001). "Les structures des relations intergouvernementales dans les systèmes fédéraux." *Revue internationale des sciences sociales*, no. 167, March: 131–138.

Cameron, D. and R. Simeon (2002). "Intergovernmental Relations in Canada: The Emergence of Collaborative Federalism." *Publius*, vol. 32, no. 2, Spring: 49–71.

Canada (2010). *Intergovernmental Relations in the Canadian Context*. Privy Council Office. Online at <http://www.pco-bcp.gc.ca/aia/index.asp?lang=eng&page=relations&doc=context/context-eng.htm>.

De Witte, B. (2000). "Fédération." In O. Duhamel and Y. Meny (eds.), *Dictionnaire constitutionnel*. Paris: Presses universitaires de France.

Delpérée, F. (2000). *Le fédéralisme en Europe*. Paris: Presses universitaires de France.

Deschouwer, K. (2005). "Belgium: Ambiguity and Disagreement." In R. Blindenbacher and A. Ostien (eds.), *A Global Dialogue on Federalism Booklet Series: Dialogues on Constitutional Origins, Structure, and Change in Federal Countries*, vol. I. Montreal and Kingston: McGill-Queen's University Press: 10–13.

Dumont, H., S. Van Drooghenbroeck, N. Lagassé, and M. Van Der Hulst (2005). "Belgium: Continuing Changes in a New Federal Structure." In R. Blindanbacher and A. Ostien (eds.), *Dialogues on Distribution of Powers and Responsibilities in Federal Countries*, vol. II. Montreal and Kingston: McGill-Queen's University Press: 6–9.

Hrbek, R. (2002). "Germany (Federal Republic of Germany)." In A. Griffith and K. Nernberg (eds.), *Handbook of Federal Countries, 2002*. Montreal and Kingston: McGill-Queen's University Press: 148–161.

Jenkin, M. (1983). *The Challenge of Diversity: Industrial Policy in the Canadian Federation*. Ottawa: Science Council of Canada, Minister of Supply and Services Canada.

Johns, C. M., L. O'Reilley, and G. J. Inwood (2007). "Formal and Informal Dimensions of Intergovernmental Administrative Relations in Canada." *Canadian Public Administration*, vol. 50, no. 1, Spring: 21–41.

Katz, E. (2005). "The United States of America: A Federal Government of Limited Power." In R. Blindenbacher and A. Ostien (eds.), *Dialogues on Distribution of Powers and Responsibilities in Federal Countries*, vol. II. Montreal and Kingston: McGill-Queen's University Press: 33–36.

Knopff, R. and A. Sayers (2005). "Canada." In J. Kincaid and A. Tarr (eds.), *A Global Dialogue on Federalism*, vol. 1: *Constitutional Origins, Structure, and Change in Federal Countries*. Montreal and Kingston: McGill-Queen's University Press: 103–143.

Krane, D. and D. S. Wright (1998). "Intergovernmental Relations." In J. M. Shafritz (ed.), *International Encyclopedia of Public Policy and Administration*. Boulder: Westview: 1168–1176.

Lagasse, C.-E. (2003). *Les nouvelles institutions politiques de la Belgique et de l'Europe*. Namur: Érasme.

Leach, R. (1976). "Interprovincial Co-ordination." In D. J. Bellamy, J. H. Pammett, and D. C. Rowat (eds.), *The Provincial Political System. Comparative Essays*. Agincourt: Methuen: 381–397.

Leclair, J. (2005). "The Supreme Court of Canada's Understanding of Federalism: Efficiency at the Expense of Diversity." In J.-F. Gaudreault-Desbiens and F. Gélinas (eds.), *Le fédéralisme dans tous ses États. Gouvernance, identité et méthodologie – The States and Moods of Federalism. Governance, Identity, and Methodology*. Cowansville: Yvon Blais: 383–415.

Lecours, A. (2002). "Belgium (Kingdom of Belgium)." In A. L. Griffiths and K. Nerenberg (eds.), *Handbook of Federal Countries, 2002*. Montreal and Kingston: McGill-Queen's University Press: 59–73.

Leton, A. (2009). "Le partage des compétences et les relations intergouvernementales: la situation en Belgique." In B. Fournier and M. Reuchamps (eds.), *Le fédéralisme en Belgique et au Canada. Comparaison sociopolitique*. Brussels: De Boeck: 97–105.

Macintyre, C. and J. Williams (2005). "Australia: A Quiet Revolution in the Balance of Power." In R. Blindenbacher and A. Ostien (eds.), *Dialogues on Distribution of Powers and Responsibilities in Federal Countries*, vol. II. Montreal and Kingston: McGill-Queen's University Press: 3–6.

Massart-Piérard, F. (2005). "Une étude comparée des relations entre entités fédérées au sein du système de politique extérieure en Belgique francophone." *Revue internationale de politique comparée*, vol. 12, no. 2: 191–205.

Massin, G. (2002). *La contribution des antifédéralistes des origines à la théorie constitutionnelle américaine.* Research thesis submitted to Faculté des sciences juridiques, politiques et sociales of Université du Droit et de la Santé de Lille II.

McRoberts, K. (1985). "Unilateralism, Bilateralism, and Multilateralism: Approaches to Canadian Federalism." In R. Simeon (ed.), *Intergovernmental Relations.* Toronto: University of Toronto Press: 86–87.

Ontario (2006). *The Protocol.* Ministry of Intergovernmental Affairs. Online at <http://www.ontla.on.ca/library/repository/mon/14000/263297.pdf>, retrieved on June 30, 2010.

Opeskin, B. R. (2001). "Mécanismes régissant les relations intergouvernementales dans les fédérations." *Revue internationale de sciences sociales,* no. 167, March: 139–148.

Parti libéral du Québec (2001). *Un plan d'action. Affirmation, autonomie et leadership.* Comité du Parti libéral du Québec sur l'avenir politique et constitutionnel de la société québécoise.

Pelletier, R. (2002). *Intergovernmental Mechanisms: Factors for Changes?* Discussion Paper no. 29, Commission on the Future of Health Care in Canada.

Pelletier, R. (2005). *Le Conseil de la fédération, un premier bilan.* Presentation prepared for the symposium "Bilan des réalisations du gouvernement Charest," Quebec City, December 9–10.

Pelletier, R. (2008). *Le Québec et le fédéralisme canadien. Un regard critique.* Quebec City: Les Presses de l'Université Laval.

Pelletier, R. and M. Tremblay (2000). *Le parlementarisme canadien.* Quebec City: Les Presses de l'Université Laval.

Poirier, J. (2002). "Formal Mechanisms of Intergovernmental Relations in Belgium." *Regional and Federal Studies*, vol. 49, no. 3: 24–54.

Poirier, J. (2005). "Les ententes intergouvernementales et la gouvernance fédérale: aux confins du droit et du non-droit." In J.-F. Gaudreault-Desbiens and F. Gélinas (eds.), *Le fédéralisme dans tous ses États. Gouvernance, identité et méthodologie – The States and Moods of Federalism. Governance, Identity, and Methodology.* Cowansville: Yvon Blais: 441–472.

Poirier, J. (2009). "Le partage des compétences et les relations intergouvernementales: la situation au Canada." In B. Fournier and M. Reuchamps (eds.), *Le fédéralisme en Belgique et au Canada. Comparaison sociopolitique.* Brussels: De Boeck: 107–122.

Polet, R. (1995). "La Belgique fédérale: une construction complexe, mais équilibrée." *Eipascope,* no. 1.

Prince, M. J. (2001). "Canadian Federalism and Disability Policy Making." *Canadian Journal of Political Science*, vol. 34, no. 4: 791–817.

Quebec (2004). *Le Conseil de la fédération. Un premier pas vers une nouvelle ère de relations intergouvernementales au Canada.* Quebec City: Secrétariat aux affaires intergouvernementales canadiennes.

Quebec (2008). *Le nouvel espace économique du Québec.* Quebec City: Gouvernement du Québec.

Reuchamps, M. and F. Onclin (2009). "La fédération belge." In B. Fournier and M. Reuchamps (eds.), *Le fédéralisme en Belgique et au Canada. Comparaison sociopolitique.* Brussels: De Boeck: 21–40.

Rocher, F. (2006). "La dynamique Québec-Canada ou le refus de l'idéal fédéral." In A.-G. Gagnon (ed.), *Le fédéralisme canadien contemporain.* Montreal: Les Presses de l'Université de Montréal: 93–146.

Saunders, C. (2002). "Australia (The Commonwealth of Australia)." In L. Griffiths and K. Nerenberg (eds.), *Handbook of Federal Countries, 2002.* Montreal and Kingston: McGill-Queen's University Press: 32–46.

Saunders, C. and K. Leroy (2006). "Commonwealth of Australia." In C. Saunders and K. Leroy (eds.), *Legislative, Executive, and Judicial Governance in Federal Countries.* Montreal and Kingston: McGill-Queen's University Press: 37–71.

Schneider, H.-P. (2005). "Germany: Länder Implementing Federal Legislation." In R. Blindenbacher and A. Ostien (eds.), *Dialogues on Distribution of Powers and Responsibilities in Federal Countries,* vol. II. Montreal and Kingston: McGill-Queen's University Press: 15–18.

Simeon, R. (2006). *Federal-Provincial Diplomacy. The Making of Recent Policy in Canada – with a new preface and postscript.* Toronto: University of Toronto Press.

Smiley, D. V. (1976). *Canada in Question: Federalism in the Seventies,* 2nd ed. Toronto: McGraw-Hill Ryerson.

Smiley, D. V. (1987). *The Federal Condition in Canada.* Toronto: McGraw-Hill.

Smiley, D. V. and R. L. Watts (1985). *Intrastate Federalism in Canada.* Ottawa: Supply and Services Canada.

Swenden, W. and M. T. Jans (2006). "Will It Stay or Will It Go? Federalism and Sustainability of Belgium." *West European Politics,* vol. 29, no. 5, November: 877–894.

Tiernan, A. (2008). "The Council for the Australian Federation: A New Structure of Australian Federalism." *Australian Journal of Public Administration,* vol. 67, no. 2: 122–134.

Vergniolle de Chantal, F. (2008). *Fédéralisme et antifédéralisme.* Paris: Presses universitaires de France.

Vile, J. (1977). "Federal Theory and the 'New Federalism'." *Australian Journal of Political Science,* vol. 12, no. 2: 1–14.

Warhurst, J. (1983). *Central Agencies, Intergovernmental Managers, and Australian Federal-State Relations.* Canberra: Centre for Research on Federal Financial Relations, Australian National University.

Warhurst, J. (2008). "Patterns and Directions in Australian Politics over the Past Fifty Years." *Australian Journal of Politics and History,* vol. 50, no. 2: 163–177.

Wanna, J. *et al.* (2009). *Common Cause: Strengthening Australia's Cooperative Federalism. Final Report to the Council for the Australian Federation.* Council for the Australian Federation, May.

Watts, R. L. (2008). *Comparing Federal Systems,* 3rd ed. Montreal and Kingston: McGill-Queen's University Press.

Wheare, K. C. (1963). *Federal Government,* 4th ed. London: Oxford University Press.

2. INTERGOVERNMENTAL RELATIONS BETWEEN CIVIL SERVANTS

JEAN-FRANÇOIS SAVARD

In their chapter, Rocher and Gilbert describe the various institutions in Germany, Australia, Belgium, the United States, and Canada that structure intergovernmental relations in these federations. This comparative analysis shows, among other things, that in Canada intergovernmental relations are characterized by what is called *executive federalism*. In other words intergovernmental relations in Canada at both the federal and provincial levels are structured mainly around relationships between and among the elected representatives who form the executive branch. This leaves no room for elected members of legislative assemblies who are not ministers. In contrast, in the United States relations between the federated states and the federation are part of a complex web of federal and state executive and legislative bodies (Bakvis and Brown 2010).

However, according to Laforest and Montigny,

[la] *majeure partie du volume des échanges entre les différents niveaux de gouvernements repose ... sur des discussions entre les fonctionnaires. Bien qu'elles se déroulent généralement dans l'ombre, ces délibérations administratives permettent notamment d'harmoniser l'application de certaines politiques, d'assurer un certain partage de l'expertise et de préparer les rencontres de niveaux supérieurs. Pour y parvenir, les deux ordres de gouvernement se sont dotés de structures administratives, et ce, sur le plan tant interne que communautaire* (2009: 142).

Executive federalism is therefore largely contingent on the support of a government apparatus. But as Magali Marc (2005: 35) points out, "fewer studies have focused on how [civil servants] manage their relationship in areas where two orders of government are involved." We can add that studies of how civil servants manage their interprovincial relations are just as rare, if not more so.

This chapter is to provide a better understanding of the context in which these intergovernmental relations are carried out. To this end, we will first present two theoretical approaches—administrative federalism and coherent federalism—with a view to shedding light on intergovernmental relations between civil servants. We will then examine the policy coordination mechanisms found in the European Union, which should provide a better understanding of the situation in Canada. We will then present an analysis of the data on intergovernmental meetings and agreements (two policy coordination mechanisms found in Canada) with a view to better understanding the characteristics of intergovernmental relations between civil servants in Canada. Lastly, based on this empirical analysis, we will determine which approach best describes the intergovernmental relations between civil servants.

I.   ADMINISTRATIVE FEDERALISM

Bearing in mind that the concept of *executive federalism* refers to intergovernmental relations between elected officials in the executive branch, our first reflex might be to qualify intergovernmental relations between civil servants as *administrative federalism*. This concept was evoked in 1993 by Prime Minister Jean Chrétien when he asserted in the wake of his election that Canadians were tired of hearing about the constitution and that it was time to usher in an era of administrative federalism (which he contrasted with the idea of constitutional federalism). In the prime minister's opinion, this administrative federalism made sense because it was designed to help prevent Canada from getting mired in endless constitutional disputes by instead promoting administrative agreements between the central and provincial governments in all sectors (especially sectors under provincial jurisdiction), rather than constitutional reform. The prime minister believed this would make the Canadian federation work better. According to Johns *et al.* (2007), this approach has borne fruit, since the transition to a non-constitutional approach is indeed what characterizes intergovernmental relations today. Concretely this approach has resulted in hundreds of meetings each year between civil servants in different governments, the negotiation of multimillion dollar agreements each month, and countless informal contacts between civil servants (*ibid.*).

1.1. Defining Administrative Federalism

At first glance *administrative federalism* would appear to be a useful concept to better understand the relations between civil servants in different governments. However, it is important to define what we really mean by administrative federalism.

According to Schwager (1999a), administrative federalism is generally defined as a federal structure in which the central government has legislative functions, while the governments of federated states have administrative functions. More specifically, in administrative federalism the central government sets out and imposes the standards of quality with which public projects must comply, while the governments of federated states decide on the projects they wish to undertake (Schwager 1999a, 1999b). Bakvis and Brown (2010) add that in administrative federalism the federal (or central) government orchestrates all policy and program development, while the federated state governments are responsible for implementing and administering these policies and programs.

The concept of administrative federalism would help explain the complexity of federal relations in countries such as Germany, Austria, Mexico, Brazil, the United States (Congress sets standards and the state governments enforce them), and perhaps even the European Union, although it must be acknowledged that in the EU even though the European government can set standards, member states are free to decide whether or not to enforce them (Bakvis and Brown 2010). Canada, however, is characterized by a different federal dynamic that may instead be qualified as legislative federalism (Fenna 2007), which is to say that in Canada the action of governments is limited to the jurisdiction conferred on them, with little coordination between governments or levels of government. While Canada does offer a good example of the concept of legislative federalism where each level of government is responsible for developing *and* implementing the programs and policies under its jurisdiction (Bakvis and Brown 2010), the fact remains that some aspects of Canada's federal dynamics seem more akin to administrative federalism than legislative federalism, as shown in the following section.

1.2. How Administrative Federalism Works

According to Schwager (1999a), in many federations, most legislation is determined by the central government (this of course does not apply to Switzerland or Canada). For example, in Germany, despite a constitution that assigns specific roles to the *Länder*, the federal government has nonetheless taken responsibility for the vast majority of legislative functions. According to Schwager and Bakvis and Brown, this is a perfect example of administrative federalism.

How does administrative federalism work in practice? According to Schwager, in administrative federalism the central government sets minimum standards (usually through specific legislation) to fund or support by other means the implementation of various initiatives in a wide range of sectors (e.g., health, education, agriculture). The central government also determines the overall budget for initiatives in these sectors. The central government therefore assumes responsibility for developing policies and programs, but leaves the federated state governments responsible for administering how the resulting projects are implemented (Schwager 1999a, 1999b).

Why would a central government, which has the legislative and financial means to implement policies and programs, want to let federated states implement projects? According to Schwager, direct implementation of policies and programs by the central government would inevitably be hindered by the difficulty in accessing full and relevant information. What's more, the federated state governments are thought to be in closer contact with the population than the central government and therefore to have access to better information, allowing for more efficient implementation (Schwager 1999a).

Accordingly, in administrative federalism, the central government puts in place a legislative and financial framework to support a fixed number of projects, but the federated state governments decide which projects they want to implement based on the framework established by the central government (Schwager 1999a). With regard to the legal aspect, Schwager (1999b) notes that it is up to the federated state governments to decide whether they want to apply federal legislation or not; the central government cannot require them to do so.

Unlike a decentralized or devolved governmental structure, administrative federalism does recognize a certain level of autonomy of the federated state governments. More concretely, in a decentralized governmental structure the local or regional governments serve only one purpose, that of managing the legislation and programs adopted by the central government. However, in administrative federalism, the federated state governments are always free to choose which laws and programs to implement in their jurisdictions and how to do so (Schwager 1999a). For example, a federated state government that has received funds from the central government to implement a program may decide to refrain from certain parts of the program, so as to better fund those it wants to implement instead of reducing overall allocations for program components (Schwager 1999b). A federated state government can therefore decide whether or not to invest in a project (hence the recognition of a certain level of autonomy), but any investment must adhere to the financial framework put forward by the central government (hence constraints on federated states). Moreover, if the central government attempts to impose a legislative or financial framework that may harm the federated state government, the latter may simply refuse to implement such a framework and block it completely (Schwager 1999a).

Administrative federalism therefore presupposes that although the central government exercises some power over the federated state governments, the latter do have a certain level of autonomy and are not completely subject to the constraints imposed by the central government. The reality is that in administrative federalism the relationship between the central government and the federated state governments is marked by constant negotiation. On the one hand the central government has the legislative and financial means to carry out policies and programs, but not the information or authority required to implement them. On the other hand the federated state governments have the authority and information required to implement policies and programs, but not the means to develop projects the central government is willing and able to support. There results in a balancing act between the will of the central government and the freedom of federated states (Schwager 1999a). Schwager also notes (1999b) that the objective of the central government in a context of administrative federalism is not to increase the number of tools it has to act on behalf of the population, but rather to allocate these tools to the government authorities that are in the best position to use them.

Does the concept of administrative federalism accurately describe the context of Canadian intergovernmental relations? The answer is both yes and no. Yes, because since the 1990s relations between the federal and provincial governments would appear to have taken on a form that corresponds closely to the concept of administrative federalism. This is what Bakvis and Douglas affirm when they assert that

> In more recent years, Ottawa and the provinces have tried to follow a path . . . where the two orders of government are seen as partners rather than as competitors with neither subservient to the other, a much less hierarchical relationship in other words. One such development was the Agreement on Internal Trade of 1995 in which the federal government is treated as a party identical to the others (provinces and territories). A "Social Union Framework Agreement" was hammered out in 1999, which established basic parameters and ground rules for launching new federal–provincial programs and for tackling problems such as interprovincial barriers to labor mobility (2010: 492).

The agreements mentioned by Bakvis and Brown are fully in keeping with the logic of administrative federalism so dear to Prime Minister Chrétien and were proposed to the provinces based on what is referred to in Canada as spending power. However, spending power only exists between the federal and provincial governments, which means that administrative federalism only accounts for a single dimension of intergovernmental relations in Canada, i.e., federal–provincial relationships. Consequently, administrative federalism does not help explain or describe the intergovernmental relations between provinces. In the following section, we will see how the concept of coherent federalism can better account for the intergovernmental relations between provinces.

2.   COHERENT FEDERALISM

According to Johns *et al.* (2007), the increasing number of intergovernmental agreements and partnerships in recent years signals an intensification of intergovernmental activities in all public sectors. These activities have intensified to such an extent that according to Bakvis and Brown (2010), intergovernmental policy coordination represents the greatest intergovernmental relations challenge in modern federations. They add that under the current circumstances, policy coordination between provincial governments or between provincial and federal governments has become a necessity, or at least very desirable (*ibid.*). But what exactly do they mean by "policy coordination"?

Bakvis and Brown propose two definitions. According to the first, borrowed from Webb (1995), policy coordination is a mutual adjustment that leads governments to implement policies they would not have developed had they been able to act unilaterally. According to the second, borrowed from Bakvis and Juillet (2004), policy coordination is a harmonization of structures and activities to meet horizontal objectives, reduce overlap, and ensure that the actions of one or more governments do not prevent horizontal objectives from being met.

These definitions have the merit of showing that intergovernmental relations extend far beyond a mere federal–provincial dimension, but they do not take into account the full complexity of intergovernmental relations in a multidimensional context. According to D'Agostino (2009), the public policy process is based on mechanisms that link federated state governments and their apparatuses to central governments and their apparatuses. Moreover, the objective of these relations is not only to avoid overlap between public policies but also to create a synergy among them that is mutually reinforcing. The challenge therefore goes beyond simply coordinating public policies and instead becomes a matter of ensuring coherence. In Canada, this principle of public policy coherence is reflected in a set of structures, institutions, and practices that truly constitute what we would call *coherent federalism*. But before delving deeper into our discussion of coherent federalism, we must first define what is meant by public policy coherence (the basis of coherent federalism).

2.1. Defining Public Policy Coherence

To begin, we can define public policy coherence by asserting that it involves harmonizing a policy's objectives and implementation activities. However, this first definition provides a limited view of coherence, which may be conceived in a much broader sense. According to the OECD (2005), the pursuit of coherence consists of ensuring that the attainment of a government's policy objectives or results is not hindered by other policies developed by the same government or other governments. We therefore see that the concept of coherence does not dismiss the idea of policy coordination advanced by Bakvis and Douglas but rather embraces it as an integral part of policy coherence. This OECD definition is compelling because it goes well beyond the previously mentioned definition by linking the objectives and results of multiple public policies. According to the Development Assistance Committee (DAC), different policies are coherent if they are mutually reinforcing and create synergy (OECD 2005).

Jones (2002) lends credence to this notion by asserting that public policy coherence occurs when the objectives of one policy do not contradict those of other policies. Understood in this way, coherence is a concept that is not limited to the analysis of a single policy, as the first definition suggests, but instead includes a set of linked policies. However, it remains to be specified which policies can be linked. For May *et al.* (2005), coherence refers to the harmonization of different components that are associated with the same policy sector and share a common set of ideas and objectives. This is what Jordan and Halpin (2006) express when they assert that coherence is the integration of different activities (within the same sector, but carried out by different governments) under a common framework, with a view to achieving the desired results.

Forster and Stokke propose a definition of policy coherence that integrates all these elements rather well. They see a coherent policy as "one whose objectives, within a given policy framework, are internally consistent and attuned to objectives pursued within other policy frameworks of the system—as a minimum, these objectives should not be conflicting" (1999: 23). In a report published in 2005, the European Union (Studies in European Development 2006) took an in-depth look at the issue of coherence. According to these experts, policy coherence requires two essential virtues: efficiency and quality. Efficiency is important because the pursuit of coherence must make it possible to improve the effects of policies in a context where funding is limited, while quality refers to the inherent need to identify interference or incompatibility between policies. The notion of quality also refers to the complementarity between policies during their implementation and to the synergy of their effects (*ibid.*). This brings us closer to a more functional definition of coherence that allows us to better grasp how the above-mentioned normative aspects may take shape in a public policy process.

The OECD defines coherence as an effort to ensure that the expected objectives and results of policies developed by a government are not in contradiction with or hindered by other policies of the same government (OECD 2005). From a more operational standpoint, coherence can be understood as a policy development approach whereby governments adopt a complete, comprehensive vision of their actions to ensure that these actions do not cause any internal conflict. Ideally, the objective of policy coherence should be to find the most efficient and inexpensive ways to meet governmental and intergovernmental public policy objectives and prevent overlap, contradiction, and interference. Coherence therefore implies improving the quality of collective actions between public and intergovernmental institutions (Studies in European Development 2006). Thus we see how the two essential virtues mentioned above (efficiency and quality) come into play in a public policy process.

The pursuit of coherence seems, in theory, to be a rather simple undertaking. After all, as the European Union stresses (*ibid.*), it should simply be a matter of paying enough attention to governmental action to detect and eliminate contradictions. However, nothing is so simple, and instead a minimum threshold of incoherence would appear to be necessary. The experts at the Studies in European Development Centre do in fact uphold that a certain degree of incoherence may be desirable: "It might be the result of responding simultaneously to a wide range of legitimate interests, on which governments have to act even though actions may be partly contradictory" (2005: 17). In this regard, Bakvis and Brown show the great complexity of governmental relations in Canada, where each government has different interests to protect and constitutional powers to defend these interests. They affirm that despite this complexity it is still possible to attain a certain degree of coherence through the implementation of various mechanisms. In the next section, we will see which mechanisms make it possible to seek policy coherence in the context of a federation. We will start by showing how the principles supporting coherent federalism fit together and thus give effect to coherence-building mechanisms.

2.2. Principles and Mechanisms of Coherent Federalism

The experts at the Studies in European Development Centre (2006) assert that policy coherence is only fully attainable within a conceptual triptych of policy coordination, complementarity, and coherence. I would therefore suggest that coherent federalism is based on this triptych of organizing principles whereby coordination and complementarity serve the central normative principle of coherence. This idea is in keeping with the previously examined definitions of coherence, where coherence is an ideal to strive for through coordination mechanisms that ensure the pursuit of harmony and complementarity in public policy objectives.

We must now qualify Bakvis and Brown's assertion that policy coordination poses the greatest challenge for federations in terms of public policy, and that this challenge is in fact one of coordination and coherence. The triptych demonstrates that coordination and complementarity are the organizing principles that give effect to policy development and implementation mechanisms in coherent federalism, while coherence is the normative principle that motivates the development of these policies. In other words, in coherent federalism governments seek to establish coordination and complementarity mechanisms in order to ensure the highest possible degree of coherence.

According to the Studies in European Development Centre (2006), the Confederation already boasts a number of mechanisms that make the quest for coherence possible. These mechanisms are based on how public decisions are made and implemented and do not necessarily concern policy content itself. They generally meet three criteria: a strong political commitment to the pursuit of coherence, institutional architecture that allows adequate coordination, and good analytical capability combined with efficient information transmission systems (*ibid.*).

Let us examine these criteria individually. First, a strong political commitment to the pursuit of coherence means that public decision makers strive to clearly define policy objectives and priorities while taking into account the criteria that will be used to evaluate policies following their implementation. Next, the institutional architecture must enable adequate coordination between governments by putting in place flexible and transparent structures that allow them to adapt to constantly changing political environments, quickly identify incoherencies, and promote dialogue between them in order to quickly resolve any administrative disputes related to different organizational cultures or differing interpretations of objectives or priorities. In other words, these mechanisms must promote intergovernmental cooperation. Lastly, the governments must have the analytical capability and information transmission systems needed to be able to identify, document, and analyze contradictions between policies so that they can be resolved. These components (analytical capability and information transmission system) also serve to evaluate the human and financial resources governments will need to meet coherence objectives (Studies in European Development 2006).

These criteria are part of a vast set of mechanisms that can be grouped into three categories: overall policy and political decision-making, government institutions and administration, and assessment and advisory capacity. Overall policy and political decision-making aim to integrate the objectives of one sector (e.g., international development) in other policies or programs that might have an impact on the sector. These mechanisms take the form of dialogue or cooperation between governments and government departments conducive to a horizontal approach that makes it possible to involve a broad range of ministries in the development of public policies aimed at a specific sector, not only the specific ministry responsible for it. Government institutions and administration are designed to influence public decision makers inside the machinery of government. These mechanisms may take various forms including formal coordination processes (e.g., interministerial committees) and informal gatherings of senior government officials. Lastly, assessment and advisory capacity are a way to include both governmental and nongovernmental expertise in policy development and leverage the research, knowledge, and experience of both governmental and nongovernmental actors with a view to defining objectives that harmonize well within a sector (Studies in European Development 2006). In addition to public consultations, these mechanisms may take other forms such as advisory committees and issue tables.

Although it is fairly easy to see how the mechanisms of policy coherence can be categorized, listing individual mechanisms is another challenge. In its 2006 study, the Studies in European Development Centre emphasizes that only mechanisms that are formally established and explicitly aimed at policy coherence are easily identifiable. All other mechanisms are difficult to identify, regardless of whether they are informal or unintentionally contribute to the pursuit of coherence (Studies in European Development 2006: 25), and require more in-depth study that is beyond the scope of this chapter. What's more, the institutional context also plays a role in identifying coherence mechanisms. Even within a federation there are cultural differences between federated states, and this multiplies the forms coherence mechanisms can take, especially informal mechanisms. It is therefore necessary, to the extent possible, to take into account states' cultural realities and the institutional frameworks they yield to properly identify a state's coherence mechanisms.

The Studies in European Development report (2006) provides a number of examples in the international aid sector that clearly illustrate these coherence mechanism categories. With regard to policy mechanisms, Estonia has a set of principles that promote a holistic approach to developing public polices and require decision makers to consider as a whole any policies likely to influence a given sector. In Poland and Slovakia, the governments have a cooperation strategy that requires decision makers to adopt a comprehensive approach to policy development. In international development in Austria, the government passed legislation requiring public decision makers to take into account international development objectives and principles in all policy development processes.

Institutional and administrative mechanisms generally take rather similar forms. In the Czech Republic, Belgium, and France, the governments regularly set up interdepartmental committees or working groups tasked with developing coherent polices between ministries within the same sector. The Czech Republic even has an interdepartmental work commission that coordinates activities between ministries—and greatly facilitates horizontal work. In Greece the government has interdepartmental committees to which officials from various ministries contribute and that ensure policy coherence and complementarity, but they meet infrequently and do not constitute a true "operational" mechanism for the pursuit of coherence. Lastly, in international aid, Spain offers an instructive approach, especially for federations. Its government set up an interdepartmental committee on international cooperation that coordinates the efforts of Spanish ministries whose actions may have an impact on international development, and an interterritorial committee that coordinates, negotiates, and cooperates with various levels of government and government officials with a view to ensuring coherent international intervention (Studies in European Development 2006).

We will continue with the example of international aid to illustrate consultative mechanisms aimed at public policy coherence. In Denmark the government recently adopted a policy on development in Africa. This policy was the fruit of consultation with public and private stakeholders interested in the matter. The consultation was carried out in three phases: first during open and public debates, then as part of a public hearing, and lastly through an electronic consultation whereby citizens were invited to submit their comments electronically. All the data and viewpoints collected were incorporated into the analysis that led to the development of the Danish policy. The Netherlands took a different approach, with less emphasis on public consultation and more on informal exchanges between Dutch ministers and their European counterparts. Lastly, it should be noted that a mechanism establishing a network on policy coherence for development serves as an information sharing and consultation platform for European civil servants to discuss research reports or impact reports on international development issues (Studies in European Development 2006). This network makes it easier to integrate data and analyses from a variety of European experts.

3. THE CASE OF CANADA
AND QUEBEC–ONTARIO RELATIONS

The key point in the Studies in European Development report is that some states have mechanisms explicitly aimed at the pursuit of public policy coherence and others that promote coherence without being explicitly designed to do so. To a certain extent, this latter situation prevails in Canada, where two main coordination mechanisms promote the development of coherent policies between governments, even though they have not been explicitly developed for this purpose. These mechanisms fall essentially under the category of government institution and administration.

Intergovernmental conferences, one of the main coordination mechanisms in Canada, are of different natures (Pelletier and Tremblay 2009), but usually take the form of prime ministers' conferences, which are convened by the federal prime minister to discuss issues defined by him or her. The agendas of these conferences are therefore set by the federal government. It was in reaction to this dominance by the central government that in 2003 the provincial governments created the Council of the Federation, which aims to act as a counterweight to federal power. In theory the Council of the Federation helps intensify interprovincial relations and maintain an ongoing dialogue between the provinces so they can assert their autonomy vis-à-vis a dominant federal government. However, although this forum is alive and well, it has not yet been able to act as a counterweight to the federal government's influence. Lastly, intergovernmental conferences may take the form of interdepartmental meetings that bring together sectorial ministers and their civil servants with a view to discussing specific issues.

As Bakvis and Brown (2010) point out, these mechanisms are relatively institutionalized. The Canadian constitution does not provide for the creation of intergovernmental forums, but they have arisen on their own since the 1960s. However these forums have grown prominent enough that several Canadian governments have seen fit to create agencies responsible for intergovernmental relations. These agencies are generally at the heart of the government machinery and maintain close ties with sister organizations in all government departments (special units of various departments that coordinate intergovernmental activities and liaise with central agencies) (Johns *et al.* 2007). In Quebec, Secrétariat aux affaires intergouvernementales canadiennes (SAIC), a component of Ministère du Conseil exécutif, is the agency responsible for intergovernmental relations, while in Ontario and the federal government, the departments of intergovernmental affairs constitute these agencies. It should be noted, however, that at the federal level Intergovernmental Affairs (IGA) is a component of the Privy Council Office, a similar structure to that adopted in Quebec.

According to Johns *et al.* (2007), intergovernmental relations agencies provide monitoring, coordination, and counsel. They must continuously stay abreast of issues of concern to the member governments of the Confederation, in all policy sectors. They are also tasked with preparing intergovernmental conferences, developing and negotiating the conference agendas, and defining the key messages for political leaders. In addition these agencies coordinate the negotiation of intergovernmental agreements (we will return to this point in the following paragraph). It should be noted that intergovernmental relations agencies are not solely responsible for these functions, as they mainly play a role of coordination between the central agencies and ministries involved, either through intergovernmental conferences or through the negotiation of intergovernmental agreements. Lastly, intergovernmental relations agencies advise prime ministers on pressing issues through monitoring and consultation work with other departments.

Intergovernmental agreements, the second mechanism for coordination between Canadian governments, take two forms: federal–provincial–territorial agreements, where the federal government generally imposes conditions, and interprovincial agreements that take provincial autonomy more fully into account, since they are negotiated on an equal footing. According to Johns *et al.* (2007), these agreements usually serve to harmonize policies between jurisdictions, reduce overlap and duplication, and improve the quality of services offered by governments, notably by resolving problems that require joint action.[1]

---

1. One example is the Quebec–Ontario agreement on construction worker credentials.

Magali Marc (2005) gives the example of labour force training, where a federal–provincial agreement provided for joint management of the sector, thereby helping to avoid intergovernmental conflict.

It would be wrong to think that Canada has only two coordination mechanisms. Intergovernmental conferences and agreements are certainly the most visible but, as Johns *et al.* point out, behind these more formal mechanisms is a myriad of networks and relationships:

> which link officials to each other across departments, sectors, and governments, and to others such as political staff, international and municipal governments, and nongovernmental organizations and groups. These informal networks and relations are not easily studied. They consist of unstructured, sporadic personal meetings, contacts, telephone and conference calls, e-mails, lunches and the like which are virtually impossible to catalogue, aggregate, or track (2007: 34).

Marc confirms this finding and notes that, despite policy disagreements between elected officials, civil servants stay in constant contact and maintain their networks, which contributes to policy coordination efforts. In this regard she points out that civil servants "spent a lot of time meeting each other, coordinating their efforts, harmonizing their interventions, and readjusting their programs to take into account what the other order of government is doing" (2005: 44). However, Johns *et al.* qualify Marc's remarks, stressing that civil servants are ultimately accountable to elected officials, and the policies they develop must therefore follow the direction set out by these officials. The coordination work of civil servants through informal networks, although very important to coherence, remains at the mercy of the wishes of elected officials.

These two coordination mechanisms—intergovernmental conferences and agreements—show how, structurally, civil servants play a central role in Canadian intergovernmental relations, because not only do civil servants themselves take part in intergovernmental conferences (there are a number of intergovernmental forums for senior civil servants in Canada), but they must also provide secretarial services for intergovernmental conferences of departments and prime ministers. It should be noted that although elected officials determine the thrust of intergovernmental agreements, civil servants are the ones who negotiate the more concrete points of these agreements and who ultimately implement them.

Although at the structural level we can identify the central role civil servants play in intergovernmental relations, it remains to be seen whether in practice this role is as crucial as the structure suggests.

In other words, are the relations between civil servants from different governments strong enough to play the central role one generally imagines?

To answer this question, we analyzed data compiled by SAIC, which collects information on all intergovernmental meetings and agreements and publishes this information each year. For the purposes of this chapter, our analysis was limited to meetings held in the decade of 2000–2010 and to agreements signed in the same period. It should be noted that this analysis concerns only meetings in which the Government of Quebec took part and agreements to which it was party.

Our analysis reveals that from 2000 to 2010 the Government of Quebec took part in 1,108 intergovernmental meetings, 582 of which brought together senior civil servants and 526, elected officials (ministers or prime ministers). This shows that from 2000 to 2010, more than 52% of intergovernmental meetings involved civil servants, and more than 65% of these meetings were of a federal–provincial nature. We therefore see a predominance of vertical linkages (federal–provincial) in Canadian intergovernmental relations. That said, a more detailed analysis reveals that nearly 50% of interprovincial meetings were aimed at civil servants, whereas this was the case in 54% of federal–provincial meetings. The central role played by civil servants in intergovernmental relations is therefore just as significant between the federal government and the provinces as it is between the provincial governments. What is of particular interest in this data is the multilateral nature of intergovernmental meetings. Bilateral interprovincial (Quebec and another province) and bilateral federal–provincial (Quebec and the federal government) meetings account for a mere 1% of these events. Moreover, with regard to the specific purpose of this chapter, we should point out that in ten years there were only five bilateral interprovincial meetings between Quebec and Ontario, and these five meetings brought together ministers or premiers. This is not to say that Quebec–Ontario relations are practically nonexistent. This data rather suggests that Quebec–Ontario relations—especially those between civil servants—play out on two main stages, i.e., multilateral meetings and informal networks.

With regard to intergovernmental agreements, the SAIC data paints a picture quite similar to that of the intergovernmental meetings. The data supports our arguments because, although it does not explicitly mention the role played by civil servants, these agreements are a good indicator of the strength of their contribution since, as we noted earlier, civil servants are always involved in negotiating and implementing them. Between 2000 and 2010, Quebec signed 867 intergovernmental agreements, two-thirds (66.3%) of which were of a federal–provincial nature, while only 8% were of an interprovincial nature (the other agreements were signed with aboriginal communities or U.S. states). Again, we see a clear predominance of vertical relations. However, a more detailed analysis reveals that half of the Government of Quebec's interprovincial agreements were signed with Ontario. This fact is noteworthy because it supports the hypothesis in the previous paragraph: Quebec–Ontario relations are alive and well (otherwise there would not be so many agreements signed between the two governments) and play out on stages that mask the existence of these relations, namely multilateral meetings and informal networks. Unfortunately, more research is needed to further explore this hypothesis.

A more detailed analysis might allow us to qualify our remarks—we could, for example, further examine the nature or content of interprovincial and federal–provincial agreements—but for now the key point is that the SAIC data empirically confirms the central role civil servants play in Canadian intergovernmental relations (Laforest and Montigny are therefore absolutely right). This data shows that vertical relations are predominant (federal–provincial relations are much more intense than interprovincial relations) and that Quebec's biggest provincial partner is Ontario, thereby supporting the hypothesis that bilateral Quebec–Ontario relations play out in multilateral forums and informal networks, which is consistent with what is asserted by Marc (2005), Bakvis and Brown (2010), and Johns *et al.* (2007).

At the beginning of this chapter, we noted that our main objective was to better understand the context in which civil servants carry out intergovernmental relations. We presented two theoretical approaches that we believe best describe these relations: administrative federalism and coherent federalism. It is now time to identify which of these two approaches allows a better understanding of the context of intergovernmental relations between civil servants in Canada.

Our analysis of data on intergovernmental meetings and agreements reveals a clear predominance of vertical (federal–provincial) relations, which ultimately shows that intergovernmental relations between civil servants correspond to the concept of administrative federalism. That being said, there are two reasons such a statement must be qualified. First, our analysis illustrates that relations are not only federal–provincial—there are in fact many interprovincial meetings and, since 2003, the provinces have had the Council of the Federation. Moreover, 8% of the intergovernmental agreements adopted by the Government of Quebec have been of an interprovincial nature. Since we know that the Canadian provinces do not really have the means to impose specific conditions among themselves (as the federal government does), we can infer that interprovincial relations are carried out on an equal footing. This is an intergovernmental relations context that does not correspond to administrative federalism, even though the latter recognizes provincial autonomy. Second, as we mentioned previously, our analysis did not take into account the content of the agreements. However, it would not be overstepping the bounds to hypothesize that some federal–provincial agreements are mainly to harmonize policies or practices, while others really aim to impose federal conditions on the provincial governments. The question then is how to identify the proportion of each type.

It is therefore clear that although intergovernmental relations between civil servants are mainly in a context of administrative federalism, some are more in line with coherent federalism. We can thus conclude that intergovernmental relations between civil servants take place mainly in a context of administrative federalism, but also coherent federalism. More research is now needed to identify to what extent intergovernmental relations can be explained by one approach or the other.

CONCLUSION

The goal of this chapter was to examine intergovernmental relations in Canada from a different angle by focusing on intergovernmental relationships between civil servants. To better understand these relations, we first discussed the two theoretical approaches likely to explain the context in which they are conducted, i.e., administrative federalism and coherent federalism. We then reviewed coordination mechanisms that promote coherence in member states of the European Union.

We were thus able to determine that Canada has two main intergovernmental coordination mechanisms that promote the pursuit of coherence: intergovernmental meetings and agreements. We then carried out an empirical analysis of intergovernmental meetings and agreements based on data published by SAIC, which allowed us to empirically demonstrate the significance of the role civil servants play in Canadian intergovernmental relations. Moreover, our analysis revealed general trends characteristic of the intergovernmental relations of civil servants. First, intergovernmental relations between civil servants are marked by a predominance of federal–provincial relations. Next, bilateral relations between provincial civil servants—which include Quebec–Ontario relations—are mainly through multilateral forums and informal networks. Lastly, although interprovincial relations and agreements account for only a small part of intergovernmental relations in Quebec, the fact is that Quebec civil servants nonetheless maintain abundant interprovincial relations and their main partners are their Ontario counterparts.

To conclude, we believe that intergovernmental relations between civil servants are more in a context of administrative federalism than coherent federalism—the predominance of federal–provincial relations is the main indicator. However we must qualify this a bit. Despite the predominance of federal–provincial relations, the provinces also maintain relations among themselves through interprovincial meetings and agreements. Moreover, the provinces have also established the Council of the Federation, which seeks to be a counterweight to the federal–provincial conferences. Accordingly, although it is true that intergovernmental relations between civil servants are mainly conducted in a context of administrative federalism, some do in fact take place in a context more akin to coherent federalism.

Many of the authors cited in this chapter stress that civil servants play a key role in intergovernmental relations, but few studies have really examined this point. Although this chapter aims to address the issue, much more work is needed to fully grasp the nature of intergovernmental relations between civil servants.

BIBLIOGRAPHY

Bakvis, H. and D. Brown (2010). "Policy Coordination in Federal Systems: Comparing Intergovernmental Processes and Outcomes in Canada and the United States." *Publius: The Journal of Federalism*, vol. 40, no. 3: 484–507.

Bakvis, H. and L. Juillett (2004). *The Horizontal Challenge: Line Departments, Central Agencies and Leadership*. Ottawa: Canada School of Public Services.

D'Agostino, M. (2009). "Securing an Effective Voice for Citizens in Intergovernmental Administrative Decision Making." *International Journal of Public Administration*, vol. 32, no. 8: 658–680.

Fenna, A. (2007). "The Malaise of Federalism: Comparative Reflections on Commonwealth–State Relations." *Australian Journal of Public Administration*, vol. 66: 298–306.

Forster, J. and O. Stokke (1999). *Policy Coherence in Development Co-operation*, Portland: Frank Cass.

Johns, C., P. O'Reilly, and G. Inwood (2007). "Formal and Informal Dimensions of Intergovernmental Administrative Relations in Canada." *Canadian Public Administration*, vol. 50, no. 1: 21–41.

Jones, T. (2002). "Policy Coherence, Global Environmental Governance, and Poverty Reduction." *International Environmental Agreements: Politics, Law and Economics*, vol. 2, May: 389–401.

Jordan, G. and D. Halpin (2006). "The Political Costs of Policy Coherence: Constructing a Rural Policy for Scotland." *Journal of Public Policy*, vol. 26, no. 1: 21–41.

Laforest, G. and É. Montigny (2009). "Le fédéralisme exécutif: problèmes et actualités." In R. Pelletier and M. Tremblay (eds.), *Le parlementarisme canadien*. Quebec City: Les Presses de l'Université Laval: 129–162.

Marc, M. (2005). "Federal-Provincial Overlap and Civil Servants: The Case of Occupational Training in Quebec and Ontario." *Canadian Public Administration*, vol. 48, no. 1: 35–52.

May, P. J. *et al.* (2005). "Policy Coherence and Component-Driven Policy Making: Arctic Policy in Canada and the United States." *The Policy Studies Journal*, vol. 33, no. 1: 37–63.

OECD (2005). *Policy Coherence for Development: Promoting Institutional Good Practice*. Paris: OECD.

Pelletier, R. and M. Tremblay (eds.) (2009). *Le parlementarisme canadien*, 4th ed. Quebec City: Les Presses de l'Université Laval.

Schwager, R. (1999a). "Administrative Federalism and a Central Government with Regionally Based Preferences." *International Tax and Public Finance*, vol. 6, no. 2: 165–199.

Schwager, R. (1999b). "The Theory of Administrative Federalism: An Alternative to Fiscal Centralization and Decentralization." *Public Finance Review*, vol. 27, no. 3: 282–309.

Studies in European Development (2006). *European Union Mechanisms that Promote Policy Coherence for Development*. Amsterdam: Aksant Academic Publishers.

Webb, M. C. (1995). *The Political Economy of Policy Coordination: International Adjustment since 1945*. Ithaca: Cornell University Press.

3. FROM THE CONFEDERATION OF TOMORROW TO THE PATRIATION OF THE CONSTITUTION
Quebec–Ontario Relations in Transition

ALAIN-G. GAGNON
and FRANÇOIS LAPLANTE-LÉVESQUE

Quebec–Ontario relations have often been defined by ties of solidarity, especially when the two provinces have confronted the federal government over the distribution of powers. Union National leader Maurice Duplessis (1936–1939, 1944–1959) and Liberal Mitchell Hepburn (1934–1942) were without doubt the two premiers who best embodied the culture of opposition to federal intrusions into provincial jurisdiction during the 20th century. Their collaboration was particularly notable during the Rowell–Sirois Commission (1937–1940). Hepburn's successor George Drew also cooperated with Maurice Duplessis during the 1945 and 1946 conferences on reconstruction, which established a Quebec–Ontario axis (Bryden 2000). Like Hepburn, Drew defended provincial rights in reaction to the heavy centralization imposed by Ottawa beginning in the late 1930s, making him a valuable ally of Quebec in its negotiations with the federal government. Despite this agreement on constitutional matters, Hepburn was otherwise quite scornful of Quebec, as revealed in this excerpt from a 1944 letter to a friend in Alberta:

I think the longer we appease the isolationists in Quebec, the surer we are of civil war. I think if we act now and leave no doubt about the determination of the English speaking part of Canada, whether of Anglo-Saxon stock or otherwise, to preserve British traditions and maintain the

British connection, then we will have laid the foundations of unity . . . Anything else simply means a steady trend toward a Quebec-dominated Canada. That I for one am not prepared to accept. I believe in the British connection and all it means. And I would much rather see my children grow up as citizens of the United States than to be citizens of a Canada which was reduced to the low ethical and moral standard of the people of Quebec (Bryden 2000: 385).

It was not until the 1960s that the close cooperation of the Duplessis–Hepburn era would arise again between the premiers of the central provinces, this time during the reign of Conservative premier John Robarts (1961–1971) and the Union Nationale's Daniel Johnson (1966–1968) (Hopkins 1977). This cooperation came at a time when Quebec was seeking to assert itself by creating the conditions for cultural, economic, political, and social development necessary to carve out a better position for itself within Confederation and the continental economy. Ontario's influence on the Quiet Revolution is not well known, but it is worth taking a second look and drawing our own conclusions. The decision by Premier Leslie Frost (1949–1961) in 1960 to strike a commission to examine the province's pension funds and study the possibility of making them transferable between provinces certainly influenced the Jean Lesage government's decision to explore the matter in 1963. Ottawa saw an interest and moved rapidly to get involved in this provincial jurisdiction. After intense discussions between Ottawa and the provinces in 1963 and 1964, a pan-Canadian program was proposed on a voluntary participation basis. Quebec was the only province to opt for its own pension plan. This set the scene for asymmetrical federalism as a management approach and also provided the best demonstration of a province exerting a definite influence on priorities identified by the federal government.

The 1960s were marked by national movements on a massive scale. Quebec rode this wave of affirmation and decolonization to give momentum to its vast plan of reform in a number of fields, starting with policies in matters of education, culture, and the economy as well as society. The Quiet Revolution was in full swing. The decade was also characterized by major tensions between the Quebec government and the federal government (Gagnon and Montcalm 1990). These tensions were documented by various inquiry commissions, including the Laurendeau–Dunton Commission and the Gendron Commission (Gagnon and Latouche 1991). Several studies have already explored the close ties between the governments of Quebec and Ontario during the Laurendeau–Dunton Commission (1963–1968) (Montigny and Chambers 2000; Vipond 1991).

This chapter will mainly focus on Quebec–Ontario relations during a transition phase (1971–1981). This period covers the years between the 1971 Victoria Charter and the patriation of the Constitution ten years later. These were two key moments because they illustrate a shift in interests in Quebec–Ontario relations. During this period, relations between the two provinces grew strained. Ontario's position increasingly shifted away from the defence of provincial rights as it sought to align its own political and economic future with that of Canada. According to economist Thomas Courchene (1998: 17), this shift in interest on the part of Ontario was the predictable reaction of a central region whose future was tied to that of the central government.

I.   THE VICTORIA CONFERENCE

To really understand the changing relations between the governments of Quebec and Ontario during the negotiations surrounding the proposed Victoria Charter, we must return to the early 1960s, when Quebec, in full political, economic, and social transition, shifted its position with regards to the Constitution. With the election of Jean Lesage's Liberals in 1960, Quebec moved towards modernization and sought more earnestly than ever a certain form of equality between the two founding peoples (McRoberts 1999: 60). Debates between Canada's anglophones and francophones became increasingly centred around Quebec, and the increased role played by the state in Quebec fuelled the perception that it was not a province like the others. The new breed of Liberal Quebec nationalists pushed for major constitutional changes and insisted that Canada's political life should better reflect the country's dual nature. They also wanted Quebec's central role in Canada to be recognized.

Against this background of empowerment, Jean Lesage revived the premiers' conferences (the last of which had been held in 1926). Lesage's goal was to "encourage interprovincial cooperation, without creating a negative attitude towards Ottawa on the part of the provinces" (Morin 1972: 11). He also insisted on increasing the number and frequency of intergovernmental meetings and discussions in order to encourage federal–provincial cooperation. In fact, the 1960s saw more intergovernmental conferences than ever before (Morin 1972). During this period however, relations between Ottawa and Quebec City were quite strained. Quebec's constitutional demands, its refusal to back the 1966 Fulton–Favreau formula, and the rise of the sovereignty movement (with the creation of the Mouvement Souveraineté-Association in 1967) caused worry, even incomprehension, in Ottawa and the provincial capitals (Roy 1978: 137).

As mentioned in the introduction, Ontario was the first English province to take a serious interest in intergovernmental relations in the postwar years. During the 1960s, Ontario stepped up its initiatives in areas such as law, culture, language, society, and the economy (McWhinney 1979: 78). During his first term, Premier John Robarts (1961–1971) undertook major government reforms, developing paragovernmental organizations like the Ontario Advisory Committee on Confederation, which was active from 1965 to 1971. This nonpartisan body made up of professionals from various backgrounds acted as an advisory body to the Ontario government on the role the province could play within Confederation. It was also tasked with identifying constitutional changes to be pursued by the province (Ontario Advisory Committee on Confederation 1967: ix).

The release of the first report of the Laurendeau–Dunton Commission on Bilingualism and Biculturalism in 1965 plunged Canada into a constitutional crisis that would have unimaginable repercussions. When Daniel Johnson took up office as premier of Quebec in 1966, he quickly took stock of the shocking assessment described in the commission's first report regarding the state of Canada's federation and the relations between its French- and English-speaking citizens. A vast movement in favour of greater autonomy for Quebec was born (Martin 1974: 49).

Within weeks of coming to power, Johnson reestablished the legislative committee on the Constitution and, in his first speech from the throne, revisited the idea of a pact between two nations, calling for fundamental changes to the Constitution in order to create an equal partnership between the two nations (Roy 1978: 137). The other provinces, however, had little desire to get involved in a major constitutional reform. In reaction to Quebec's increasingly isolated position on this issue, Ontario Premier John Robarts convened an intergovernmental constitutional conference in November 1967.

The main objective of the conference, dubbed "The Confederation of Tomorrow," was to give Johnson an unprecedented opportunity to present his province's demands to the entire country (McRoberts 1978: 227). Here is how Johnson described Quebec's main demands to the other premiers at the interprovincial conference. According to Johnson, it had to be recognized that

> la constitution [canadienne] actuelle comporte encore des éléments valables en ce qui concerne l'organisation d'un Canada à dix, il faut bien admettre que cet autre Canada, le Canada à deux reste largement à inventer. Voilà sans doute pourquoi notre pays est resté jusqu'à maintenant le Canada des deux solitudes.

[...] *Il est fondamental que la Constitution reconnaisse les droits collectifs des deux communautés culturelles ... Voilà pourquoi notre gouvernement a reçu le mandat de militer de toutes ses forces en faveur d'une constitution nouvelle consacrant l'égalité juridique et pratique de nos deux communautés nationales. ... Il y a donc un rôle que seul le Québec peut jouer pour assurer l'égalité de la nation canadienne-française. C'est pourquoi, il a besoin de pouvoirs accrus* (1967: 17).

The conference opened a new chapter in Canada's constitutional debate, culminating 15 years later in the patriation of Canada's Constitution—over the objections of the Quebec's National Assembly (White 1985: 289). In addition to proving that the provinces could discuss constitutional reform with one another, it also confirmed Robarts' leadership role among the premiers and convinced Quebec that its aspirations were not entirely falling on deaf ears in English Canada. Thanks to Robarts' initiative, Ontario had played a decisive role in giving Quebec the opportunity to be heard across Canada. Certain political figures even claimed that Robarts' openness and goodwill played a role in convincing Johnson that Quebec should remain within Confederation (Martin 1974: 50). Bolstered by this interprovincial alliance, Quebec and Ontario maintained close ties until the election of the Parti Québécois in November 1976.

Ontario and the other English provinces had sent Ottawa a clear message: they were sympathetic to Quebec's position, and if the federal government took no initiative on constitutional negotiations, the provinces would follow Ontario's lead and pursue discussions among themselves, to the detriment of Ottawa's leadership in constitutional talks (*ibid.*). It was an effective way of forcing the hand of the federal government, which responded to Ontario's announcement of an interprovincial conference by hurriedly announcing that it would hold a federal–provincial conference of its own. This meeting was held in Ottawa in February 1968, paving the way for a round of constitutional negotiations that culminated in the failure of the Victoria Conference in 1971.

In a way, the February 1968 conference eschewed the major issues of the Confederation of Tomorrow conference. Then federal justice minister Pierre Elliott Trudeau put forth a three-step plan for constitutional negotiations. The first was a debate on a topic of great importance to Prime Minister Lester B. Pearson—the protection of human rights (including language rights)—followed by a discussion on the central institutions of the Canadian federation. Only after these two steps were complete would the division of powers be addressed (McRoberts 1999: 198), even though this issue had been at the very heart of the discussions during the Confederation of Tomorrow. The federal government's plans did not sit well with the premiers. Quebec, Ontario, and the other provinces opposed the idea of a constitutionally enshrined charter of rights. The question of French language rights, however, was better received, and Quebec–Ontario ties were strengthened by the promise of Premier Robarts to provide bilingual government services, which drew praise from Johnson (Martin 1974: 51). Nevertheless, the federal–provincial conference allowed the federal government to assert its authority by pushing its own agenda and stripping Ontario of its leadership role on the constitutional front.

It was Johnson's successor Jean-Jacques Bertrand who attended the February 1969 federal–provincial conference. He was determined to see constitutional talks continue and succeed. However, Quebec was the only province seeking radical changes to the Constitution. The governments of Ontario, Prince Edward Island, and New Brunswick may have expressed cautious sympathy for Quebec, but in the end they would side with Ottawa (Roy 1978: 181–182).

For Pierre Elliott Trudeau, prime minister of Canada since April 20, 1968, Canada was one nation made up of individuals who aspired to speak two languages from coast to coast. He saw this vision as the basis for building and protecting the rights of citizens. In contrast, Bertrand, like his predecessor Daniel Johnson, saw Canada as a country composed of two nations, which could not be reduced to "agglomerations of individuals with identical rights" (Roy 1978: 181). In Bertrand's eyes, these two nations had to be considered entities in and of themselves, with rights that went well beyond the exclusive recognition of individual rights. He refused to recognize Canada's linguistic duality as defined in the federal government's project, arguing instead in favour of political recognition of a national duality, made tangible through the recognition of special status for Quebec. The governments of all nine English provinces (and the federal government) were unanimous in rejecting the idea of formal special status for Quebec. However, Ontario and Manitoba said they could be open to accepting "certain practical accommodations that would grant Quebec *de facto* special status without formal recognition" (Roy 1978: 182; Gagnon and Garcea 1988). The premiers left the conference without reaching an agreement on a formula that made Quebec feel at home in the federation. They expressed a desire to carry out a more in-depth study of the changes to make to Canada's Constitution in order to help the country move forward.

The December 1969 meeting of the premiers proved extremely frustrating for all parties. Bertrand continued pushing his constitutional agenda, whereas Ontario and the western provinces felt that negotiations were hindering progress in areas such as taxation and the economy and had taken on too much importance (Martin 1974: 52). The decision was made that the next federal–provincial conference would not deal with constitutional issues and that no constitutional negotiations would take place until after the April 1970 general election in Quebec. The parties present were worried about Quebec's political climate, and they wanted to avoid giving ammunition to either Bourassa's Liberals or Lévesque's Parti Québécois, both of which were vying for power in Quebec.

With the election of the Liberals in 1970, Quebec's position shifted somewhat. Shortly after taking office, Robert Bourassa declared that his government would prioritize the economy and take a pragmatic approach rather than focus on constitutional issues that the average citizen cared little about (*ibid*.: 53). Ontario premier John Robarts, effectively freed from his commitments to Quebec, could not help but breathe a sigh of relief.

That did not mean relations between Quebec and Ontario were all sweetness and light, however. Premier Robarts wanted the provinces to be able to deal directly with Ottawa on an individual basis on specific issues and he no longer seemed willing to back Quebec as systematically as in the past. There was even a certain level of indifference between the two provinces. It must be noted, however, that the idea of bilateral negotiations held out certain advantages for Quebec in its ongoing tug-of-war with Ottawa by enabling it to play provincial legitimacy off against federal legitimacy within Quebec's borders. The idea of bilateralism therefore became a more prominent feature of the landscape of federal–provincial relations as of this period.

This is the climate in which the June 1971 Victoria Conference was held. The conference spawned a draft charter that would apply across Canada. The Quebec government still wanted to take advantage of Ottawa's desire to patriate the Constitution in order to revisit the division of powers. Quebec repeated the same arguments it had made during the meetings leading up to the Victoria Conference. As Robert Bourassa pointed out in his 1995 memoir:

> the federal government's desire to patriate the Constitution was an opportunity for Quebec to leverage its position within the federation . . . According to the Quebec government, the federal government would only get what it wanted if, at the same time, a new balance of power was struck between the federal government and the provinces (1995: 91).

This charter, which included an amending formula and articles dealing with political and language rights, also contained provisions regarding the Supreme Court, the powers of disallowance and reservation, regional disparities, and federal–provincial consultations

(Roy 1978: 155–156). Before this major plan for reforms could go forward, the Victoria Charter had to be ratified by all parliaments, in accordance with one of the basic rules of the British constitution, which states that "what touches all should be agreed to by all – *quod omnes tangit ab omnibus comprobetur*" (see Tully 1999: 120).

The ultimate goal of the Victoria Conference was the patriation of the Constitution. The core issue was obviously the amending formula (Martin 1974: 54). Ontario's new premier Bill Davis, who was attending his first conference, was hoping that the issue of the amendment formula would be resolved quickly in order to make room for more important topics such as the division of powers and the revenues available to the provinces. Negotiations were tough. The federal government was nevertheless able to obtain the support of Alberta, British Columbia, and Ontario. In the end Bourassa bowed to pressure from Quebec civil society and refused to sign. Trudeau was prepared to resume work on the file again at a later date, preferring to wait for a more auspicious moment before acting. Davis did his best to act as a mediator between Ottawa and Quebec, but to no avail (Martin 1974). The conference ended in failure.

2.   THE LEADUP TO PATRIATION

The 1970s were defined by profound transformations in Canada's political landscape and a shift in Ontario's position in reaction to Quebec's desire to rethink its relationship with Canada after the November 1976 victory of the Parti Québécois. Rather than review the entire history of federal–provincial tensions in detail, this section will examine the development of Quebec–Ontario relations at a key moment in Canadian history when, a few years later, Quebec was forced to fall back in line following the failed May 1980 referendum.

In his book *Le fédéralisme canadien*, jurist Gil Rémillard relates the history of the negotiations leading up to the patriation of the Constitution. He identifies two phases: the period of the federal–provincial meetings held in the wake of the failed referendum, and the period following the Supreme Court's opinion on the legality of the federal government's patriation resolution (Rémillard 1985: 111). These key events in the history of federal–provincial relations revealed major changes in the Quebec–Ontario dynamic.

Shortly after the May 1980 referendum, Prime Minister Trudeau committed himself to reforming and patriating the Constitution and adapting Canadian federalism to better reflect a changing Canadian society (*ibid.*). Despite some gestures of openness, such as the September 8, 1980 federal–provincial conference, the premiers were convinced that Trudeau was prepared to proceed with the unilateral patriation of the Constitution if negotiations with the provinces failed. It was simply a matter of time.

The thorniest subject of the negotiations was a constitutionally enshrined charter of rights. Seven provinces were firmly opposed to Trudeau's plan. Bill Davis agreed with the principle, but refused to see Ontario become a constitutionally bilingual province. René Lévesque fiercely opposed the idea of a new charter, because Quebec already had its own charter of human rights and freedoms (Rémillard 1985: 115). In order to create some leverage with Ottawa, Quebec minister of intergovernmental affairs Claude Morin drafted a common position for the provinces, which he presented to the premiers for discussion on the last day of the conference. Morin addressed the various points on the agenda, presenting for each one a position that reflected the past positions adopted by the provinces at previous conferences. He included the demands the provinces felt were most important. These propositions were adopted by the premiers as the basis of the provincial position. Trudeau rejected them immediately. The conference ended in failure, and a few days later the federal cabinet announced its intention to unilaterally patriate the Constitution.

Five provinces—British Columbia, Alberta, Manitoba, Newfoundland, and Quebec—agreed to challenge the patriation in their respective Courts of Appeal, and ultimately before the Supreme Court of Canada (*ibid.*). By February 28 of the following year, only two provinces—Ontario and New Brunswick—still supported patriation as envisioned by Trudeau. Quebec and Ontario had chosen their respective sides.

The eight other provinces presented Trudeau with a compromise offer on April 16, 1981, declaring that they would accept patriation without constitutional amendment in exchange for an amending formula. To arrive at this compromise, René Lévesque, who had recently been re-elected despite the unsuccessful 1980 referendum, had to accept certain concessions previously nearly unthinkable for Quebec, including the notion of provincial equality. Under the proposed amending formula, any change to the constitution would have to be approved by the federal government and two-thirds of the provinces, representing at least 50% of Canadians. For changes regarding provincial powers, the provinces would have the right to opt out with full financial compensation. Prime Minister Trudeau deemed this offer by the premiers to be unacceptable. It was yet another deadlock.

Negotiations remained at a standstill until after the Supreme Court had ruled on the legality of Trudeau's patriation resolution. In the end, despite the Supreme Court ruling in his favour, Trudeau did not completely close the door to federal–provincial negotiations (Rémillard 1985: 154). For their part, the eight recalcitrant provinces questioned the legitimacy of patriation, which they felt was contrary to the most elementary democratic principles of a federation. On October 18, the provincial delegations met to touch base and decide how to proceed. The premiers of Ontario and New Brunswick, who disagreed with the rest of the group, quickly left the meeting. The eight other provinces agreed to meet with Trudeau on November 2 for a final round of negotiations. Relations between Quebec and Ontario and Quebec and New Brunswick became severely strained during this period. The strong ties which had formerly bound these three provinces had visibly deteriorated since the mid-1970s.

At the very start of the meeting, Ontario premier William Davis offered to give up his province's veto, and New Brunswick premier Richard Hadfield suggested a charter with two categories of rights: those that were mandatory across the country, and those that required the approval of provincial legislatures. Some of the provinces found the idea interesting, but Quebec, Manitoba, and Alberta were against it. They challenged Trudeau to submit the idea to a referendum.

Premier Davis, still trying to play the role of peacemaker, suggested a compromise. The eight recalcitrant provinces would accept Trudeau's charter if he agreed to their amending formula. However, no consensus emerged. Saskatchewan premier Allan Blakeney accepted the idea of enshrining language rights if it led to a compromise. René Lévesque could sense that the common front between the provinces in opposition was starting to fall apart (Rémillard 1985: 157–158). He immediately struck an agreement with Trudeau to continue constitutional talks for two years and submit the results of these discussions to a Canada-wide referendum. The English provinces categorically rejected the idea of a referendum, arguing that "we have the mandate to govern and the public cares little about these questions" (*ibid.*: 158). The premiers would not forgive Lévesque for his "betrayal," and one by one, they abandoned Quebec. This sounded the death knell of the constitutional negotiations and was, arguably, the very outcome Trudeau had been hoping for, as he finally succeeded in breaking provincial solidarity.

This gave Trudeau the complete freedom to act by aligning himself as needed with Ontario or New Brunswick—two provinces with large francophone populations—or with the poorer provinces, who needed the assistance of the federal government to put in place a wide range of services while balancing their budgets. The issue of patriation was very important to Ottawa because it would allow the capital to reassert the leadership it had lost during the Ontario-led Conference of Tomorrow. That initiative by the Robarts government had had unexpected repercussions and had propelled Quebec to the centre of the constitutional debates of 1968 to 1981. By the end of this period, however, Ontario had redeemed itself in federal government eyes by aligning its policies with the interests of Canadian unity.

CONCLUSION

The study of these two key periods in the history of Canada's constitutional politics reveals a major change in the relations between the governments of Quebec and Ontario. These two members of the federation represent the economic, political, and cultural heart of the country, accounting for nearly 75% of Canada's population. Their leaders have frequently agreed on issues of importance to their residents. In constitutional matters, one cannot help but conclude that Ontario's Robarts government played a major role in ensuring that Quebec was able to remain centre stage in Canadian politics for so long. Robarts remained loyal in his support for Quebec, as revealed by the Task Force on Canadian Unity (1977–1979), known as the Pepin–Robarts Commission (Wallot 2002). The years following the departure of John Robarts from the political stage saw the two provinces drift apart as the government of Ontario realigned its policies with the wishes of the federal government.

The election of David Peterson (1985–1990) constituted a return of sorts to the political vision of John Robarts, but it would be a brief interlude. Peterson's job was made somewhat easier by the Quebec government, which had rethought its constitutional position, reaching out to English Canada at the end of Lévesque's second term by suggesting a *beau risque* with the rest of Canada. When Robert Bourassa's Liberals came to power in December 1985, this new openness set the stage for the Meech Lake adventure (1987–1990) with the support of Ontario. During this new round of constitutional talks, that support remained solid, and the two provinces entered a new era of collaboration.

The next round of constitutional talks on the Charlottetown Accord did not bring Quebec and Ontario any closer together. Since then, relations between the two provinces have remained stable. Their premiers have been more interested in defending the economic interests of their electorate than helping each other in the tug-of-war that originally led to the common front against federal intrusion into their exclusive jurisdictions (health, education, infrastructure). Jean Charest (2003–) and Dalton McGuinty (2003–) have yet to revive the Quebec–Ontario cooperation that characterized the era when Maurice Duplessis and Mitchell Hepburn, and later Daniel Johnson and John Robarts fought as allies to defend provincial rights.

BIBLIOGRAPHY

Bourassa, R. (1995). *Gouverner le Québec*. Montreal: Fides.

Bryden, P. E. (2000). "The Ontario-Quebec Axis. Postwar Strategies in Inter-governmental Strategies." In E.-A. Montigny and L. Chambers (eds.), *Ontario since Confederation: A Reader*. Toronto: University of Toronto Press: 382–408.

Courchene, T., with C. R. Telman (1998). *From Heartland to North American Region State: The Social, Fiscal and Federal Evolution of Ontario*. Toronto: University of Toronto Press.

Gagnon, A.-G. and J. Garcea (1988). "Quebec and the Pursuit of Special Status." In R. D. Olling and M. W. Westmacott (eds.), *Perspectives on Canadian Federalism*. Scarborough: Prentice-Hall: 304–325.

Gagnon, A.-G. and D. Latouche (1991). *Allaire, Bélanger, Campeau et les autres*. Montreal: Québec Amérique.

Gagnon, A.-G. and M. B. Montcalm (1990). *Quebec: Beyond the Quiet Revolution*. Toronto: Nelson Canada.

Hopkins, P. D. (1977). *Daniel Johnson and the Quiet Revolution* (Master's Thesis). Burnaby: Department of Political Science, Simon Fraser University.

Johnson, D. (1967). In *Le Devoir*, November 28: 17.

Martin, J. (1974). *The Role and Place of Ontario in the Canadian Confederation*. Toronto: Ontario Economic Council.

McRoberts, K. (1978). "An Overview of Ontario–Quebec Interprovincial Rela-tions." In *Les relations économiques Québec-Ontario: document de référence et compte rendu du colloque*. Quebec City: École nationale d'administration publique.

McRoberts, K. (1999). *Un pays à refaire. L'échec des politiques constitutionnelles canadiennes*. Montreal: Boréal.

McWhinney, E. (1979). *Quebec and the Constitution 1960-1978*. Toronto: University of Toronto Press.

Montigny, E.-A. and L. Chambers (2000). *Quebec Ontario since Confederation: A Reader*. Toronto: University of Toronto Press.

Morin, C. (1972). *Le pouvoir québécois… en négociation*. Montreal: Boréal Express.

Ontario Advisory Committee on Confederation (1967). *Background Papers and Reports*. Toronto: The Queen's Printer of Ontario.

Rémillard, G. (1985). *Le fédéralisme canadien*, t. II: *Le rapatriement de la Constitution*. Montreal: Québec Amérique.

Roy, J.-L. (1978). *Le choix d'un pays. Le débat constitutionnel Québec-Canada, 1960-1976*. Ottawa: Leméac.

Tully, J. (1999). *Une étrange multiplicité: le constitutionnalisme à une époque de diversité*. Quebec City: Les Presses de l'Université Laval.

Vipond, R. (1991). *Liberty and Community: Canadian Federalism and the Failure of the Constitution*. Albany: State University of New York.

Wallot, J.-P. (ed.) (2002). *Le débat qui n'a pas eu lieu: la commission Pepin-Robarts vingt ans après*. Ottawa: Ottawa University Press.

White, R. (1985). *Ontario 1610-1985. A Political and Economic History*. Toronto: Dundurn.

4. FROM FRENCH CANADIAN SOLIDARITY TO SHATTERED REFERENCES
The Transformation of Québécois and Franco-Ontarian Identities

MICHEL BOCK

The current differentiation between Québécois and Franco-Ontarian identities can sometimes lead even the best-intentioned observer to forget that there was a time, not so long ago, when such a distinction between these two groups would have seemed strange and meaningless. This period, characterized by the French Canadian national project, has posed something of a problem to the collective memory of both Quebec and French-speaking Ontario since the 1960s, when the heady intellectual and political atmosphere of the Quiet Revolution swept aside many of the old convictions and replaced them with new ones. In our resolutely modern age, the traditionalism of the French Canadian national vision engenders a kind of malaise, not only among present-day actors, but also among certain researchers, whose interpretations of Quebec and Franco-Ontarian history tend to significantly underplay the importance of the French Canadian identity, if not ignoring it outright (Bock 2008). Yet as we will see, this traditionalism helped rally French Canadians in Quebec and Ontario behind a common national project and created a solidarity that transcended local, regional, and provincial cleavages for generations.

The nature of this French Canadian project has been the topic of much debate among historians over the last half century. The debate itself reveals the full extent of the social changes that have swept French-speaking Canada and Quebec since the Quiet Revolution.

In the 1950s and 1960s, historians argued that the "economic inferiority" of French Canadians had been caused by the traditionalism of the religious and secular elite, though there were serious differences of opinion as to the origins of the problem (Brunet 1958; Ouellet 1966). In the 1970s and 1980s, a younger generation of historians who had come of age during and immediately after the major reforms of the Quiet Revolution used the newly developed tools of social history to reveal the deep roots of Quebec modernity. As demonstrated by Ronald Rudin (1997), these historians set about presenting Quebec as a "normal" society whose historical experience matched that of other societies across North America and the Western world. Whereas earlier historians saw the traditionalism of French Canadian society as a constraint to be overcome in order for French Canadians to enter the modern age, their successors virtually ignored this traditionalism in favour of a new vision that placed modernity at the very heart of Quebec's historical experience. In both cases, modernity is defined almost entirely in terms of urbanization, industrialization, economic progress, and the rejection of traditionalism. In both cases, the issue of the French Canadian diaspora and its ties to what had long been referred to as "the old province"— an issue closely tied to French Canadian traditionalism—went largely unheeded by researchers, who refocused their analysis on Quebec and its territory (Bock 2004).

Only since the 1990s has a "*nouvelle sensibilité*" (Kelly 2003) arisen among researchers interested in the Quebec/French Canadian national question, largely thanks to a generation of historians and sociologists who were born after the Quiet Revolution and never experienced the so-called "*Grande Noirceur.*" This new generation has sought to escape the confines of the old traditional/modern dichotomy, taking a fresh and perhaps more dispassionate look at French Canadian traditionalism through its cultural, institutional, and religious expressions. This phenomenon has been accompanied by a new wave of intellectual and political history that helped restore a certain respect for the national question after thirty years of disinterest by social historians. This study is rooted in this "*nouvelle sensibilité.*" In the following pages, we will show how the ties that linked Quebec and French-speaking Ontario prior to the Quiet Revolution stemmed from a traditionalist view of the French Canadian national "reference," a concept introduced nearly twenty years ago by Fernand Dumont (1993), who defined it as an overall representation of a national identity founded on a common memory and giving meaning to a social organization as diverse, coherent, and politically autonomous as possible. For the purposes of this study, the Church and the countless institutions in its orbit provided French Canada's social organization with its institutional and political structure, indeed its basic framework, at least until the 1960s (Gould 2003).

This study will be divided into five sections organized along thematic and chronological lines. After a description of the conceptual considerations guiding our approach, the next two sections will examine the conditions that fostered the emergence of a national French Canadian "reference" after the failure of the Lower Canada Rebellions of 1837—a reference that would also come to include the French Canadians who had emigrated to what, after 1867, would become Ontario. The following section will examine the factors that, at the turn of the 20th century, further strengthened the ties of "national" solidarity between French Canadians in Ontario and Quebec, ties indelibly marked by the Regulation 17 crisis—the last major postconfederation school crisis. The last section will look at how this French Canadian reference broke down after the Second World War, as well as how it has since been reformulated. These processes culminated at the time of the Quiet Revolution, when the social structuring role played by the Church for over a century was largely taken over by the state in both Quebec and French-speaking Ontario. As a result, the solidarity of the past was questioned, and new identities emerged on both sides.

I.   BASIC CONCEPTS

In his seminal work, *Genèse de la société québécoise*, which explores the emergence of the national consciousness of French-speaking Quebec, Fernand Dumont proposes three theoretical models of human "gathering" or "grouping"—"belonging," "integration," and "reference" (1993: 337–352). The first model designates a type of gathering in which relations are essentially personal, with members staying in direct contact without any intermediary. This contact maintains the group as an object (e.g., a sports team, a small village). The second model is based on an organization structured in a more complex manner and within which roles and status are attributed in a more formal way. Dumont offers the example of a company whose essentially interchangeable members are not identified on a personal level, but rather according to their role and status. The reference group, or nation, is a form of organization that is more difficult to define but no less real. Dumont explores how it can be possible for two individuals unaware of each other's existence, living far apart in very different environments, to claim the same membership in an organization as abstract as a nation? How are they aware of belonging to the same national collectivity, and on what do they base their shared agreement as to what distinguishes them from neighbouring nations? The answer lies in the concept of "reference," which Dumont defines as a symbolic representation of society that transcends the life experiences of each member on an empirical level. The nation is there-fore more than the simple sum of individual aspirations competing in social space. Through the construction of a "reference" it manages, or at least attempts, to convince its members of its own existence as a collective subject.

It would be a mistake, therefore, to see a reference as nothing more than a reflection of the "primary" cultural reality of its members, i.e., their customs or ethnic characteristics. On the contrary, it operates on a different level, that of the national "consciousness," and requires those same members to voluntarily subscribe to it in a gesture that is essentially political in nature. A reference is not a "natural" feature of the social environment. It is the result of a collective "imaginary" construct. According to Dumont, a reader of Durkheim, this process stems from ideology, historiography, and literature. Here we find that Dumont's ideas share a commonality with the classic work of Benedict Anderson (1983). Creation of the reference occurs essentially in the discursive sphere. The reference penetrates the consciousness of indi-viduals and secures their allegiance by way or through the mediation of an institutional structure that collectively unites them and instils in them a desire to be *of* the nation and to share in its imaginary world, its traditions, and its *memories*, i.e., the story of its birth, development, and destiny. In the Western world over the last two centuries, one of the main institutions generating an awareness of the nation has been, of course, the school system. Before the introduction of social constructivist teaching methods, schools strived to "raise" children up to a supposedly superior cultural condition that was both higher and more profound, while instilling a sense of belonging to a collective *national* entity that transcended the boundaries of their initial (or pri-mary) *community* of belonging. Its mission was to level or homogenize local cultural differences, which were seen as obstacles to the creation of a nation as a collective subject (Thériault 2007). By constructing a reference incarnating this national consciousness, it was hoped that children would be emancipated and extirpated from the limits of the *local* so that they could consider themselves as an integral part of the collective subject, the nation, thereby attaining the *universal*.

Dumont freely recognizes that his concept of "reference" is essen-tially an abstract construction, a symbolic reality stemming from dis-course. Nevertheless, his interpretation of the national question stands in sharp contrast to certain others, like that of Marxist historian Eric Hobsbawm, who famously argued that tradition is nothing more than an "invention" by the elite for the sole purpose of supplanting class consciousness with national consciousness in the minds of the masses and the working class in order to distract them from the fundamental social and material inequalities of society (Hobsbawm 1990; Hobsbawm and Ranger 1983). Dumont does not see the national reference as a weapon used by the bourgeoisie to mask or legitimize the socio-economic alienation of the proletariat. He sees it instead as a powerful creator of solidarity insofar as it has the ability to convince perfect strangers that they share a common destiny. This conviction can lead to the type of collective action which, by definition, is the cornerstone of any societal project worthy of the name:

> An individual either chooses to take refuge in the cocoon of private life, believing that it represents freedom, and thus abandons the task of interpreting history to anonymous agents, or he chooses to contribute to the creation of a *habitable* reference by other means than outdated customs. In doing so, he becomes what had been predicted: a citizen of a country, an agent of a history, and a participant in the collective imagination (Dumont 1993: 352).

These preliminary observations on Dumont's reference group model help illustrate how the rise of the idea of nation, which started in the 18th century in the West, should not be disassociated from modernity, or even democracy (Thériault 2002). Dumont's ideas also challenge the validity of the Manichean opposition between the concepts of "civic" and "ethnic" nationalism, which continue to frame the debate over the national question in Quebec today. Membership in a nation as defined by Dumont is not based on blood or "ethnicity," contrary to what some researchers and intellectuals have suggested (Bouchard 1999). Rather, one wilfully chooses to become a member of the nation by adopting its memory and participating in its supporting institutions. Again, this shared memory gives meaning to a historic experience we tell ourselves is unique and of sufficient value to extend through collective mobilisation. This concept echoes Renan's definition of the nation as a "daily plebiscite," while at the same time rejecting the limits of the "nation as contract," which reduces society to nothing more than a space in which individual aspirations are perpetually negotiated. The nation is therefore much more than a compromise. It is both a heritage and a project.

2. THE CREATION OF THE FRENCH CANADIAN NATIONAL PROJECT

The rise of French Canada as a national project or "reference group" is closely linked to the troubled context of the Lower Canada Rebellions of 1837 and the coming into effect of the 1841 *Act of Union*. It was from this point on that a truly "French Canadian reference" developed, largely in reaction to the ideology of the Patriotes of the 1830s, which has also been the subject of an interesting historical debate in recent decades. For example, in the 1960s, Fernand Ouellet argued that Louis-Joseph Papineau and the Parti Patriote were proponents of a backwards ideology and an Old Regime mentality (Ouellet 1968). In the early 1990s, Allan Greer (1997) was still arguing that this insurrection movement was more like a traditional *jacquerie* than an attempt at revolution in the modern political sense. Recently, however, new interpretations of the Rebellions have come to view these events as an authentic revolutionary phenomenon inspired by political liberalism (Lamonde 2000; Bellavance 2004) or American republicanism (Bouchard 2001; Harvey 2005). According to both interpretations, the Patriote ideology did not conceive of Lower Canadian society as a durable phenomenon stemming from tradition or rooted in common memory. For Gérard Bouchard, Yvan Lamonde, and Louis-Georges Harvey, the Patriote enterprise of the 1830s was the Lower Canadian manifestation of the fundamental principle of Americanism, which rejected European traditions and colonialism as chains from which the societies of the New World—where everything would begin anew—had to free themselves. In the political consciousness of Lower Canada, the past had no intrinsic value. On the contrary, it was seen as a burden to be thrown off and perhaps even forgotten entirely in order to fully embrace universal truths. In other words, this project rejected the key components of reference grouping—the desire to prolong a common history and the promotion of the elements that made it unique and distinct from all other collective historical experiences.

However, the failure of the Patriotes and their liberal/republican aspirations had a major impact on the intellectual and political landscape of Lower Canada. In an effort to snuff out the remaining embers of the Lower Canada insurrection movement, the British colonial authorities turned to the famous Durham Report. Convinced that the insurrection was an ethnic conflict rather than a struggle for democracy, republicanism, or an end to colonialism, Lord Durham recommended uniting Upper and Lower Canadas in order to make the *Canadiens* (i.e., French Canadians) a minority, and thereby ensure their political, linguistic, and cultural assimilation into British society. Durham insisted that this assimilation was not a form of reprisal. On the contrary, the English aristocrat was convinced that the best thing for French Canadians was to become wholly British in order to avoid cultural and socioeconomic isolation on a continent that History had irrefutably destined for Anglo-Saxon hegemony. In a now infamous phrase, he described the French Canadians as "a people with no history and no literature." Durham's words have raised the ire of generations of intellectuals and polemists, but it must be said that they were not entirely inaccurate. What he really had identified was the absence of an authentic *Canadien* "reference." Indeed, at the time of the rebellions, there was very little in the way of French Canadian history writing or literature (Dumont 1993; Ducharme 2006). Without a "reference," without a tradition of literature and historiography, without *memory*, any claim to nationhood by French Canadians was tenuous at best. Durham concluded that, having been cut off from the traditions of France since the Conquest, they must either embrace the British traditions (i.e., "reference") or resign themselves to marginalization and mediocrity.

There was, however, a third option available to the French Canadians. They could construct their own tradition, an authentic national reference stemming from a collective desire to construct their own society (Thériault 2007) on the North American continent. Shortly after the Union, numerous writers set to work, laying the foundations of a French Canadian reference. Chief among them was historian and poet François-Xavier Garneau (1809–1866), widely considered the greatest French Canadian writer of the 19th century. The publication of his monumental *Histoire du Canada depuis sa découverte jusqu'à nos jours* in four volumes between 1845 and 1852 earned him the title of French Canada's first "national historian." Piqued by Durham's stinging remarks, Garneau diligently set about the task of providing the complete story of the birth and development of the French Canadian nation, which he presented as a perpetual struggle for survival. His message was clear: the national experience of French Canada was worth pursuing and protecting from the assimilationist intentions of Durham and the British oligarchy (Ducharme 2006; Gasbarrone 2002).

Writers such as Rameau de Saint-Père, Faillon, Casgrain, Fréchette, and Gérin-Lajoie followed in Garneau's footsteps. While their respective bodies of work differed, each contributed to defining the new reference (Beaudoin 1989; Biron *et al.* 2007). French Canadians were henceforth represented as a people who had come into being with the founding of New France—the inheritors of the providential mission of spreading the Catholic faith and French civilization in America. Of course, the 19th century provided fertile ground for all sorts of messianic ideologies, even in societies generally associated with modernity, like France, Great Britain, and the United States. French Canada would be no exception. At the same time, there was an undeniably powerful conservative and traditionalist shift (in the philosophical sense) on the part of intellectuals during this period. Despite the persistence of a minority liberal undercurrent, this shift towards traditionalism contributed to the process of institutional clericalization seen in French Canada after the Union of 1841 (Dumont 1993; Lamonde 2000; Perin 2008). The "religious awakening" of the 1840s and 1850s was made possible by a remarkable increase in the ranks of the clergy, which was due in part to recruitment from Europe. For decades, European clergy members had been barred from settling in the province, but the colonial authorities lifted this ban, seeing in the Church an effective force for neutralizing whatever revolutionary impulses might linger from the 1837 events (Sylvain and Voisine 1984). Moreover, many of these clergymen were recruited from the most ultramontane and counter-revolutionary corners of Europe, which also played a large role in curbing revolutionary zeal throughout French Canada after 1841.

The expansion of the clergy and the *modus vivendi* that the Church arrived at with the French Canadian political class, dominated at first by the reformers until the "Bleus" took over, allowed the Church to consolidate its influence over much of the social sphere, including basic and higher education, hospital care, charities, orphanages, and part of the press, in addition, of course, to a rapidly growing network of dioceses and parishes. This institutional structure supported and spread the French Canadian reference which, in turn, gave it meaning and justified its expansion. The national reference eventually became inextricably linked to the religious reference, to the point where there was almost no differentiation, leading some researchers to conclude that though there has never been a French Canadian nation-state, there had been a "nation-church" which successfully structured and legitimized French Canadian social organization for over as century (Gould 2003; Warren 2007).

3. QUEBEC, ONTARIO, AND FRENCH CANADIAN EMIGRATION

The French Canadian nation as conceived of after 1841 did indeed have borders, but they were not those of Lower Canada or, later, Quebec. Instead, they corresponded to the more "virtual" boundaries of the French Canadian institutional structure, the backbone of which was the Catholic Church. This "church-nation" extended far beyond the St. Lawrence Valley and was quick to follow and steer the flow of migrants, if not at times precede them outright. In the mid-nineteenth century, a massive wave of emigration swept Lower Canada. Exceptional population growth coupled with an underdeveloped manufacturing sector resulted in a massive outflow of half a million French Canadians, a movement that ended only with the Great Depression of the 1930s (Roby 1990; Lavoie 1973; Frenette 1998; Gervais 1993). The majority of these emigrants swelled the growing population of the industrial cities of New England, where the textile industry's appetite for unskilled labour seemed bottomless. The intellectual and clerical elite of Lower Canada certainly did not rejoice at this emigration. On the contrary, they first reacted with contempt, dismissing those who left as rabble abandoning the motherland to be swallowed up in the maw of the great American behemoth, traitors to the agricultural and spiritual vocation of their forefathers (Roby 1987). There was more to this reaction, however, than a simple rejection of modernity. It also reflected a genuine defence of the French Canadian "reference," which the elite saw—and understandably so—as being threatened by the forces of North American industrialization, largely dominated by Anglo-Saxon capital.

This reaction would quickly be tempered, however, by the strength and cultural vitality of the "Little Canadas" springing up all across New England. Since this vitality obviously stemmed from the French Canadian institutions that these new Franco-Americans had recreated in their adopted country, the French Canadian elite adjusted its take and began to see emigrants as "missionaries" rather than "corrupt strays." Emigrants were answering the apostolic vocation that Providence had bequeathed to the French Canadian nation—to keep alive the flames of the Catholic faith and "French" civilization (Roby 1987).

Given a choice, however, the elite preferred to see French Canadian émigrés relocate to Ontario or the Western provinces after 1867 (Lalonde 1979). Throughout the 19th century, French Canadian colonization of Ontario progressed steadily, thanks in large part to the famous "colonizer priests," who wanted to see the province become a link in the human chain connecting Quebec to French-speaking Manitoba (Dussault 1983; Coulombe 1998; Bernard 1988). In 1842 the French Canadian population of Upper Canada was 14,000. Thirty years later, there were 75,000 French Canadians in Ontario, and by 1911, that number would rise to 202,000 (Gervais 1993: 51, 100). The common driving force behind these migratory movements was economics. Migrants were drawn to Ontario by agriculture, mining and forestry, or manufacturing depending on the economic structure of the three main regions in question (the south, east, and northeast). As in New England, the institutional structure of French Canada moved along with them to provide a societal framework for the population and maintain its connection to the French Canadian reference. This made Ottawa Ontario's main French Canadian center, on par with Montreal and Quebec City as one of French Canada's leading cultural, intellectual, and political metropolises. Originally founded as a lumber camp called Bytown in 1826, Ottawa attracted the Missionary Oblates of Mary Immaculate in 1844, only three years after they had arrived to

Montreal. They founded the diocese of Ottawa in 1847, Bytown College (which would later become the University of Ottawa) the following year, dozens of parishes, and many other institutions. The congregation of the Grey Sisters of the Cross joined the Oblates in Ottawa in 1845 and proceeded to expand the network of French Canadian "national" institutions (e.g., schools, hospitals, boarding schools, orphanages). But it was the designation of Ottawa as the capital of the United Province of Canada in 1857 and, ten years later, of the new Canadian Confederation, that allowed for the emergence of a secular elite made up of politicians, civil servants, and journalists. In fact, Upper Canada's first French language newspaper, *Le Progrès*, was founded in 1858. Some forty more would spring up across the province over the next half century (Gervais 1993: 62). This new secular elite would in turn found numerous associations in Ottawa, including the third chapter of the Saint-Jean-Baptiste Society in 1851 (after Montreal in 1834 and Quebec City in 1842), Institut canadien-français d'Ottawa in 1852, and Union Saint-Joseph in 1863, just to name a few. They would lay the foundation for a vibrant and diverse literary, cultural, and intellectual community (Gervais and Bock 2004).

Elsewhere in the province, French Canadian ecclesiastic institutions pursued their efforts. The Jesuits, for example, who had been allowed to return by the British authorities after the Rebellions, founded parishes in several communities, as well as classical colleges in Windsor (1857) and Sudbury (1913). Numerous women's religious orders rounded out the portrait to make French Canada a concrete social reality with both its own institutional structure and identity (Choquette 1984; Savard 1993). The growth of the French Canadian population in Ontario (and elsewhere), the role of clerical (or at least Catholic) institutions, and the emergence of a secular elite educated primarily in Church institutions lent considerable credence to the notion that the French Canadians were a people without literal borders, defined primarily not by a shared territory, but by common traditions. By this we mean a shared adherence to a distinct collective memory, or in other words, a national reference relatively independent of other processes of *nation-building* at work in the social environment.

4.   THE COMPACT THEORY OF CONFEDERATION AND THE REGULATION 17 CRISIS

During the negotiations in the Parliament of Westminster surrounding the adoption of the *British North America (BNA) Act*, none of the architects of the legislation were concerned about protecting the cultural and language rights of the French Canadian and Acadian minorities outside the newly created province of Quebec. In fact, aside from a small minority of opponents associated mainly with the Parti rouge and the Institut canadien de Montréal, the intellectual, political, and religious elite of Lower Canada was in favour of Confederation and rejoiced at the idea that Quebec would regain, if not full independence, at least a large part of the political autonomy it had lost in 1841 (Bellavance 1992; Lamonde 2000). At most, the "Fathers of Confederation" wanted to ensure the protection of the educational rights of *religious* minorities, without any consideration for language. Section 93 of the *BNA Act* stipulated that Protestants in Quebec and Catholics in other provinces could have their children educated in "separate" schools. In essence, they tended to see Confederation as a pact between contracting provinces that were considered sovereign in their respective jurisdictions as defined by the new constitution. This at least appeared to be the consensus among the Grits and, to a lesser extent, the Bleus. The Tories however, had much more centralist conception of the federal government (Romney 1999).

Towards the end of the nineteenth century, however, a new interpretation made significant headway among intellectuals and certain politicians in French Canada. According to this new interpretation, the *BNA Act* was not a pact between a group of autonomous provinces, but between "two founding peoples" (Silver 1982). This phenomenon was due to the emergence of the French Canadian nationalist movement, which became a powerful public voice in Quebec in the aftermath of the hanging of Métis leader Louis Riel in 1885 and the Manitoba schools crisis, which was triggered when the provincial government abolished funding for separate (and French) schools in 1890. This "discovery," as it were, of Canada's French Catholic minorities helped cement the union between the new French Canadian nationalism and the old messianic and traditionalist ideology that had spread since the 1840s. As one of Canada's "two founding peoples," French Canadians had the right to reside anywhere in the country without having to renounce their identity or their cultural, religious, or language rights. However, their rights as founders were conferred not so much by virtue of their contribution to the 1867 "pact," but by their long-standing presence in America and the missionary work they had undertaken since the time of their arrival at the dawn of the French Regime (Bock 2008). The idea of founding peoples may not have carried much legal or constitutional weight, but politically, it was extremely powerful. The idea that Canada had been founded by two distinct nations was a powerful rhetorical weapon in the hands of nationalists, who could now simultaneously rally to the defence of Quebec's provincial autonomy within the federation and of French Canadian minorities struggling against the assimilation tactics of the Anglo-Protestant majority. From the late nineteenth to the mid-twentieth century, numerous nationalist activists and intellectuals would rank the defence of minorities as one of the main responsibilities of Quebec. Their position was consistent with their organic and cultural vision of a French Canadian nation for whom the "old province" represented the "homeland" or epicentre.

While there were many well-known French Canadian national-ist leaders, two in particular are worth mentioning— politician Henri Bourassa (1868–1952) and priest and historian Lionel Groulx (1878–1967). The first founded the newspaper *Le Devoir* in Montreal in 1910, using it from the outset to support causes such as the nationalist move-ment and the defence of French Canadian minorities outside Quebec. The second was appointed as the first chair of Canadian history at Université Laval's Montreal campus in 1915. In 1920, he became the head of the monthly publication *L'Action française*, rocketing to the forefront of the nationalist movement and replacing Bourassa himself as its leading voice. Groulx was without a doubt the most visible and most influential nationalist of the first half of the 20th century and he would have a major influence on generations of intellectuals. He spent his long career as a historian and a polemist developing a philosoph-ically traditionalist definition of French Canadian national identity and elaborating, better than anyone had done before him, the idea of "two founding peoples" of Canada, or in other words the country's binational character (Bock 2004). His nationalist convictions natur-ally led him to work to foster closer ties between Quebec and North America's scattered French Canadian minority communities, whose presence he saw as a testament to the ancestral mission of the French Canadian nation and as a form of living memory.

Of all the minority communities on the continent, the Franco-Ontarians were by far the ones to whom Canon Groulx paid the most attention. Franco-Ontarians held a unique position in Groulx's mind not only because of the geographic proximity of Canada's two cen-tral provinces, but also because of the close relations he personally maintained with members of French-speaking Ontario's nationalist elite. When, in 1912, the Ontario government adopted the infam-ous Regulation 17 prohibiting the use of French in the province's so-called "bilingual" schools, the French Canadian minority enjoyed unfailing support from Groulx, who repeatedly spoke in support of the Franco-Ontarian resistance movement throughout the crisis and worked tirelessly to encourage his nationalist allies to do the same. The school conflict is sometimes presented in both the historiography and collective memory of French-speaking Ontario as the founding event of a Franco-Ontarian identity distinct from that of Quebec or French Canada (Grisé 1982; Dionne 1995). This interpretation ignores the fact that Regulation 17 actually sparked an unprecedented outpouring of solidarity among French Canadians in Ontario and Quebec (Savard 1993; Gervais 1996; Bock 2004), testimony to their deep collective attachment to a national reference powerful enough to incite them to action and strengthen their ties. The Regulation 17 incident, like the Manitoba school crisis of 1890 and other events, took on truly "national" proportions in the French Canadian sense of the term. An attack against Franco-Ontarians became an attack against the entire French Canadian nation. From this point of view, Quebec, as homeland of the nation, owed a duty of solidarity to its "brothers" in Ontario. Failure to fulfill this duty meant risking the spread of national "apostasy" to Quebec itself. The campaign in support of the Franco-Ontarian cause orchestrated by the nationalists was very successful. It kept the school crisis in the forefront as a major political issue for a number of years, so much so that Quebec premier Louis-Alexandre Taschereau agreed to discuss it with his Ontario counterpart Howard Ferguson in an attempt to persuade him to change his government's policy. Eager to shore up Quebec's support in its undeclared war against the federal government over the issue of increased political autonomy, Ferguson agreed (Gervais 1996). In 1927 Ontario abolished Regulation 17, bringing the crisis to an end.

5. QUEBEC, FRENCH-SPEAKING ONTARIO, AND THE REDEFINITION OF THE FRENCH CANADIAN REFERENCE

The school conflict highlighted the need for a more coordinated effort on the part of the numerous French Canadian associations active within the various Canadian provinces. By the 1930s, Association catholique de la jeunesse canadienne-française, established with the help of Lionel Groulx himself at the turn of the twentieth century, had founded chapters across Quebec and Ontario to instill in young people a sense of belonging to a larger whole and to overcome regional divisions and the isolation facing many communities. In 1926 the nationalist elite in Ottawa took an additional step by founding Ordre de Jacques-Cartier. This secret society managed to infiltrate the main components of the vast network of French Canadian (and even Franco-American) institutions and associations with the explicit goal of influencing them through the promotion of its own nationalist and traditionalist ideology (Robillard 2009). In the 1930s and 1940s, other organizations were founded to strengthen ties between Quebec and French Canadian minorities. Franco-Ontarians played a major role in the establishment of these organizations, which included Comité permanent de la survivance française (1937), Mouvement Richelieu (1945), Association canadienne d'éducation de langue française (1948), and Conseil de la vie française en Amérique (1952) (Savard 1993). This fast-growing associative network in turn nurtured the French Canadian reference and added even more substance to the idea of a French Canada founded more on shared tradition than on a clearly defined territory.

This conception of the French Canadian identity would not survive the twentieth century, however. By the end of the 1930s, cracks had begun to appear in the conceptual foundations of this idea, which had taken decades to build. On one hand, many of the younger nationalists were arguing that Quebec should abandon the French Canadian minorities and demand full political independence. At the same time, the French Canadian episcopacy took the controversial decision of prohibiting the Specialized Catholic Action movement (e.g., Jeunesse ouvrière catholique, Jeunesse agricole catholique, Jeunesse indépendante catholique, etc.) from promoting nationalism on the grounds that Catholicism was universal by definition and should transcend secular matters by staying away from politics. Nationalists from the Groulx camp were vigorously opposed to this attempt to dissociate what in their view was indissociable—the spiritual and cultural dimensions of French Canada's national identity—but to no avail (Bock 2009). It was after the Second World War, however, that the French Canadian reference, as long conceived, came in for its most virulent criticism, one that would ultimately lead to its demise with the onset of the Quiet Revolution of the 1960s. In the postwar era, as the West entered an era of unprecedented economic progress spurred by the growth of the secondary and tertiary sectors, a new generation of nationalist intellectuals took aim at French Canadian traditionalism. Their final verdict was damning. The traditionalists were found guilty of abandoning Quebec's economic development to Anglo-Saxon capital and of spreading compensatory "myths" about the "providential mission" of the French Canadian nation and the spiritual reconquest of the continent. Criticism of French Canadian traditionalism and messianism led neo-nationalist intellectuals to call on the Quebec state to become an agent of economic development so that French Canadians could take their rightful place in the economy of their own province (Behiels 1985; Bock 2004). By presenting the Quebec state as the only real hope for the French Canadian nation, these young reformist intellectuals echoed the Keynesian themes popular throughout the Western world since the 1930s but vigorously resisted by the Union nationale government of Maurice Duplessis (1936–1939, 1944–1959). In this new nationalist cosmology, French Canadian minorities, deprived of the potential benefits of the Quebec state, appeared to be doomed to slow and painful extinction (Martel 2000).

French Canadian traditionalism was also the target of attacks by a group of anti-nationalist intellectuals centered around the journal *Cité libre*, founded in 1950 by Pierre Elliott Trudeau and Gérard Pelletier. Inspired largely by the ideas of French personalism, which encouraged laypeople to live a more authentic spiritual experience by empowering themselves within both the Church and society at large, the "*cité-libristes*" vigorously denounced what they saw as the archaism and religiosity of traditional French Canadian Catholicism as well as the authoritarianism of a certain sector of the clergy on the grounds that these were obstacles to reaching one's full personal potential as a believer and a citizen (Meunier and Warren 2002; Gauvreau 2005). The work of the Vatican II Council (1962–1965) would soon reveal that the personalist philosophy had permeated even the highest level of the international ecclesiastical hierarchy, prompting the Church to subsequently limit its actions to the spiritual and pastoral spheres, essentially leaving secular matters to civil society (Meunier 2007). The combined effects of these internal and external factors seriously diminished the role of the Catholic Church as a fundamental institution of French Canadian society. This phenomenon is what truly lies at the heart of the Quiet Revolution, which essentially constituted a "transfer" of the Church's works and societal structuring role to the state, replacing the French Canadian nation-church with the Quebec nation-state (Gould 2003).

It was inevitable that this structural change would cause a redefinition of the French Canadian reference. As the focus shifted to Quebec, French Canadian minority communities outside the province's borders were left out in the cold. The erosion or transformation of the French Canadian national reference effectively sounded a death knell for the national solidarity that had existed till then, as symbolized by two key events. In 1965, Ordre de Jacques-Cartier self-destructed over a conflict between its Quebec members and the leadership in Ottawa. Then came the Estates General of French Canada in Montreal, which drew hundreds of delegates from across the country between 1966 and 1969 to debate the future of the French Canadian nation against the agitated backdrop of the Quiet Revolution. When a wave of *indépendantiste* sentiment swept over almost the entire Quebec delegation, Franco-Ontarian representatives walked out, boycotting the 1969 proceedings and declaring the French Canadian national project officially dead (Martel 1997; Gervais 2003). These events were not taken lightly. For Franco-Ontarians, the split with Quebec was traumatic. The Church had lost its influence as a secular institutional force, and the attitude of the *"vieille province"* now seemed reduced to one of disquieting indifference. The future seemed quite uncertain.

Fortunately, or so it seemed at first, a wind of change was blowing through political circles in English Canada, which had been thrown completely off balance by Quebec's independence movement. Franco-Ontarians could now count on provincial and federal government support for help in strengthening their institutional structures. The province created new institutions in the vital fields of education and culture and the federal government adopted the 1969 *Official Languages Act*, under which it would provide millions of dollars to the associations and institutions of "official language" minority groups (Carrière 1993). In that sense, the state replaced the Church for Franco-Ontarians as well. However, their minority status made them more vulnerable, leaving them largely dependent—with the exception of the educational rights enshrined in Section 23 of the *Canadian Charter of Rights and Freedoms* in 1982 (Behiels 2005)—on the unpredictable turn of political events and the good will of politicians. Furthermore, the logic behind the Trudeau government's new language policies did not clearly recognize the *national* and societal duality of Canada (i.e., the theory of two founding peoples). According to Trudeau's vision, the French language was in no way conceived as part of an autonomous national historic community with its own social organization and shared common memory. Instead, it was given meaning through bilingualism, which was transformed by the magic stroke of the lawmaker's pen into the common heritage of all Canadians. Indeed, the federal government went to great effort to convince Canadian anglophones to recognize their "Canadian-ness" by enrolling their children in French immersion schools, which it heavily subsidized (Hayday 2005). In keeping with this idea, the federal government also unequivocally rejected the notion of biculturalism and national duality in favour of a multiculturalist policy geared towards ensuring Canadian social unity (Guindon 1993).

Federal intervention did indeed make huge contributions to the cultural vibrancy of Franco-Ontarians in the 1970s and 1980s. Nevertheless, Franco-Ontarian leaders continued to reject the reasoning behind official bilingualism and multiculturalism and to demand official recognition of not only the French language, but also of the society (i.e., grouping by reference) that nourished it and drew on it for its social cohesion (Savard 2008). The fear was that, by refusing to give Franco-Ontarians (and the rest of French Canada) "national" minority status, they would be reduced, under multiculturalism, to a simple ethnic or linguistic minority "like any other."

CONCLUSION

Historical research into the identity representations of Franco-Ontarians and their ties to Quebec after the "fracturing" of French Canada in the 1960s is still in its infancy.[1] However, sociology has revealed the emergence, among a certain segment of Franco-Ontarian youth, of a sort of cultural "hybridity" based on bilingual identity (Heller 2004; Gérin-Lajoie 2004; Dallaire 2004). Some believe this situation to be the partial result of the phenomenon of assimilation gnawing away at French-speaking Ontario (Bernard 1994), but it is also evidence of the challenges Franco-Ontarians face in maintaining the French Canadian reference without the support of the social organization that Church institutions had provided for centuries. In the wake of the Quiet Revolution, while French-speaking Quebec was gearing its national aspirations towards greater political autonomy, federal government language policies may have been among the factors contributing to the denationalization of Franco-Ontarian and French Canadian identity (Bock 2010). By making bilingualism the cornerstone of the symbolic recasting of Canada (Igartua 2006), Canadian politicians were in effect legitimizing the hybridity and "bilingualism" of the Franco-Ontarian identity. Could the increased structural integration of the Franco-Ontarian community into overall Canadian society since the 1960s have resulted in its "symbolic" integration as well, i.e., partial or total abandonment of the French Canadian national reference in exchange for membership in a new bilingual and multicultural "Canadian" reference? This hypothesis, which sheds new light on the many struggles of Franco-Ontarian leaders for greater political autonomy over the years (Cardinal 2008; Foucher 2008; Poirier 2008), deserves further investigation. Since the 19th century, French-speaking Ontario has demanded and justified the expansion of its institutional space based on the conviction that, along with Quebec, it was part of a comprehensive, autonomous, and self-referential society—French Canada. In the current context, the future may not seem so certain.

---

1. See, however, Anne-Andrée Denault (2008), who has studied the positions of Quebec's political parties towards minority francophone communities since the 1970s. In recent years the Quebec government has taken concrete measures to attempt to rebuild ties with minority francophone communities. These measures include the adoption of the Politique en matière de francophonie canadienne (2006) and the creation of the Centre de la francophonie des Amériques, which was officially opened in 2008.

BIBLIOGRAPHY

Anderson, B. (1983). *Imagined Communities. Reflections on the Origin and Spread of Nationalism*. London: Verso.

Beaudoin, R. (1989). *Naissance d'une littérature. Essai sur le messianisme et les débuts de la littérature canadienne-française (1850-1890)*. Montreal: Boréal.

Behiels, M. (1985). *Prelude to Quebec's Quiet Revolution. Liberalism versus Neo-nationalism, 1945-1960*. Kingston and Montreal: McGill-Queen's University Press.

Behiels, M. (2005). *La francophonie canadienne. Renouveau constitutionnel et gouvernance scolaire*. Ottawa: Les Presses de l'Université d'Ottawa.

Bellavance, M. (1992). *Le Québec et la Confédération: un choix libre? Le clergé et la constitution de 1867*. Quebec City: Septentrion.

Bellavance, M. (2004). *Le Québec au siècle des nationalités. Essai d'histoire comparée*. Montreal: VLB.

Bernard, R. (1988). *De Québécois à Ontarois. La communauté franco-ontarienne*. Hearst: Le Nordir.

Bernard, R. (1994). "Du social à l'individuel: naissance d'une identité bilingue." In Jocelyn Létourneau (ed.), *La question identitaire au Canada francophone: récits, parcours, enjeux et hors-lieux*. Quebec City: Les Presses de l'Université Laval: 155–163.

Biron, M., F. Dumont, and É. Nardout-Lafarge, with M.-E. Lapointe (2007). *Histoire de la littérature québécoise*. Montreal: Boréal.

Bock, M. (2004). *Quand la nation débordait les frontières. Les minorités françaises dans la pensée de Lionel Groulx*. Montreal: Hurtubise HMH.

Bock, M. (2008). "Se souvenir et oublier: la mémoire du Canada français, hier et aujourd'hui." In J. Y. Thériault, A. Gilbert, and L. Cardinal (eds.), *L'espace francophone en milieu minoritaire au Canada. Nouveaux enjeux, nouvelles mobilisations*. Montreal: Fides: 161–203.

Bock, M. (2009). "Apogée et déclin du projet national groulxiste: quelques réflexions autour de *Directives* (1937)." In Y. Lamonde and D. Saint-Jacques (eds.), *1937: un tournant culturel*. Quebec City: Les Presses de l'Université Laval: 27–38.

Bock, M. (2010). "Quelle histoire nationale pour les minorités canadiennes-françaises?" In É. Bédard, S. Cantin, and D. Lefeuvre (eds.), *L'histoire nationale en débat. Regards croisés sur la France et le Québec*. Paris: Riveneuve: 115–133.

Bouchard, G. (1999). *La nation québécoise au futur et au présent*. Montreal: VLB.

Bouchard, G. (2001). *Genèse des nations et cultures du Nouveau Monde. Essai d'histoire comparée*. Montreal: Boréal.

Brunet, M. (1958). "Trois dominantes de la pensée canadienne-française: l'agriculturisme, l'anti-étatisme et le messianisme." In *La présence anglaise et les Canadiens*. Montreal: Beauchemin: 112–166.

Cardinal, L. (2008). "Les minorités francophones hors Québec et la vie politique au Canada: comment combler le déficit démocratique?" In J. Y. Thériault, A. Gilbert, and L. Cardinal (eds.), *L'espace francophone en milieu minoritaire au Canada. Nouveaux enjeux, nouvelles mobilisations*. Montreal: Fides: 385–429.

Carrière, F. (1993). "La métamorphose de la communauté franco-ontarienne, 1960-1985". In C. Jaenen (ed.), *Les Franco-Ontariens*. Ottawa: Les Presses de l'Université d'Ottawa: 305–340.

Choquette, R. (1984). *L'Église catholique dans l'Ontario français du dix-neuvième siècle*. Ottawa: Les Presses de l'Université d'Ottawa.

Coulombe, D. (1998). *Coloniser et enseigner. Le rôle du clergé et la contribution des Sœurs de Notre-Dame du Perpétuel Secours à Hearst, 1971–1942*. Ottawa: Le Nordir.

Dallaire, C. (2004). *"Fier de qui on est... nous sommes francophones!* L'identité des jeunes aux Jeux franco-ontariens." *Francophonies d'Amérique*, no. 18: 127–147.

Denault, A.-A. (2008). "Abandon ou solidarité? Les positions des partis politiques du Québec à l'égard des communautés francophones de 1970 à 2007." In J. Y. Thériault, A. Gilbert, and L. Cardinal (eds.), *L'espace francophone en milieu minoritaire. Nouveaux enjeux, nouvelles mobilisations*. Montreal: Fides: 431–462.

Dionne, R. (1995). "1910. Une première prise de parole collective en Ontario français." *Cahiers Charlevoix*, no. 1: 15–25.

Ducharme, M. (2006). "Se souvenir de demain: réflexions sur l'édification des mémoires collectives au Canada-Uni." *Mens. Revue d'histoire intellectuelle de l'Amérique française*, vol. 7, no. 1: 9–46.

Dumont, F. (1993). *Genèse de la société québécoise*. Montreal: Boréal.

Dussault, G. (1983). *Le Curé Labelle. Messianisme, utopie et colonisation au Québec, 1850–1900*. Montreal: Hurtubise HMH.

Foucher, P. (2008). "Droits et lois linguistiques: le droit au service du Canada français." In J. Y. Thériault, A. Gilbert, and L. Cardinal (eds.), *L'espace francophone en milieu minoritaire au Canada. Nouveaux enjeux, nouvelles mobilisations*. Montreal: Fides: 431–511.

Frenette, Y. (1998). *Brève histoire des Canadiens français*. Montreal: Boréal.

Gasbarrone, L. M. (2002). "Narrative, Memory, and Identity in François-Xavier Garneau's *Histoire du Canada*." *Quebec Studies*, no. 34: 31–46.

Gauvreau, M. (2005). *The Catholic Origins of Quebec's Quiet Revolution, 1931–1970*. Montreal and Kingston: McGill-Queen's University Press.

Gérin-Lajoie, D. (2004). "La problématique identitaire et l'école de langue française en Ontario." *Francophonies d'Amérique*, no. 18: 171–179.

Gervais, G. (1993). "L'Ontario français, 1821-1910." In C. Jaenen (ed.), *Les Franco-Ontariens*. Ottawa: Les Presses de l'Université d'Ottawa: 49–125.

Gervais, G. (1996). "Le Règlement XVII (1912–1927)." *Revue du Nouvel-Ontario*, no. 18: 123–192.

Gervais, G. (2003). *Des gens de résolution. Le passage du Canada français à l'Ontario français*. Sudbury: Prise de parole.

Gervais, G. and M. Bock (2004). *L'Ontario français. Des Pays-d'en-Haut à nos jours.* Ottawa: Centre franco-ontarien de ressources pédagogiques.

Gould, J. (2003). "La genèse catholique d'une modernisation bureaucratique." In S. Kelly (ed.), *Les idées mènent le Québec. Essais sur une sensibilité historique.* Quebec City: Les Presses de l'Université Laval: 145–174.

Greer, A. (1997). *Habitants et patriotes. La Rébellion de 1837 dans les campagnes du Bas-Canada.* Montreal: Boréal.

Grisé, Y. (1982). "Ontarois: une prise de parole." *Revue du Nouvel-Ontario*, no. 4: 81–88.

Guindon, H. (1993). "L'État canadien: sa minorité nationale, ses minorités officielles et ses minorités ethniques: une analyse critique." In J. Lafontant (ed.), *L'État et les minorités.* Saint-Boniface: Éditions du Blé and Presses universitaires de Saint-Boniface: 261–272.

Harvey, L.-G. (2005). *Le printemps de l'Amérique française. Américanité, anticolonialisme et républicanisme dans le discours politique québécois, 1805-1837.* Montreal: Boréal.

Hayday, M. (2005). *Bilingual Today, United Tomorrow: Official Languages in Education and Canadian Federalism.* Montreal and Kingston: McGill-Queen's University Press.

Heller, M. (1994). *Crosswords: Language, Education and Ethnicity in French Ontario.* Berlin: Mouton de Gruyter.

Hobsbawm, E. (1990). *Nations and Nationalism since 1780.* Cambridge: Cambridge University Press.

Hobsbawm, E. and T. Ranger (eds.) (1990). *The Invention of Tradition.* Cambridge: Cambridge University Press.

Igartua, J. (2006). *The Other Quiet Revolution: National Identities in English Canada, 1945–1971.* Vancouver: University of British Columbia Press.

Kelly, S. (ed.) (2003). *Les idées mènent le Québec. Essais sur une sensibilité historique.* Quebec City: Les Presses de l'Université Laval.

Lalonde, A.-N. (1979). "L'intelligentsia du Québec et la migration des Canadiens français vers l'Ouest canadien, 1870-1930." *Revue d'histoire de l'Amérique française*, vol. 33, no. 2: 163–185.

Lamonde, Y. (2000). *Histoire sociale des idées au Québec*, vol. 1: *1760–1896.* Montreal: Fides.

Lavoie, Y. (1973). "Les mouvements migratoires des Canadiens entre leur pays et les États-Unis au XIXᵉ et au XXᵉ siècle: étude quantitative." In H. Charbonneau (ed.), *La population du Québec. Études rétrospectives.* Montreal: Boréal: 73–88.

Martel, M. (1997). *Le deuil d'un pays imaginé. Rêves, luttes et déroutes du Canada français.* Ottawa: Les Presses de l'Université d'Ottawa.

Martel, M. (2000). "*Hors du Québec, point de salut!* Francophone Minorities and Quebec Nationalism, 1945–1969." In M. D. Behiels and M. Martel (eds.), *Nation, Ideas, Identities. Essays in Honour of Ramsay Cook.* Toronto: Oxford University Press: 130–140.

Meunier, E.-M. (2007). *Le pari personnaliste. Modernité et catholicisme au XXᵉ siècle.* Montreal: Fides.

Meunier, E.-M. and J.-P. Warren (2002). *Sortir de la «Grande Noirceur». L'horizon «personnaliste» de la Révolution tranquille.* Quebec City: Septentrion.

Ouellet, F. (1966). *Histoire économique et sociale du Québec, 1760–1850.* Montreal: Fides.

Ouellet, F. (1968). "Les insurrections de 1837–1838: un phénomène social." *Histoire sociale/Social History*, vol. 1, no. 2: 54–82.

Perin, R. (2008). *Ignace de Montréal. Artisan d'une identité nationale.* Montreal: Boréal.

Poirier, J. (2008). "Au-delà des droits linguistiques et du fédéralisme classique: favoriser l'autonomie institutionnelle des francophonies minoritaires du Canada." In J. Y. Thériault, A. Gilbert, and L. Cardinal (eds.), *L'espace francophone en milieu minoritaire au Canada. Nouveaux enjeux, nouvelles mobilisations.* Montreal: Fides: 513–562.

Robillard, D. (2009). *L'Ordre de Jacques-Cartier, 1926–1965. Une société secrète pour les Canadiens français catholiques.* Montreal: Fides.

Roby, Y. (1987). "Les Canadiens français des États-Unis: dévoyés ou missionnaires?." *Revue d'histoire de l'Amérique française*, vol. 41, no. 1: 3–22.

Roby, Y. (1990). *Les Franco-Américains de la Nouvelle-Angleterre, 1776-1930.* Quebec City: Septentrion.

Romney, P. (1999). *Getting It Wrong. How Canadians Forgot Their Past and Imperilled Confederation.* Toronto: University of Toronto Press.

Rudin, R. (1997). *Making History in Twentieth Century Quebec.* Toronto: University of Toronto Press.

Savard, P. (1993). "Relations avec le Québec." In C. Jaenen (ed.), *Les Franco-Ontariens.* Ottawa: Les Presses de l'Université d'Ottawa: 231–263.

Savard, S. (2008). "Pour une politique globale, précise, cohérente et définitive de développement: les leaders franco-ontariens et les encadrements politiques fédéraux, 1968-1984." *Politique et sociétés*, vol. 27, no. 1: 129–155.

Silver, A. I. (1982). *The French Canadian Idea of Confederation, 1864–1900.* Toronto: University of Toronto Press.

Sylvain, P. and N. Voisine (1984). *Histoire du catholicisme québécois*, vol. 2: *Réveil et consolidation (1840–1898).* Montreal: Boréal Express.

Thériault, J. Y. (2002). *Critique de l'américanité. Mémoire et démocratie au Québec.* Montreal: Québec Amérique.

Thériault, J. Y. (2007). *Faire société. Société civile et espaces francophones.* Sudbury: Prise de parole.

Warren, J.-P. (2007). "L'invention du Canada français: le rôle de l'Église catholique." In M. Pâquet and S. Savard (eds.), *Balises et références. Acadies, francophonies.* Quebec City: Les Presses de l'Université Laval: 21–56.

5. "ULTIMATE FIGHTING," CANADIAN STYLE
The Battle Surrounding the Creation of a National Securities Commission

IAN ROBERGE

The regulation of the financial services sector is inherently political, especially in Canada. The regulation of financial markets, as per most policy fields in Canada, is of divided jurisdiction. The federal government is responsible for chartered banks and parts of the insurance industry. Provinces are responsible for the regulation of the securities market (though this is evolving, as is discussed in this chapter), parts of the insurance industry, cooperative banking, and trusts. Globalization, market developments, and the evolution of the regulatory environment have brought about the desegmentation of financial services sector industries, further blurring the lines of jurisdictional authority. Coleman (2002) suggests that the desegmentation of markets has led to a centralization of authority, strengthening the hand of the federal government.

There has been a long-standing debate in Canada about the need to create a national securities commission, going back to the Porter Commission in 1964 which first made the recommendation. There have been four major attempts to foster the creation of a national regulator since the turn of the century. In January 2009 the Expert Panel on Securities Regulation, put together by federal Minister of Finance Jim Flaherty, released its final report in which it recommended the creation of a national securities commission. The panel suggested that the federal government move forward on the project with willing provinces. In response, Minister Flaherty established the Canadian Securities Regulator Transition Office to assist in writing federal securities legislation and in working out organizational and administrative matters. The federal government presented the *Canadian Securities Act* in May 2010, referring the proposed legislation to the Supreme Court of Canada to assess its constitutionality. Quebec and Alberta are challenging the legislation through their respective courts of appeal. At the time of writing, the federal government still expects to have a fully functioning system in place by 2012.

At the provincial level, there are two camps on this issue, one led by Ontario and one led by Quebec, with support from Alberta and Manitoba. Ontario has strongly lobbied in recent years for the creation of a national securities commission. Proponents of a national regulator model suggest that Canada's regulatory infrastructure has long been outdated and inefficient, impeding the growth of Canadian securities markets. They also argue that the federal government is within its right to pursue such a project as part of the trade and commerce clause of the Canadian constitution. In the past, the federal government has, however, hesitated to act for fear, among other considerations, of offending Quebec sentiments. For Quebec and other opponents, provincial jurisdiction over the securities industry allows the regulator to better respond to local needs while also fostering regulatory innovation. They argue that securities regulation falls under contract law and is a provincial responsibility.

This chapter's objective is to go beyond the arguments for and against the creation of a national securities commission. The chapter is to focus on the political dynamics, the forces, and the actors at play in this policy field. How have the varying perspectives of Canadian federalism played themselves out in the debate about a national securities regulator? What has the four-decades-old battle taught us about the practice of federalism in Canada? What has it told us about Ontario–Quebec relations? In this chapter, we argue that Ontario and Quebec have distinct policy preferences based on each actor's specific interests as they pertain to the creation of a national securities regulator. For instance, the Ontario government seeks to promote Toronto as Canada's financial capital; the Quebec government is trying to safeguard Montreal as the financial and economic engine of the province. Each province, in turn, has opted for different models of regulatory competition in order to promote their selected policy option. Ontario favours processes of competitive federalism, where federal policy decisions can be imposed to reduce negative externalities. From this perspective, Canada's position as the only major state without a national regulator inflicts unnecessary costs on the country's securities markets. The creation of a national securities commission serves as the only viable policy option to correct the distortion. Quebec, on the other hand, supports processes of reflexive harmonization, in which units work together towards an acceptable compromise. The adoption of the passport model, the alternative to the national commission, is representative of this process. Ontario and Quebec prefer diverging processes since they allow the actor to push for their option—the option that best fits their particular political and economic interests.

The chapter is divided into three sections. First, we rapidly review the literature on Canadian federalism. Second, we review in detail the debate surrounding the creation of a national securities commission. Third, we highlight the different actors involved, the interests that are being promoted, and the extent to which the contention is about the accommodation of these varying interests.

I.   COMPETITION AND CANADIAN FEDERALISM

The study of Canadian federalism has evolved alongside its practice and the issues of the day. There have been ebbs and flows—periods when the topic of Canadian federalism drew a lot of attention due to particular political occurrences, and times when the topic seemed to generate fatigue and a malaise. We propose in this section to view Canada as a disaggregated whole. We argue that the federal government and the provinces have fundamental political and economic interests at stake, which get to be played out in the federal arena. Private sector and non-governmental actors also promote their own agenda through all available channels. The challenges of Canadian federalism are often best understood when we account for the multiplicity and the clashes of interests in the federation.

The literature on Canadian federalism is extensive, focusing on constitutional politics, federal–provincial diplomacy, the country's ethnic–linguistic divide and its multinational nature, fiscal federalism, the Canadian welfare state, institutional arrangements including inter- and intrastate structure, courts and the legal system, multilevel governance and the role of municipalities in the federation, and more recently open federalism as pegged by the Harper Conservatives in the 2006 election. There has also been research on comparative federalism. One of the distinct features of the study of Canadian federalism is its attempt to provide some understanding of how Canada works or, at the very least, how it might be made to work better. Canada can thus be seen as a good example on how to accommodate different people and regions, or as being somewhat dysfunctional, providing suboptimal public policies and outcomes. In either case, we are shown a holistic view of Canada.

Federations, however, are not by definition coherent entities, or political authority would more than likely be centralized. They are evolving compromises in which political and private actors promote their own interests. In Canada, the federal government has its own interests to defend, as do the provinces. Federal–provincial diplomacy in Canada is often about conflict and dispute resolution. Provinces clearly do not always share the same policy preferences; political actors across the country have different incentive structures. Alliances form and collapse. Conflicts abound in diverse policy fields including, among many: economic developments, fiscal policy, equalization payments, environmental policy, social policy, and even foreign policy. The position of the federal and provincial governments in these cases often reflects the actors' own perceptions and preferences. The federal government, or another actor for that matter, can claim to speak for the whole of the country or the so-called national interest. But the priorities expressed are not necessarily shared by all involved. The Canadian federation is at best disjointed, at worst fractured.

How is the competition among the constituent parts of Canada to be understood? The picture of Canadian federalism begins to change when we account for negotiation and processes of integration. There are many theories and approaches that can be used to understand the complex relationships inherent to a federal system. The approaches in question are often based on rational analysis. Bakvis (2009) suggests that Canadian public policy be studied through actor-centred institutionalism, focusing on the actors, their interests, and their resources in the making of policy. Sproule-Jones (1993), from a public choice perspective, long ago focused on the rules shaping actors' perceptions and actions.

The joint-decision trap (Scharpf, 1988), first elaborated to study policy making in the German federal state and the European Community, can also be used in the Canadian context, providing some insights into the national securities regulator debate. It argues that in a federal-type system, where all or a great majority of regional actors have a policy veto, the result will be suboptimal policy outcomes, due to the inability to obtain consensus between all players. As such, potential national programs can be stymied if only one of the regional actors feels that the current situation is more advantageous to its interests than the newly proposed policy would be. The trap has many weaknesses (Peters, 1997) and it clearly does not apply to every situation in Canada. The joint-decision trap, however, partially explains the policy issue under study. The creation of a national securities commission represents high politics and key provinces are attempting to use a veto to block the creation of a national body. The federal government, in turn, is trying to show some leadership, circumventing the established channels of federal–provincial diplomacy in this field to work with some of the willing provinces. The joint-decision trap, though, fails to fully capture what is at stake. Most importantly, the optimal policy is not clear. There remains serious contention about the merits of a centralized regulatory regime versus a decentralized one. Recalcitrant provinces do not necessarily favour the status quo, as shown by the introduction of the passport system (to be described later on), and they actually believe that the best regulatory arrangements can be established through provincial cooperation, rather than that which is to be imposed by the federal authority. Depoliticizing the issue, lowering the stakes could facilitate a resolution to the impasse, though it is not clear that doing so is possible.

The debate surrounding the creation of a national securities regulator can be further understood by taking into account principles of regulatory competition. According to Deakin (2006), there are two models of regulatory competition: competitive federalism and reflexive harmonization. Deakin suggests that the United States follows the first model, while the EU prefers the second. In competitive federalism, regional governments and citizens try to match supply and demand of services, with the understanding that citizens may choose to exit when unhappy with current arrangements. Harmonization takes place to reduce negative externalities, and potentially to pursue strategies of common interest. Harmonization attempts to bring about the "one best" solution. The attempt by the federal government, supported by Ontario, regarding the creation of a national securities commission fits this model relatively well. The perceived numerous inefficiencies with the current regulatory arrangements (negative externalities) must be addressed and the best, if not the only solution, is the creation of a national securities commission. The second model, reflexive harmonization, presents an opposite view of regulatory completion.

> This begins with the idea that competition is not so much a state of affairs in which welfare is maximised, but a process of discovery through which knowledge and resources are mobilised, the end point of which cannot necessarily be known. This type of competition depends on norms that establish a balance between "particular" and "general" mechanisms between, that is, the autonomy of local actors, and the effectiveness of mechanisms for learning based on experience and observation. One essential prerequisite is the preservation of local-level diversity, since without diversity, the stock of knowledge and experience on which the learning process depends is necessarily limited in scope (Deakin 2006: 444).

Reflexive harmonization speaks well to the position of Quebec and other recalcitrant actors; it describes the process taking place for the implementation of the passport model based on intraprovincial collaboration.

As each actor, especially Ontario and Quebec, elaborates its policy preference based on its own interests, the deliberation on the appropriate regulatory structure for the securities industry in Canada reflects different perspectives on regulatory competition and processes of integration. The process of regulatory competition is a means to an end, therefore each actor favours a different process to advance its cause. It is a fair question to ask why Ontario would prefer competitive federalism and Quebec reflexive harmonization. Though more of a hypothesis than an assertion, it is possible that power status partly dictates such a choice. Ontario remains a dominant political and economic actor, even though power in the Canadian federation has, in recent years, partly shifted westward. Quebec prefers the process of reflexive harmonization because it allows for the preservation of provincial autonomy. Competitive federalism, thus, is favoured by stronger actors and reflexive harmonization by relatively weaker jurisdictions. Quebec's political and economic elites generally adhere to consensual processes of decision making, which is inherent to reflexive harmonization. Quebec can only advance its interest through coalition building. Ontario, a slightly more powerful actor, can disguise its interest by using the discourse of the national imperative. For reflexive harmonization, national interest cannot be assumed and is to be built along the way through consensus and the establishment of shared practices and norms. Quebec has an interest in not having a national regulator and in playing a leadership role in the establishment and the success of the passport model as a viable alternative. Actors determine their policy preferences based on their interests; the actors' choice of the regulatory competition model reflects their understanding of the means available to them to pursue and achieve their policy of choice.

2. THE NATIONAL SECURITIES COMMISSION (ONTARIO) VERSUS THE PASSPORT MODEL (QUEBEC)

2.1. The Road to a National Securities Commission

This section presents the recent history relating to the creation of a national securities commission, highlighting key arguments in favour of and against such a model.

Above and beyond the broad forces acting upon financial markets worldwide at the turn of the millennium, such as the globalization of financial markets, there were three sets of circumstances particular to Canada that helped to usher the return on the policy agenda of the topic of a national securities commission. First, the federal government made major revisions to the *Bank Act* in 2001. Bill C-8 sought, among other objectives, to foster competition in the banking industry and to address the issue of bank mergers. The federal government could, following the adoption of Bill C-8, focus on other existing priorities in the governance of financial services sector markets. Second, the Ontario government reviewed, starting in 2001, the *Act governing the Ontario Securities Commission*. The committee that it set up to do so spent the first chapter of its interim report arguing in favour of a national securities commission. Third and last, there had been in 1999 a ten-year agreement among the exchanges to rationalize activities. Among other changes, Toronto became the dominant exchange for primary and secondary trading, and Montreal specialized in the exchange of derivatives. The time, therefore, seemed right to review in full the regulatory environment for securities markets across Canada.

The federal government established in 2002 the Wise Persons' Committee (WPC) under the guidance of Michael Phelps, an established industry insider, with the mandate to review and make recommendations pertaining to the regulatory structure of Canadian securities markets. The Committee's report, titled *It's Time*, enthusiastically endorsed the creation of a national regulator, with regional offices across the country. The report stated:

> This is not the first time that Canadians and their governments have considered whether to reform Canada's securities regulatory structure. Unlike prior efforts, however, there is now an unprecedented opportunity—and a necessity—for change. Issuers, investors and financial intermediaries across Canada are united in their call for change. Markets around the world and their regulatory structures are rapidly changing. Other countries are finding ways to achieve competitive advantage through their securities regulatory structure. Canada should do no less (WPC 2003: 13).

It appeared momentum existed in favour of the creation of a national securities commission. The federal government never acted, however, on the recommendations of the WPC, never making it a political priority.

Following on the quasi-failure of the WPC, the Ontario government put together the Crawford Panel on a Single Canadian Securities Regulator which emitted its final report, *Blueprint for a Canadian Securities Commission*, in June 2006. The panel was chaired by Purdy

Crawford, another well-connected industry insider. The panel was to work independently from government and to propose both a national regulator model and the route to implementation. To keep politics out of it and to minimize the risk that the national commission be dominated by the interest of one or a few provinces, the panel recommended that provinces pool their jurisdiction, and create together a national commission. The result of the Crawford panel seemed anticlimactic following the work of the WPC and did not create much of a stir.

The Investment Dealers Association, which has now been replaced by the Investment Industry Regulatory Organization (the IDA merged with Market Regulations, Inc., the self-regulatory organization that supervised market behaviour), put together the Task Force to Modernize Securities Regulation in Canada, which also emitted its final report in 2006. As the title suggests, the initiative largely focused on processes and content of securities regulation in Canada.

Proponents of the national regulator model, however, were not easily deterred. Previous efforts had not achieved success largely because the federal government did not have the political will to push the project forward. Federal Minister of Finance Jim Flaherty decided that the time had come for the central government to fully back the creation of a national securities commission. The federal government put together the Expert Panel on Securities Regulation, which delivered its final report in January 2009, after ten months of work. The panel was chaired by Tom Hockin, former minister of state (Finance), and was composed of various established experts. The panel carried out its work at a time of market upheaval. The global financial crisis that spread from the United States outward was felt in Canada with stock market indexes dropping rapidly in the fall of 2008. Canadian market actors, under the guidance of governments, sought resolution to the asset-backed commercial paper (ABCP) crisis which had hurt both large institutional investors and small individual ones. Hard times in financial markets served as the backdrop for yet another discussion about the creation of a national securities regulator.

The Hockin report recognized that previous attempts failed and that it needed to propose a concrete and detailed map for implementation. The panel recommended a single commission, and a single securities act across Canada. Provinces would opt in to the regime by adopting the harmonized legislation, thus respecting provincial autonomy, and regulatory oversight would be consistent across the country. If a sufficient number of provinces failed to partake in the initiative, the federal government could then move to offer issuers and registrants direct access to the new regime. The panel proposed a draft securities act. Minister Flaherty enthusiastically endorsed the recommendation, and since the report's release, has worked towards implementation.

There are many established arguments in favour of the creation of a national securities commission. The arguments are largely a critique of the existing system, with the understanding that a single national regulator will be able to overcome these existing flaws. They can be structured around three axes: 1) the effectiveness and the efficiency of the regulatory structure, 2) the need for greater transparency and accountability though simplification, and 3) the international imperative. There are many components to each argument. The Hockin report questioned the effectiveness of current arrangements by stating that the content of securities regulation had fallen behind international standards and best practices. The Panel stressed the need to measure the performance of securities regulation in Canada, and to move towards more principles-based regulation (British Columbia adopted principles-based legislation in 2004, but never carried through with implementation). Put simply, provincial governments and provincial regulators are not doing a good enough job to ensure a fair and efficient market, an objective which all can agree on. The current regulatory structure is also said to be costly, with the need to support thirteen different regulators across Canada. In turn, the industry is said to be subjected to extra costs due to the need to respond to different regulators, an argument that has been contested by some who argue that the cost for emitters in Canada is not necessarily much more than that in other jurisdictions (Suret and Carpentier 2003).

Greater transparency and accountability is sought on at least two levels. First, the Canadian system is said to be complicated for outside firms and investors, discouraging possible involvement in Canadian markets. Second, market enforcement is said to be at the very least uneven, if not simply wanting in Canada. There is, thus, a need to better protect small investors. The complaint-handling and redress mechanisms which employ a mix of provincial securities commissions, self-regulatory organizations, and even the RCMP if criminal matters are involved, is said to be burdensome and opaque. Provincial securities commissions are accused of being lax and of not putting enough resources into compliance. Many publicized cases have been tried in the United States, such as that of Conrad Black, before being close to coming to court in Canada. The creation of an Adjudicative Tribunal, independent from the Commission, proposed in the Hockin report is in response to such concerns.

Finally, proponents of a single regulator argue that Canada would be best represented internationally by a national body. Generally, provincial regulators from Ontario and Quebec represent Canada at the International Organization of Securities Regulators. Canada, it is suggested, would be in a better position to collaborate if it spoke with a single voice.

The policy story fits the competitive federalism model. The current arrangements are costly, creating negative externalities. Financial services sector actors potentially shy away from emitting and investing in Canada because of the country's complex and, according to some, outdated regulatory structure. There are, however, disagreements, especially among governments, on how to resolve the issue, and so there cannot be a negotiated agreement on the one best policy option, the creation of a national regulator. The federal government is thus forced to step in with the unequivocal backing of Ontario to provide the framework for the creation of a national securities commission. Provinces are to wilfully opt in to the scheme, which makes it appear as though the policy is not being imposed, yet it forces the opposing faction into a tight corner. Market participants who prefer the national regulator scheme will more than likely be drawn to operate in jurisdictions that have opted in. Provinces that do not opt in and continue with provincial regulation could potentially be less competitive.

2.2. The Alternative: The Passport Model

There is, however, a radically different position, championed by Quebec, Alberta, and Manitoba, which until recently had also been supported by British Columbia, and generally draws consideration across provinces. Quebec occupies a unique place when considering Canadian financial markets. Big banks dominate across Canada, except in Quebec where the Mouvement Desjardins is the big player. There are unique financial institutions, to name only one, the Caisse de dépôt et placement. Montreal has long been a financial capital, and the Montreal exchange (now part of the TMX Group) has a long and storied history. In the West, Winnipeg has a long history of activities in the securities industry. It hosted the Winnipeg Commodities Exchange, which in 2007 was bought out by Intercontinental Exchange (ICE), a leading global player in the field of futures, options, and the over-the-counter (OTC) market. ICE Futures Canada has offices both in Calgary and Winnipeg. For its part, Calgary is seen as a rising financial capital. Big money is needed to finance oil and gas projects. The Alberta and Vancouver stock exchanges merged in 1999 to form the

Canadian Ventures Exchange, now part of the TMX Group and called the TSX Venture Exchange. Canadian securities markets are small by international standards. Toronto is unmistakably the country's financial capital, in large part due to the dominance of the TMX Group. There is, however, plenty of activity elsewhere in the country.

The provinces established, starting in 2003, the Provincial–Territorial Securities Initiative under the guidance of the Council of Ministers of Securities Regulation; its purpose was to reform the Canadian securities system. In 2004 the Council agreed on an action plan which called on participating provinces to adopt and implement the passport system. The passport model is imported from Europe, where it has been used extensively across pillars to favour financial services sector integration. Simply put, the passport system operates through the principle of mutual recognition and legal delegation. Without the passport system in place, market participants who want to operate cross-country need to fulfill the regulatory requirements of all provinces and territories. With the adoption of the passport system, now fully implemented, market participants work through only one jurisdiction, the primary jurisdiction of their choice, and they are allowed to operate in all participating jurisdictions. The Action Plan also called on provinces to pursue legislative and regulatory harmonization, which is essential for the proper functioning of the passport system. All provinces and territories have signed on, except Ontario.

There are many arguments in favour of the passport model and in opposition to the creation of a national securities regulator. The most cited argument, especially from Quebec, is that current arrangements respect the Canadian constitution as traditionally understood, whereas securities regulation is of provincial jurisdiction.

The second argument that is put forward is that the current system works and that it is safe. Canadian markets are structured around small firms with local interests which are better served by local regulators who have inside knowledge of specific industries. Proponents of the passport model also note regularly in their press releases that Canada scores well when ranked by international organizations.

Third, the passport model has many advantages. It reduces costs for market participants, since they deal with a provincial regulator, not a country-wide regulatory mammoth; it allows local markets to flourish; and it facilitates market innovation. There is, in fact, no guarantee that a national regulator is going to do better. The US and the UK systems were hit much more severely by the turmoil in financial markets post-2007. Canadian markets and firms fared relatively well in light of the turbulence. A national regulator will not necessarily lead to lower regulatory costs, especially because it will still need to be present across the country. A national regulator could actually be too big, a heavy and hard-to-manoeuvre bureaucracy.

Fourth, Canadian markets have flourished and internationalized with the current system, and provincial regulators are very active internationally when needed.

Fifth and last, Canada may be one of the rare countries without a national regulator, but its arrangements are not unique in and of themselves. As mentioned previously, the passport model is borrowed in parts from the EU financial services sector integration process. The argument has also been made that the Canadian regulatory structure is not different, for instance, from the regime for corporate law in the US (Carpentier and Suret 2003).

Proponents of a national securities regulator believe that the passport model simply does not go far enough. They see it as a step in the right direction, but as something that is too timid. Supporters of the passport model suggest in turn that the project responds to the specificities of the Canadian situation. If the passport model has not achieved its full potential, they point out it is because Ontario has refused to join. Reflexive harmonization speaks to a bottom-up exercise focused on consensus building. In adopting the passport model, provinces have shown that they can make changes to improve the system. The end result is not predetermined and there is a lot of flexibility for change. The process respects provincial autonomy. The passport model demonstrates what provinces can achieve, working together without the perceived unwarranted intervention of the federal government.

3. THE ACTORS, THEIR RATIONALE, AND POLICY PREFERENCES

The previous subsection makes it clear: there are fundamental differences pertaining to the policy to be adopted and to the process to be followed. Above and beyond the rhetoric, how are actors' rationales and interests to be understood? There are, clearly, serious political and economic considerations at play.

The table below presents where the major actors stand as regards the creation of a national securities commission. It is worthy of note that the majority of market actors support the creation of a national securities commission. The Expert Panel on Securities Regulation received 75 written submissions, which are available on its website (Expert Panel on Securities Regulation, 2009b). The vast majority of the submissions came from market actors, with a few submissions from government, regulatory, and self-regulating organizations. Based on our observations, there were 55 submissions clearly in favour of the creation of a national securities commission. There were five submissions clearly against, and fifteen submissions that were noncommittal or dealt with the topic in a different way. The five submissions that opposed the creation of a national regulator were those from the Autorité des marchés financiers (the Quebec regulator), the British Columbia Securities Commission (the British Columbia government no longer opposes the federal proposal), the Chambre de la sécurité financière, the Fédération des chambres de commerce du Québec and the Mouvement des caisses Desjardins. Thus, the only market actors clearly opposed to the creation of a national securities commission come from Quebec. The Mouvement Desjardins is the only large financial institution that speaks out against the creation of a national regulator. From the outside looking in, it is unclear to which extent Desjardins is opposed on principle, or whether its management has deemed it politically advantageous to align itself with the provincial government. It should be pointed out that provincial securities regulators are reluctant to partake in the project. Provincial regulators' hesitation can likely be understood as reflecting their own self-interest and that of their employees. Overall, there is a strong base of support for moving forward with the creation of a national regulator.

Table 1
Policy Preferences

National Regulator	The Passport System
1) The federal government	1) The Quebec, Alberta, and Manitoba governments and some provincial regulators
2) The Ontario government	
3) A majority of market actors (financial firms, professional associations such as the Canadian Bankers Association, the TMX, emitters, large institutional investors, pension plan operators, etc.)	2) A few market actors (often from Quebec: Mouvement des caisses Desjardins, Chambre de la sécurité financière, Fédération des chambres de commerce du Québec)
4) Consumer groups and small investors	

There are three key considerations in trying to explain Ontario's position versus that of Quebec. First and foremost, Ontario and Quebec's economic interests are at odds. The clash is particularly evident when considering Toronto's role as Canada's financial centre. The head office for a national regulator may not necessarily be in Toronto and there will more than likely be regional offices across the country, but the concern remains that the commission is going to be Toronto-centric. At the time of writing, there is even some consideration being given to the creation of a commission without a head office, so as to avoid alienating a province or a city. It remains unclear how the national regulator would work in practice without established headquarters. Whether or not there is a head office, and irrespective of where it may be, the regulator will have no choice but to focus on Toronto, the country's financial capital. Canada's premier exchange, the TMX, is in Toronto and there is vast expertise in the city. There are few financial centres that matter around the world and they are quite prestigious. From a Canadian and an Ontario perspective, there is a definitive interest in preserving and promoting Toronto as such a centre (Bryant 2010). Building Toronto as a global financial centre helps ensure that Canada be perceived as a major economic player. The Ontario economy is moving away from extracting and manufacturing and towards service industries. The financial services sector creates a number of well-paying jobs in the heart of the city and it can help sustain the transformation of the Ontario economy.

Toronto's prominence is, however, a problem elsewhere in the country. The Quebec government has an interest in preserving what is left of Montreal as a financial capital. Montreal is the province's economic engine and its financial sector is essential to foster indigenous economic growth. Another issue that needs to be addressed is the need to keep at home the expertise that is tied to the existence of a financial centre. Language and culture also play into this debate. It is uncertain how a Toronto-focused, largely English, national regulator would take Montreal-specific interests into account. Steps have been taken to uphold Montreal as a financial capital; in May 2008 the Montreal exchange launched the Montreal Climate Exchange, a market for environmental products. Montreal's financial profile in recent years has, however, unmistakably slipped.

The Quebec government is not the only actor concerned about Toronto's status. There is some worry in other provinces, especially in Western Canada, that their own interests would not be well protected by a national regulator. Would a national regulator, even with regional offices, really understand and work to promote local markets? What power will regional offices really have? Who will make important legislative and regulatory decisions? If local offices are simply to implement national decisions, there is bound to be friction. If local offices are given too much leeway, why not keep the current system in place?

Second, Quebec has built up its regulatory regime in recent years, while the performance of regulatory authorities in other provinces has been questioned. In 2004, Quebec streamlined its regulatory apparatus, creating a single regulator called Autorité des marchés financiers (AMF). The new super-regulator, not unlike some of its European counterparts, oversees all provincially regulated financial services sector activities. The Quebec government has taken the view that a single regulator is better positioned to supervise and regulate market activity, drawing in all regulatory expertise into one location. The AMF has taken steps to beef up enforcement and to better protect small investors. There have been well publicized cases of AMF enforcement activities, including that against Norbourg and its founder Vincent Lacroix. Despite some public criticisms levied at the AMF, the Quebec government can argue that its system works and that it is up to other provinces to modernize their regulatory authorities and to invest in investor protection. The OSC, in particular, has often been criticized for alleged lax enforcement.

The third factor at play is political, especially in Quebec. The securities regulatory structure is a relatively opaque topic and normally is of little interest to the general population (except at a time of major regulatory failure). Quebec politicians, however, have been very public about their opposition to the creation of a national securities commission. The Quebec political class is, in fact, in a difficult position. On the one hand, there is, as a matter of faith and practice, a general consensus to preserve provincial autonomy in the province whenever possible. Quebec has played a leadership role in the establishment of the passport model. Quebec politicians appear strong by opposing both Ottawa and Toronto and by proposing a conciliatory alternative. The Quebec political class is largely united in its opposition. A defection by the Quebec Liberals in particular could have serious political and electoral costs with potential questions raised about their ability and willingness to defend the interests of the province. There are, however, some potential drawbacks in not participating in the federal initiative, if and when a national regulator becomes operational. As noted earlier, the federal government is proposing an opt-in scheme so that provinces who want to participate will be able to do so, and recalcitrant provinces can keep their own regulator. Provinces that refuse to join, such as Quebec, could face a competitive disadvantage, especially because market participants largely support the creation of a national regulator. Financial services sector actors could concentrate their operations under the national regime and minimize participation in the Quebec marketplace. The same consideration may not apply in the same way to Alberta, who may have specific leverage associated with its economic prospects. For Quebec, opting in is not an option, but staying out could be costly.

There is a final issue to be addressed: why has the federal government finally decided to act on this matter after having refused to do so for so long? There are a few potential explanations, including the fact that the federal minister of finance, Jim Flaherty, has long supported the creation of a national regulator. He was the Ontario finance minister during the review of the legislation governing the Ontario Securities Commission at the turn of the century. The creation of a national commission also fits with the Conservatives' philosophy of open federalism, which sees the federal government withdraw from the social sphere, leaving it to the provinces, while being more present on the economic front (Harmes 2007). The Conservatives also seem to believe, despite the Quebec rhetoric, that their political fortunes are not to be overly affected by this confrontation. It is important to remember that the federal government sent its new securities act for review to the Supreme Court to determine its constitutionality. If the Court upholds the act, which many legal experts predict will happen, the federal government will be able to use the Supreme Court decision to speak to the legality, even to the legitimacy, of its initiative.

CONCLUSION

The establishment of a national securities regulator has been a hot political issue in Canada for more than forty years. The Supreme Court of Canada, when deciding on the constitutionality of the Canadian securities act, could be the final arbiter of this long-lasting dispute. Québec could mount a political campaign against the creation of the new regulator if it were to lose the legal battle, but it would be unable to support its arguments using what has traditionally been its trump card, the Constitution. The debate surrounding the creation of a national regulator provides valuable insights on the workings of the Canadian federation. This chapter demonstrates that the Canadian federation is often best understood when viewed as disaggregated. There is a need to identify the relevant public and private sector actors, to determine their interests, objectives, and rationale. Pertaining to financial markets, there is general agreement on the need to have fair, sound, and efficient markets. There remains disagreement on the regulatory structure to be implemented for the attainment of the broader objective. The feud is both about the best policy and the process to be followed. Provinces, Ontario and Quebec in particular, have distinct interests to defend. Canadian federalism is, indeed, competitive and contentious.

Based on a game-theoretical analysis, Anand and Green recently analyzed why it is taking so long for Canada to adopt a single national regulator. They state:

> Our analysis suggests that consensus has not been reached regarding a national regulator not only because of a lack of cooperation but also because of a lack of coordination. Indeed, it seems plausible both that provinces recognize the benefit of adopting a common standardized regulatory model; and that the source of disagreement surrounds the precise regulatory content of that common standardized model (2010: 3).

The study focused on Ontario and Alberta. The analysis provided in this paper demonstrates the extent to which political and economic interests block agreement on the creation of a national organization, beyond issues of coordination and disagreement about regulatory content.

Finally, does the rift between Ontario and Quebec pertaining to the creation of a national securities regulator represent a larger disconnect between the two provinces? As noted elsewhere in this book, there have been signs of rapprochement between the two provinces. The détente between the two provinces should not be overstated. The two jurisdictions are still often in competition, especially when it comes to economic issues. In the post-manufacturing era, Quebec and Ontario are bound to compete to attract investment to their respective province. The rhetoric may be about cooperation; such cooperation often has its limits. The conflict around the creation of a national securities commission may actually be more the norm, rather than the exception.

BIBLIOGRAPHY

Anand, A. I. and A. J. Green (2010). "Why Is It Taking So Long? The Move towards a National Securities Regulator." *University of Toronto Law Journal*, vol. 60, no. 2: 663–686.

Bakvis, H. (2009). *Contested Federalism: Certainty and Continuity in the Canadian Federation*. Don Mills: Oxford University Press.

Bryant, M. (2010). "Toronto as Centre of Global Finance?" *Global Brief*. <http://globalbrief.ca/blog/2010/10/13/how-does-toronto-become-a-top-centre-for-global-finance/> (November).

Carpentier, C. and J.-M. Suret (2003). "The Canadian and American Financial Systems: Competition and Regulation." *Canadian Public Policy*, vol. 29, no. 4: 431–447.

Coleman, W. D. (2002). "Federalism and Financial Services." In H. Bakvis and G. Skogstad (eds.), *Canadian Federalism: Performance, Effectiveness and Legitimacy*. Toronto: Oxford University Press: 178–196.

Crawford Panel on a Single Canadian Securities Regulator (2006). *Blueprint for a Canadian Securities Commission: Final Paper.* <http://www.crawfordpanel.ca/index.html>, accessed in July 2010.

Deakin, S. (2006). "Legal Diversity and Regulatory Competition: Which Model for Europe?" *European Law Journal*, vol. 12, no. 4: 440–454.

Expert Panel on Securities Regulation (2009a). *Creating an Advantage in Global Financial Markets: Final Report and Recommendations.* <http://www.expert-panel.ca/eng/documents/Expert_Panel_Final_Report_And_Recommendations.pdf>, accessed in July 2009.

Expert Panel on Securities Regulation (2009b). *Written Submissions.* <http://www.expertpanel.ca/eng/consultations/written-submissions/index.html>, accessed in July 2009.

Harmes, A. (2007). "The Political Economy of Open Federalism." *Canadian Journal of Political Science*, vol. 40, no. 2: 417–438.

Peters, G. (1997). "Escaping the Joint-Decision Trap: Repetition and Sectoral Politics in the European Union." *West European Politics*, vol. 20, no. 2: 22–36.

Provincial–Territorial Securities Initiatives (2004). *Provincial/Territorial Memorandum of Understanding Regarding Securities Regulation.* <http://www.securitiescanada.org/>, accessed in July 2009.

Scharpf, F. (1988). "The Joint-Decision Trap: Lessons from German Federalism and European Integration." *Public Administration*, vol. 66, no. 3: 238–273.

Sproule-Jones, M. (1993). *Governments at Work: Canadian Parliamentary Federalism and Its Public Policy Effects.* Toronto: University of Toronto Press.

Suret, J.-M. and C. Carpentier (2003). *Enjeux et défis de la réglementation canadienne des valeurs mobilières.* Montreal: CIRANO, Rapports Bourgogne.

Task Force to Modernize Securities Legislation in Canada (2006). *Canada Steps Up: Final Report.* <http://www.tfmsl.ca/index.htm>, accessed in July 2009.

Wise Persons Committee (WPC) (2003). *It's Time.* <http://www.wise-averties.ca/main_en.html>, accessed in July 2009.

PART TWO

QUEBEC AND ONTARIO POLICY
A Comparison

6. DISTINCT ACCENTS
The Language Regimes of Ontario and Quebec

LINDA CARDINAL
and MARTIN NORMAND

In addition to the constitutional requirements imposed on the federal government, Canadian federalism allows the federated states to adopt their own language regimes. Research carried out to date has established major distinctions between the language regimes of Canada and Quebec (e.g., Cardinal 2008; Cardinal and Denault 2007; McRoberts 2002; Laponce 2007). Canada bases its regime on the principle of legal personality, granting individuals the right to access services in the official language of their choice. Quebec focuses on the principle of territoriality, granting the francophone majority the right to live, work, and receive services in French throughout the territory, which makes Quebec's approach closer to that of Switzerland and Belgium. The issue of the coexistence of the Canadian and Quebec regimes has also been the cause of much debate on the normative basis of language policies as well as the conflict between individual and collective rights (e.g., Kymlicka and Patten 2003; Seymour 2008; Taylor 1992, 1994).

In these debates, the particularities of Ontario's regime have yet to be explored.[1] Yet the Ontario government has formally intervened in language issues since the end of the 19th century, when

---

1. New Brunswick is another province that adopted a fairly complete language regime in the 1960s. For more information see Migneault 2007.

it banned French as a language of instruction. At the time, franco-phones accounted for 8% of Ontario's population (Gervais 1993). In 2006 they numbered approximately 580,000 individuals, or 5% of Ontario's population (Office of Francophone Affairs 2010b). Beginning in the 1960s, the Ontario government developed a policy based on the principle that the province's francophone minorities would have access to services in French whenever practical and reasonable. In 1986 Ontario adopted the *French Language Services Act*, which grants the prov-ince's francophones the right to receive Ontario government services in French, but only in designated bilingual areas. Ontario appears to offer a third type of language regime in Canada's current language landscape.

This chapter will compare the language situation in Ontario and Quebec. It seeks to show that the responses to language issues in both prov-inces reflect distinct, fundamental aspects of self-representation within Canadian federalism. The comparison between Quebec and Ontario will also reveal that it is difficult to view their regimes as entirely dis-tinct from one another because they share a common history. Adding the case of Ontario to existing works on language in Canada will there-fore help shed further light on the historical and political foundations of the various regimes developed since the 1960s and how they have interacted. This comparison also offers a socio-historic or contextual approach to language.

Before addressing these issues any further, let us specify what we mean here by "language regime." This term is frequently used in works on language, but a more specific definition is in order so that we may examine and compare the key aspects of the respective regimes of Ontario and Quebec.

I.   WHAT IS A LANGUAGE REGIME?

Although there is no single, widely agreed-upon definition of a "language regime," some information about its various dimensions is available. In a doctoral thesis on the training of translators and interpreters in European Union member states, Julien Fernand (2008) identified 160 language regimes. He isolated three dimensions of a language regime: 1) functional, 2) representative/symbolic, and 3) legal/political. The functional dimension is used to understand the types of communication used in European Union proceedings and addresses how languages are used within this context. The representative/sym-bolic dimension is related to a language regime's ability to reflect and/or manage cultural aspects relating mainly to multilingualism within

European institutions. The legal/political dimension of a regime has to do with the language's level of recognition or the status it is granted by institutions (see Grin 2007 regarding institutional language regimes). A language regime therefore forms a triptych made up of obligations, representations, and planning methods. This approach is useful for classifying regimes, but it offers little insight as to how the regimes came about or the issues that gave rise to them.

Kroskrity (2000) has closely studied the ideological and political issues underlying language regimes. Drawing some inspiration from Gramsci, Kroskrity submits that language regimes are not separate from the existing power relationships within a political society. According to Sonntag (2010), languages are imposed by standards spontaneously recognized by a population. These standards give the impression that certain situations (e.g., the idea that English is a neutral language) are self-evident when in fact they mask underlying inequalities. This perpetuates linguistic ideologies (i.e., belief systems surrounding a language) that are used rationalize or justify power relations (Silverstein 1979) and special interests (Irvine 1989; Heller 2002). To echo Pierre Bourdieu (Kroskitry 2000: 27–28), these language systems give speakers access to resources used to build social and cultural capital. Linguistic ideologies structure relationships between speakers and their identities.

A language regime is more than a collection of procedures and dimensions; it is also irrevocably based on issues of power. According to Labrie, *"la politique linguistique est définie comme l'exercice du contrôle social sur le pluralisme et la variation linguistique"* (2003: 30). In some cases, these issues may even threaten the stability of the state (Laitin 2007). In other cases, a language minority may be too small to represent a real threat to the established order yet still play a major symbolic role in defining national identity (Coakley 2008). There can be as many language regimes as there are situations requiring formal intervention, but the reasons for adopting them and the power issues involved will differ depending on the context (Arzoz 2009).

To summarize, the literature on language reveals on the one hand that language regimes have three dimensions—functional, symbolic, and legal/political—and on the other hand that they are based on contexts defined by issues of power, redistribution, and hegemony. This more comprehensive theory of language regimes can be juxtaposed with the citizenship debates where attempts were also made to systematize the notion of "citizenship regimes." Writers like Dobrowolsky and Jenson (Jenson and Phillips 1996) assert that "[b]y the concept of citizenship regime we mean the institutional arrangements, rules, and understandings that guide and shape concurrent policy decisions and expenditures of states, problem definition by states and citizens, and claims-making by citizens" (2004: 156). As such, these regimes are intended to firmly establish a specific representation of citizenship within a political context in a nation-state. According to these authors, a citizenship regime defines the framework for political discourse within a specific jurisdiction. Citizenship includes values, rights, and obligations as well as governing practices that allow citizens to take part in public debate. It also defines the nation and sets out who can and cannot be a member, including national minorities.

The study of citizenship regimes led to an acute interest in the idea of changing from one regime to another. According to Jenson and Phillips (1996: 113), any citizenship regime can be modified in periods of economic and political turmoil, although such transformation is generally no easy task. Citizenship regimes change slowly. Their stability stems from the fact that they usually represent citizenship in a way that corresponds to how citizens see themselves. This means citizenship regimes manage to address the concerns of a large enough segment of civil society to build the consensus required to create stability (*ibid.*: 130). A state cannot hope to promote citizenship in a way that goes against the will of the majority of its citizens. Furthermore, if a society objects to granting minority rights, even the state could have difficulty making changes to its own citizenship regime to address the concerns of minorities. Such an approach suggests that state intervention must be backed by a broad consensus if it is to be legitimate. In other words, if the regime is based on a hegemonic approach to relations between the state and society, any changes to those regimes require a certain consensus among the majority of its citizens. Any regime or change to a regime must be recognized as legitimate by citizens. As such, Jenson and Phillips acknowledge that citizens are also actors in a regime and that a regime is not built solely on power relationships and conflicts of interest.

We must wonder, however, as to the origin of the consensus upon which the citizenship regime rests if it is more than the sum of the interests it represents. Loughlin's 2005 work on the cultural foundations of the modern state reveals the existence of normative, institutional, and political traditions from which states draw the principles that guide public policy, including policies towards minorities. We can speculate that these traditions also help to create a consensus within society and make change even harder within a citizenship or language regime. Using the example of anglophone countries, particularly the United Kingdom, Loughlin argues that there exists a tradition combining elements of pluralism and repression of languages and minorities. Welsh, for example, was systematically banned starting in 1536, but the Bible was translated into Welsh and the language was still permitted in Protestant churches (Cardinal and Denault 2007). This type of regime endured until the early 20th century—over 400 years. It was not until the 1960s that the first law would appear allowing Welsh in the public sphere.

Membership in a political community therefore also occurs within a linguistic community. In other words, citizenship regimes are developed within a political community that expresses itself in a certain language. Although majority groups do not always necessarily see language as a key condition of citizenship, regimes are nevertheless based on a certain understanding of the language. Furthermore, citizenship regimes also provide members of a community with a certain image of themselves as part of a specific language community.

The citizenship and language regimes of Canada have also been closely intertwined since the country's beginnings. These regimes were built in part on a concept of citizenship and language passed down from the British. Two notable signs of this heritage were the banning of French in all anglophone provinces in the late 19th and early 20th century but also its recognition as a language of debate in the Canadian Parliament. The creation of the 1963 Royal Commission on Bilingualism and Biculturalism[2] and the adoption of the *Official Languages Act* of 1969 laid the foundations for the transformation of Canada's citizenship and language regimes. These events made it possible to change the prevailing representation of citizenship, which was mainly British, anglophone, and Protestant, and replace it with a new—and still controversial—approach in which Canada is viewed as a country built by the meeting of two founding peoples whose members must be treated equally. The *Official Languages Act* adopted in 1969 was a key element of the new language regime, which was introduced at the same time. The act stipulates that Canadians have the right to receive federal government services in the official language of their choice

---

2. In 1963, following a series of political debates on the situation of French, the Canadian government created a royal commission on bilingualism and biculturalism (better known as the B&B commission), which was given the task of studying the relations between the two founding peoples and to make recommendations on this subject. Liberal Party leader and Canadian prime minister Lester B. Pearson appointed ten commissioners and made Quebec's André Laurendeau and Ontario's Davidson Dunton joint chairs. The commission published its first report in 1965 and pursued its work until 1970. The commission revealed major discrepancies between francophone and anglophone communities, particularly in the fields of education and employment, where francophones were victims of discrimination. The commission made a number of important recommendations to rectify the situation, some of which were accepted by newly elected prime minister Pierre Elliott Trudeau. This would lay the foundation for Canada's current language regime.

and that the federal civil service must include an equitable number of francophones and anglophones. The act also created the Office of the Commissioner of Official Languages in order to investigate citizen complaints regarding non-compliance with the act.[3]

Further changes were made to the Canadian language regime in 1982 when the federal government enshrined the constitutional right of members of minority groups in either language (francophones outside Quebec and anglophones inside Quebec) to receive an education in their mother tongue.[4] This new right bolstered francophone/anglophone equality by addressing not only the issue of services, but also the role of education in supporting these groups. The *Official Languages Act* therefore requires the state to communicate with citizens in the official language of their choice and recognizes the right to education in one's own language, thus confirming that in Canada, language, culture, and institutions are interrelated. In 1988 the *Official Languages Act* was recast, and two new sections were added. The first asserted the right of public employees to work in the official language of their choice. The second required the federal government to ensure the vitality and development of official language minorities and foster the recognition and use of both languages. The new sections were crucial, because they further enshrined bilingualism within federal institutions and cast the government of Canada as the guardian of official language minorities. Without relieving the provinces of their obligations towards minorities, the federal government would henceforth be responsible for the development of official language minorities, even within the provinces.

Jenson and Phillips highlight the differences between the citizenship regimes of Canada and Quebec. A look at their language regimes, however, reveals that despite their differences, they are also constantly interacting with one another. In Canada, the current federal regime has developed in interaction with those being implemented in the provinces. Likewise, both the Quebec and Ontario regimes have also developed in step with federal government actions in the area of official languages. Each regime has its own unique features, but none is completely independent of the other. It is especially difficult to separate them from one another since the *Official Languages Act* demands

---

3. For more information on the role of the Office of the Commissioner of Official Languages, see Office of the Commissioner of Official Languages 2010b.
4. According to Section 23 of the *Constitution Act, 1982*, parents belonging to a linguistic minority have the right to have their children educated in that minority language in homogeneous schools, which they are allowed to manage, wherever justified by sufficiently population levels. See Canada 2010b.

increasingly more federal government intervention in provincial juris-diction.[5] Canadian federalism is constantly wrestling with issues related to the recognition of official language minority rights. Implementing these rights requires an increasingly collaborative approach to federal-ism between the different levels of government.

To summarize, language regimes shed light on the type of relation-ship that exists between the state and a language in a given context. By adapting components of citizenship regimes to language, we can conclude that language regimes involve institutional arrangements, rules, and representations that guide and assist states in making deci-sions regarding public policy and state spending, identifying issues, and understanding public demands in the field of language. Regimes therefore help shape policy, establish the linguistic framework of policy debate, and identify language issues within a given context. The exist-ence of several language regimes within a single federation complicates matters further, because they are in constant interaction.

Finally, language regimes are based on four dimensions: 1) The legal/political or institutional dimension includes the constitutional and legal frameworks of the state as well as citizens' rights with regard to language acquisition and access to services in their language, as well as language in education, media, the justice system, and health care. 2) The symbolic dimension represents language or linguistic groups within a given state and its institutions. This includes the institutional and cultural foundations of policies and their influence on shaping policy as well as the presence of linguistic minorities in the political sphere. 3) The operational/functional dimension corresponds to day-to-day use of language and linguistic planning, i.e., how languages are used within their own contexts and how services are provided within institutions. 4) The governance dimension identifies the main actors involved in implementing language regimes, including opportunities to involve language groups. These four dimensions also make it more difficult to fully grasp citizenship regimes, which are inextricably tied to the languages that interact within the state. Regime development hinges on the representation of these interactions or on relations between majorities and minorities within a jurisdiction. Their development may also be intertwined with other language regimes within the same state.

---

5. Note that when amendments were made to Part VII of the *Official Languages Act* in 2005, it was stipulated that "implementation shall be carried out while respecting the jurisdiction and powers of the provinces."

2.   ONTARIO'S LANGUAGE REGIME

French presence in Ontario dates back to the era of Étienne Brûlé, who accompanied Samuel de Champlain in 1610 on one of his expeditions into what would become Ontario (Bock and Gervais 2004; Gervais 1993). From that point on, the French presence in Ontario continued to grow with the arrival of Catholic missionaries as well as military forces who built a series of forts, the first of which was Fort Frontenac in Kingston. But the first real French settlement in Ontario was in the southwest, around Fort Pontchartrain du Détroit and the Assomption Mission in the modern-day Detroit and Windsor region. The first francophone communities thus settled in southwestern Ontario nearly 400 years ago. After the Seven Years' War, Ontario's French population came under British rule. The Royal Proclamation of 1763 created the Province of Quebec and introduced common law. Then, in 1774, the *Quebec Act* was adopted in an attempt to win over the loyalty of the French Canadians.[6] Later, the British government sought to appease disgruntled Loyalists by granting them land and compensation to help them settle in lots along the shores of the St. Lawrence, in the Bay of Quinte, on the Niagara peninsula, and in the southwestern tip of Ontario. This influx of Loyalists into areas already populated by French Canadians would alter the demographic context and dynamics. The Loyalists also demanded changes to the *Quebec Act* so that they could have their own British-based political and legal institutions. The *Constitutional Act* of 1791 addressed the demands of the Loyalists. The Province of Quebec was divided into Upper and Lower Canada, each with its own government and legislative assembly. The French Canadian enclaves scattered around Upper Canada quickly became minorities and every subsequent institutional gain for francophones was hard-earned. In 1867, Section 93 of the *British North America Act* (also known as the *Constitution Act of 1867*) protected separate Catholic

---

6. The *Quebec Act* of 1774 rectified certain contentious provisions of the Royal Proclamation of 1763. The British government extended the borders of the Province of Quebec, gave the province's mainly Catholic inhabitants freedom of religion, introduced a Test Oath free of religious references, restored the French civil code, and allowed the continuation of the seigniorial system (*Canadian Encyclopedia* 2010).

school boards in Ontario and Protestant school boards in Quebec, allowing the predominantly Catholic French Canadians to continue instructing their children in French in Ontario.[7]

But at the same time, Ontario openly proclaimed its English and Protestant identity, in keeping with the British tradition. For the inhabitants of Upper Canada, the influx of French Canadians after 1840 became an issue, since these newcomers refused to assimilate into the English community. French-language instruction in the province's public and separate schools was targeted by Protestant lobbyists, particularly the Orangemen and the Canada First movement, who had the support of the Irish Catholic clergy, also opposed to the use of French in Ontario schools. Together, they managed to convince the Ontario government to ban French in the province's schools. The move came amidst a school crisis sweeping across Canada, fuelled by Anglo-Canadian nationalists and Imperialists who wanted a country founded on the English language and Protestantism (Berger 1970). In 1912 Ontario adopted *Regulation 17*, an administrative measure prohibiting instruction in French after Grade 2. The Canadian government of the day preferred not to intervene to resolve tensions between francophones and anglophones. However, in January 1915, Quebec's Legislative Assembly unanimously proclaimed its opposition to *Regulation 17*. Premier Lomer Gouin implored Ontario's Conservative premier James Whitney to respect the rights of his province's French Canadian minority (Centre de recherche en civilisation canadienne-française 2004). *Regulation 17* was not fully revoked until 1944, 32 years later. However, the school crisis was resolved in 1927 with a change to the regulation that once again allowed instruction in French.

In summary, the Ontario language regime of the day was intended more to constrain than to promote French. The government showed tolerance towards francophones by allowing them to continue to

---

7. Section 93(2) stipulates that "[a]ll the Powers, Privileges and Duties at the Union by Law conferred and imposed in Upper Canada on the Separate Schools and School Trustees of the Queen's Roman Catholic Subjects shall be and the same are hereby extended to the Dissentient Schools of the Queen's Protestant and Roman Catholic Subjects in Quebec." Section 93(3) adds that "[w]here in any Province a System of Separate or Dissentient Schools exists by Law at the Union or is thereafter established by the Legislature of the Province, an Appeal shall lie to the Governor General in Council from any Act or Decision of any Provincial Authority affecting any Right or Privilege of the Protestant or Roman Catholic Minority of the Queen's Subjects in relation to Education" (Canada 2010a).

receive some instruction in French within a separate or Catholic system —which in any case was already a constitutional right—but it was much more repressive with regard to opportunities for them to actually study in French. Ontario's francophones were considered second-class citizens because of their language and their French Canadian culture. However, that situation gradually began to change in the 1960s. Ontario's restrictive approach to its francophone minority began facing serious challenges on a number of fronts. The strongest condemnations came from Quebec, which denounced the inferior situation of French Canadians and demanded recognition of its distinct character as the home of the French language in Canada. This debate also provided an opportunity for Ontario to play a leading role in the country. In 1961 the election of John Robarts as premier of Ontario (1961–1971) marked a turning point in the province's relations with Quebec and between francophones and anglophones across the country. One of the priorities of the Robarts government was to rethink the Canadian federation in order to lay the foundation for a new partnership between the main partners characterized by the promotion of bilingualism and biculturalism. Robarts was also the first Ontario premier to work overtly in favour of building greater recognition of Ontario's francophones and granting them more services. Through his actions, he wanted to show that it was possible to live in French outside of Quebec. Robarts believed that since the country was founded as a pact between two founding peoples (anglophones and francophones), both peoples had rights as well as a duty of reciprocity towards one another as equal partners within the federation.

Robarts did not modify the current legal framework in matters of language. He did, however, initiate a major change in the symbolic foundation of the language regime by calling into question its English and Protestant character. He strove toward greater pluralism. As early as 1965, he took steps to ensure better integration of French in Ontario's public sector and created the Advisory Committee on French Language Services in order to provide services to francophone residents. He also accepted the use of French in Ontario's Legislative Assembly. In 1967 he allowed public French-language high schools to be opened. However, the existing (anglophone) school boards refused to authorize the construction of these schools. He also recognized the significance of the federal government's adoption of the *Official Languages Act* in 1969. Premier William Davis (1971–1985) succeeded Robarts and continued with his policies. On May 3, 1971, Davis made an important declaration to Ontario's Legislative Assembly, stating that "it is clear that Ontario has made a solid commitment to the principle of bilingualism as a matter of equity for our residents and as a large contribution to the continued and future strength of Canada."[8] He promoted a very specific type of bilingualism designed not to upset the anglophone majority historically resistant to gains by the francophone minority. The government would henceforth offer services in French to franco-phone residents, but only where there was sufficient demand, where it was practical and possible. The Ontario government therefore adopted a policy of controlled openness towards this minority, based on a prag-matic and specific conception of bilingualism. Ontario's new policy on providing services in French meant, among other things, that the government had to translate into French all documents intended for the public and provide French replies to inquiries written in French. It also resulted in the creation of the first designated areas, i.e., regions in which the number of francophones justified providing services in French. Ontario also accepted the principle of making its laws avail-able in French.

But Davis was less of an autonomist than his predecessor. He was more supportive of Ottawa's efforts in constitutional affairs and agreed with the project to patriate Canada's constitution. Ontario also com-plied with the stipulations of Section 23 of the *Canadian Charter of Rights and Freedoms*, which grants official language minorities, including Franco-Ontarians, the right to French publicly funded classes, schools, and school management where numbers are sufficient. Becoming an officially bilingual province, however, was out of the question (Cardinal and Lang 2007).

A major turning point in Ontario's linguistic history came in 1984. The Conservative government of the day amended its *Courts of Justice Act*, proclaiming that French and English would henceforth be the offi-cial languages of the Ontario justice system. For the first time in its history, Ontario granted a language right to its francophone residents. In 1986, after Liberal Party leader David Peterson was elected premier (1985–1990) following decades of Conservative governments, the first *French Language Services Act* was adopted. Peterson also created the Office of Francophone Affairs to oversee the application of the new act.[9]

---

8. Université d'Ottawa (UO), Centre de recherche en civilisation canadienne-française (CRCCF), Fonds Association canadienne-française de l'Ontario (C2), C2/470/18, "Ontario, ministère du Procureur général, s.d., 1922, 1975–1981 – Mémorandum du Ministère du Procureur général." June 23, 1980.
9. See the website of the Office of Francophone Affairs: <http://www.oaf.on.ca>.

This first law, which came into effect in 1989, finally gave francophone residents the right to receive services from and communicate with the government in French.[10]

In 1986 Ontario passed Bill 75, which stipulated that the government would henceforth fund Catholic secondary schools, putting an end to decades of discrimination against Catholics, a group to which most francophones belonged. Finally, in 1988 the government adopted a law recognizing that francophones had the right to manage their own schools. French-language school boards were set up in Toronto and in Ottawa-Carleton. However, Franco-Ontarians would not win the right to fully manage their own school boards until 1997, during the administration of Conservative premier Mike Harris.

In 2007 the Ontario government created the Office of the French Language Services Commissioner and appointed the first commissioner.[11] The new position was enshrined in the *French Language Services Act*, which defined the role of the Commissioner as:

> responsible for investigating whether the Act is being complied with, at his or her own initiative or in response to complaints; reporting on the results of investigations; and monitoring the progress of government agencies in providing French-language services (Office of the French Language Services Commissioner of Ontario 2008: 12).

In other words, the Commissioner was granted two powers: investigation and recommendation. However, the Commissioner reports directly to the Minister Responsible for Francophone Affairs, not to the Ontario parliament.

Finally, in 2010, the Ontario government adopted the first regulation creating French-language service planning bodies in the health sector across Ontario.[12] At least five bodies will be set up primarily to make recommendations to the Local Health Integration Networks (LHINs) regarding the development of health care provided to francophones. These bodies will also be managed by and for francophones. LHINs must also report to the government regarding French-language services. We are still waiting to see, however, if the resources allocated to these new health care planning bodies will be sufficient.

---

10. The law also required the government to translate its public and general laws when Ontario laws were overhauled in 1990.
11. See the website of the Office of the French Language Services Commissioner: <http://www.flsc.gov.on.ca/>.
12. These bodies had not yet been officially constituted at the time of writing.

These key dates constitute Ontario's political/legal framework in the field of language. In the context of the national unity debate that was going on at the time, the *French Language Services Act* was a very powerful symbol, even more so than legal bilingualism. Not only did it receive the unanimous support of all three parties represented in Ontario's Legislative Assembly, it was also offered in the spirit of reconciliation and reciprocity. In his speech during the third reading of the bill, Peterson declared that "[l]*'Ontario apporte ainsi une magnifique contribution au projet canadien de réconciliation nationale*," adding, "*les Québécois observent de très près ce que l'on fait ici, ce qui se passe à cette Législature*" (Cardinal 2001: 52). The law demonstrated, as Robarts had desired 20 years earlier, that it was possible to live in French outside Quebec. Its preamble reads, "the French language is an historic and honoured language in Ontario" and "the Legislative Assembly recognizes the contribution of the cultural heritage of the French speaking population and wishes to preserve it for future generations" (Ontario 2010).

The act did not give French full official language status. The Ontario regime that emerged changed certain past practices, but it did not completely break from its repressive approach. Official bilingualism was rejected in favour of *de facto* bilingualism, wherever justified by sufficient numbers of francophones. Furthermore, the *French Language Services Act* is an umbrella act, meaning it provides a framework for a number of existing services. It took certain measures that were already in practice in the field and enshrined them in law. The act therefore regulated a tested and proven situation, without introducing any dramatic changes.

From a functional standpoint, the act's application framework is founded on the principle of designation. That means that francophones (including newly arrived francophones) are entitled to receive services in French in 25 designated bilingual areas, or, as Davis put it, where bilingual services are practical.[13] It should be noted that 80% of the province's francophones live in these regions. That means that most of Ontario's francophones have access to provincial government services in French. Municipal governments are exempt from the application

---

13. A bilingual area is established when 5,000 francophones live in a given area or when 10% of the population is recognized as being francophone. The names of Ontario's 25 designated bilingual areas are listed on the Ontario Office of Francophone Affairs website.

of the act, as are public agencies, hospitals, and retirement homes. Municipal governments can choose to adopt French language service policies, which is the case in Ottawa.[14]

The Ontario government can designate agencies in order to ensure services are provided in French.[15] There is a tradition in Ontario of providing services through nongovernmental agencies. Not all designated bilingual agencies are managed by and for francophones. The Ontario government has also tried to "bilingualize" unilingual anglophone agencies in designated areas to get them to offer services in French. Regardless of the type of agency that is designated bilingual, they are all required to actively provide services in French, just like the government.[16]

In summary, Ontario's language regime stems from a tradition and a history of reluctance to grant rights to the francophone minority. The regime has changed gradually since the 1960s. Since the time of the Robarts government, Ontario's actions have been founded on a sense of duty towards Franco-Ontarians, partly because of their proximity to Quebec and partly because they belong to one of the two founding peoples. Ontario has acted in harmony with the federal government, which promotes the development of French outside of Quebec. The federal government intervenes in the fields of education and justice and helps fund French services. The language regimes of Ontario and Canada are thus constantly interacting and contributing to the gradual transformation of relations between the province's anglophone majority and francophone minority. However, the government must act with careful pragmatism in order to avoid upsetting the majority. French is

---

14. The City of Ottawa's bilingualism policy is available online at <http://www.ottawa.ca/city_hall/policies/bilingualism_policy/index_en.html>.

15. The Office of Francophone Affairs states that agencies may be officially designated as offering services in French if they meet four conditions: "Offer quality services in French on a permanent basis, guarantee access to its services in French, have francophones on the board of directors and in its executive, and develop a written policy for services in French that is adopted by the board of directors and that sets out the agency's responsibilities with respect to services in French" (Office of Francophone Affairs 2010a). To date, over 200 agencies have been designated bilingual. Examples include community health care centres, hospitals, preschool centres, daycares, and legal clinics.

16. Data from a study on services actively offered in French in the field of justice revealed that civil servants working in designated bilingual positions showed a clear tendency to offer services in French only when requested rather than to actively offer them, despite being aware of their obligations in this area (Cardinal, Plante, and Sauvé 2010: 17; see also Office of the French Language Services Commissioner of Ontario 2010a).

one of Canada's official languages, but the *French Language Services Act* provides for *de facto* bilingualism rather than official bilingualism. Furthermore, it does not apply to all jurisdictions or all municipalities.[17]

Finally, towards the end of the 1990s, the controversy surrounding the planned closure of Ottawa's Montfort Hospital proved to be a major test of the *French Language Services Act*. In *Lalonde v. Ontario (Commission de restructuration des services de santé)*, the Court of Appeal for Ontario not only rejected the order to close the hospital, it also recognized the restrictive nature of the principle of designation. According to the court, once an agency has been designated to provide services in French in accordance with the act, the government cannot then decide to reduce these services to a level below what it was at the time of designation.[18] Furthermore, the Court of Appeal asserted the importance of francophone institutions, including in the field of health, in helping Ontario's French-speaking communities to flourish. In the past, demands by Franco-Ontarians to manage their own services and institutions were a reaction to the government's often mediocre record in providing French-language services. From now on, these demands may instead be seen as reasonable, practical, and in accordance with Ontario's traditional pragmatism.

3.   QUEBEC'S LANGUAGE REGIME

Despite the legacy of the Conquest, French is widely used in Quebec to this day. The new British administration did not grant French any particular status, but the *Quebec Act* allowed for the continuation of the seigniorial system, the Catholic religion, and the French Civil Code.

---

17. Despite the increasingly important role played by municipal governments in providing services, the *French Language Services Act* does not specifically address this issue. When the act was adopted, opposition from anglophone politicians and lobby groups like Alliance for the Preservation of English in Canada (later renamed Canadians for Language Fairness) forced the Ontario government to exclude municipal governments from the application of the act.

18. According to the Court of Appeal, "Montfort's designation does not apply only in respect of specified services. It applies in respect of all the health care services offered by Montfort *at the time of designation*" [our italics] (paragraph 161). Further in its decision, the court adds that "Montfort's designation under the FLSA [*French Language Services Act*] includes not only the right to health care services in French at the time of designation but also the right to whatever structure is necessary to ensure that those health care services are delivered in French. This would include the training of health care professionals in French. To give the legislation any other interpretation is to prefer a narrow, literal, compartmentalized interpretation to one that recognizes and reflects the intent of the legislation" (paragraph 162). See *Lalonde v. Ontario (Commission de restructuration des services de santé)* 2001.

French was the language of everyday life in these institutions. The French Canadians and the British lived side by side in their own separate worlds, but the francophone majority could not take its language for granted. Unlike in Upper Canada, the Loyalists of Lower Canada were a numeric minority. However they had dominant status thanks to their ties to the British Crown. Thus between 1791 and 1960, linguistic debate in Lower Canada (later Quebec) was defined by the fact that the francophone majority had to 1) constantly defend its language, 2) struggle for its rightful share of power against an anglophone minority that had a negative attitude towards French and the advancement of French Canadians, 3) fight against the Canadian government on a number of fronts to introduce bilingualism into federal institutions, and 4) help defend French Canadians outside Quebec.

With the creation of the Legislative Assembly of Lower Canada in 1791, nearly 20 years after the *Quebec Act*, French Canadians constituted a majority among elected officials, but were quickly faced with a fight over the language of debate. French was allowed in practice, but the government required that all laws also be adopted in English. When the United Province of Canada was created in 1840, French was banned from the Assembly, and English was made sole official language. French would regain its status in 1867 when Canada became a federation. Section 133 of the *British North America Act* recognized the right to use English or French in debates in the federal Parliament and in Quebec's Legislative Assembly. It also stipulated that federal and Quebec laws must be published in English and French and that both languages must be used in the federal and Quebec courts. The Canadian government of the day did not provide simultaneous interpretation to ensure that elected officials could understand one another, a situation that would continue until 1959 (Delisle 2009). Section 133 did, however, protect the rights of anglophones in Quebec in Parliament and the courts.[19] This was an extension of Canada's language regime into Quebec in order to ensure the survival of English and protect the dominant status of the anglophone minority.

Quebec, for its part, was simultaneously pushing the federal government to adopt bilingualism in its federal institutions and defending francophones outside Quebec. Quebec members in the House of Commons spoke out against efforts to suppress French in

---

19. There were no equivalent stipulations to protect the rights of francophones in Ontario. In addition, when the Supreme Court was created in 1867, two of the six judges were to be from Québec, but there were no language requirements. In 1949, when the Canadian government increased the number of judges to nine, including three from Québec, there was still no mention of language.

Anglo-Canadian provinces, including Ontario's *Regulation 17*. Starting in the 1920s French Canadian elected officials in Ottawa and the Quebec government both campaigned in favour of things like bilingual postage stamps (1927), bilingual banknotes (1936) and bilingual bank cheques (1945). These measures strengthened bilingualism in federal institutions as did, ultimately, the adoption of the *Official Languages Act* of 1969.

The British approach prevailed in Quebec until the 1960s and Quebecers were on the defensive. It was a period of guarded openness toward French, punctuated by episodes of repression. Unlike Franco-Ontarians, Quebec francophones were not entirely dependent on the goodwill or sense of fairness of anglophones to secure government services. Instead they used their power in the Legislative Assembly, where they constituted the majority, to achieve their goals. However, aside from the *Lavergne Law*,[20] the Quebec government did little to promote French within the province. Yet the federal government did not hesitate to provide English with constitutional protection, although no equivalent measures existed for French in Ontario. In Quebec a laissez-faire attitude toward language prevailed that worked to the benefit of English, despite the federal government protection it already enjoyed. Paradoxically Quebecers also turned to the Canadian government to promote the status of French in Canada and end discrimination against French Canadians. The situation was therefore much more complicated than in Ontario, where the majority made the rules and the francophone minority followed them.

Starting in the 1960s, the Quebec government switched tactics. It continued to work to improve the status of French Canadians during the Royal Commission on Bilingualism and Biculturalism, but it also began laying the foundations of its own language regime. In 1961 it created its Office de la langue française as well as the Royal Commission of Inquiry on Teaching, commonly know as the Parent commission after its chairman. In 1969 the government adopted An Act to Promote the French Language in Quebec (Bill 63). In 1974 Quebec drafted its Official Language Act (Bill 22) making French the sole official language of Quebec and asserting the predominance of the French versions of Quebec laws over the English versions.[21] Finally, in 1977, the Parti québécois government adopted the Charter of the French Language,

---

20. The *Lavergne Law* was the first piece of legislation addressing language adopted by the Québec government in 1910. It required public service organizations to provide services in French and English (Gouvernement du Québec 2008).
21. A complete summary of the history of Québec's language policy since the 1960s can be found in the work by Jean-Claude Corbeil (2007).

commonly called Bill 101, which asserted the status of French as the official language of Quebec and guaranteed the rights of francophones to be educated, receive government services, and work in French. However the law was amended several times in response to court challenges. The section of Bill 101 regarding the exclusive use of French for debates in the National Assembly and in legal texts was found to be inconsistent with Section 133 of Canada's Constitution and was therefore quickly amended by the Quebec government. In 1982 Section 23 of the new *Canadian Charter of Rights and Freedoms* quashed the stipulations of Bill 101 regulating the education of the children of anglophones and granted anglophones across Canada the right to send their children to school in English. The Supreme Court did however acknowledge the legality of Bill 101 regarding the requirement that immigrants send their children to French schools. In 1988 the Quebec government was ordered by the Supreme Court of Canada to loosen its regulations pertaining to signs, which were deemed to infringe on freedom of expression. In 1993 the Liberal government of Robert Bourassa voted in Bill 86, which allowed signs in languages other than French as long as French was predominant. In 1997 the government adopted Bill 40 reinstating the Commission de protection de la langue française, which had been abolished in 1993. In 2000 Bill 71 required half of a municipality's residents to have English as a mother tongue before it could be designated bilingual. In 2002 Bill 104 blocked access to public education in English to francophones and allophones who had previously attended private anglophone educational establishments. In 2010 the Quebec government tabled Bill 103 following a decision by the Supreme Court of Canada to grant access to English schools to francophones and allophones after three years in a "bridging school" (*école passerelle*) and following a series of tests to identify the student's "genuine educational pathway" (*parcours authentique*) and eligibility.

Quebec's legal/political framework is complex. On the one hand, it seeks to empower a previously dominated majority within its own province. On the other hand, multiple court challenges up until 2002 have reasserted the place of English within Quebec's language regime and reminded the provincial government of its duty to protect the rights of its anglophone minority. Since 2002, however, legal actions have sought to overturn stipulations of Bill 101 restricting francophone and allophone access to public education in English. The Supreme Court has recognized the legitimacy and necessity of Quebec's language regime, but it is demanding greater flexibility on the part of government with regard to access to private English schools.

Symbolically the Quebec government's language actions have marked a radical departure from British tradition and the hands-off approach of earlier times. Its goal has been to reverse the situation that allowed English to maintain a dominant position for over 200 years at the expense of French. As plainly stated in the preamble to Bill 101, French is now recognized as "the distinctive language of a people that is in the majority French-speaking" and that it is "the instrument by which that people has articulated its identity." This identity therefore expresses itself in French, not in English. Bill 101 holds the National Assembly responsible for ensuring "the quality and influence of the French language" and making it "the language of Government and the Law, as well as the normal and everyday language of work, instruction, communication, commerce and business." However, its preamble also states that the National Assembly recognizes the valuable contribution of ethnic minorities to Quebec's development as well as "the right of the Amerinds and the Inuit of Quebec, the first inhabitants of this land, to preserve and develop their original language and culture." Finally, the conclusion of the preamble states that the principles of Bill 101 "are in keeping with a new perception of the worth of national cultures in all parts of the earth, and of the obligation of every people to contribute in its special way to the international community." This latter statement was clearly influenced by the fact that the party in power at the time wanted to make Quebec a sovereign country.

While Bill 101 asserted the official status of French and its community nature, it was not a call for unilingualism. On the contrary, it did nothing to discourage multilingualism. But like in Ontario, no political party wishes to make Quebec officially bilingual. All parties agree about protecting the rights of the anglophone minority. However, unlike Ontario, which follows the Canadian regime, it opposes enforcement of the *Official Languages Act* in provincial jurisdictions such as education. Successive Quebec governments have all complied with the requirements of the *Canadian Charter of Rights and Freedoms* and with the Supreme Court's decisions in matters of language, but they cannot do so unthinkingly. The Quebec government must always be careful not to undermine the legal foundations of the community dimension of language. This differs from the Canadian regime, which is based on the principle of choice, and Ontario's regime, which grants individual language rights where numbers warrant, without much concern about the role of French in the community.

Despite the legal framework protecting them, many anglophones who witnessed the introduction of the Quebec language regime chose to leave the province, triggering much uproar.[22] Some of those who stayed elected to challenge Bill 101 before the courts. They were generally successful, although they had to accept the Supreme Court's opinion regarding the legitimacy of Quebec's language regime. Another part of the anglophone community accepted its new status, since despite the predominance of French, English is obviously not threatened in Quebec. There is no indication, however, that the anglophone community has rallied behind the promotion of French.

The development of Quebec's language regime also triggered much debate between Quebec francophones and francophones in the rest of Canada. One of the side effects of Canada's language regime was to grant equal status to francophones outside Quebec and anglophones in Quebec. The *Official Languages Act* therefore eventually came to be associated with the protection of official language minorities (anglophones in Quebec and francophones elsewhere in Canada) rather than with the promotion of French in Quebec. For their part, francophones outside Quebec, caught between a rock and hard place, often allied themselves with anglophones in support of official language minority rights and education in their mother tongues. Furthermore, while the Canadian government's requirement to support official language minorities became a powerful tool in the hands of many francophones in the rest of Canada, this was always resisted in Quebec, which saw it as federal intrusion into provincial jurisdiction. In addition, measures by the federal government intended to recognize Quebec's distinct status were generally rejected by spokespersons from minority francophones communities. However, in 1969, the Quebec government adopted a policy of support for francophone life outside Quebec and made a modest contribution to promoting French. When it announced its new policy in 2003, it also signed an agreement between provinces, including Ontario, to improve French-language services.[23] Quebec also played a leading role in the Ministerial Conference on the Canadian Francophonie (MCCF),[24] but it appears to be doing less than before to

---

22. See Cardinal 2010 for more information.

23. It should be noted that the federal government has also signed agreements with the provinces to provide services in French in fields other than education. For more information, see Canadian Heritage 2007.

24. The MCCF was created in 1994 to bring together "federal, provincial and territorial ministers responsible for the Canadian Francophonie. The MCCF deals with various issues related to the Canadian francophonie issues, provides direction for intergovernmental cooperation, and plays a unifying role in support of the country's francophonie" (Ministerial Conference on the Canadian Francophonie 2010).

make federal institutions more bilingual. That fight is instead being led by the Office of the Commissioner of Official Languages, which is now in charge of overseeing the progress of bilingualism in the federal civil service. The 2009 debate in the House of Commons regarding the requirement that Supreme Court judges be bilingual did, however, lead to the unanimous adoption of a motion by Quebec's National Assembly.

In actual practice, implementation and administration of Bill 101 spurred a massive effort to standardize French-language scientific, technical, communications, and business terms. The goal was to transform the face of Quebec to make it a francophone society and influence the linguistic behaviour of its citizens such that they could integrate the use of French into their lives, i.e., their work. Quebec's ministry of Education has a major role to play regarding mother tongue education, and its ministry of Immigration is responsible for helping immigrants integrate into francophone society.

Quebec's Secrétariat à la politique linguistique and Office québécois de la langue française played key roles in the enforcement of Bill 101 and other legal measures of a linguistic nature. The Secrétariat, created in 1988, is commissioned to coordinate and consult on issues pertaining to the linguistic policy of Quebec as well as promoting it within the Québec public administration. Its responsibilities include providing advice on the implementation and consolidation of language policy and intervening in legal cases involving the Charter of the French Language. The Office, as described in the 1977 Charter of the French Language, enforces the Charter and monitors the state of language in Quebec, guiding policy with regard to official language and terminology and taking appropriate measures to promote French (Office québécois de la langue française 2010).

Ultimately the challenge in Quebec, unlike in Ontario, was to reverse a situation that had become intolerable to most francophones and to lay the foundation for a new language regime based on the principle of territoriality in order to promote the French language within Quebec's borders. Another difference is that in Ontario, the issue of bilingualism has been largely settled, whereas it remains a daily issue in Quebec. One of the most pressing concerns in Quebec is to better understand the influence of English's increasingly widespread use as the international *lingua franca* on the balance between francophones and anglophones. Will Quebec remain mostly francophone? While knowledge of French has become more important to anglophones, English is taking up more and more space in work and public life. What is most worrying to many people is the lack of solidarity in support of French on the part of younger generations, who seem more concerned with personal issues. There is also currently a debate regarding the need for a federal law recognizing the authority of Bill 101 over federal government activity in Quebec. A solution must be found to the conflict between federal and provincial laws. Some have suggested giving Bill 101 constitutional status in order to enshrine its importance and recognize its crucial role in establishing linguistic peace in Canada and Quebec.

4.   DISTINCT ACCENTS

A number of conclusions can be drawn from this chapter's contextual analysis of the language regimes of Ontario and Quebec. First, it must be recognized that from the Conquest to the 1960s, Ontario and Quebec both took an approach to the French language that was based on the British heritage of pluralism tinged with repression. In both cases the regimes that stemmed from this heritage were radically transformed. In Ontario these changes were gradual, but in Quebec they came in the form of a fundamental inversion in the relationship between the anglophone minority and the francophone majority.

Furthermore, we can see that the attitudes of the Ontario and Quebec governments to bilingualism reflect the way each province views itself within Canadian federalism. Ontario's anglophone majority rejects official bilingualism in order to protect the anglo-dominant character of the province. The goal of Ontario's policy is instead geared to ensuring *de facto* bilingualism wherever reasonable and practical, meaning in designated bilingual areas. This will never challenge the fundamentally anglophone character of Ontario. Quebec's francophone majority, for its part, has completely rejected official bilingualism and free choice in matters of language in order to protect the province's francophone character. Quebec's language policies are intended to ensure the survival of French in the province while ensuring the protection of the rights acquired by anglophones, who have gone from majority to minority status. Quebec's policies also differ from Ontario's in that they also partly extend beyond its borders—the Quebec government has a policy of support for francophone communities in the rest of Canada.

Lastly, these language regimes interact with one another. On the one hand, Canada's language regime imposes itself on the provinces in certain fields, such as education. In Quebec it also creates obligations on account of Section 133 of the Constitution. Furthermore, while the government of Canada indirectly accepts that Ontario is a unilingual English province, it does not seem willing to accept that

Quebec is predominantly French. On the other hand, the current language regimes of Ontario and Quebec are founded in part on common principles—reimagining Canada as a pact between two peoples and offering reciprocity in the field of minority rights. So what remains of these principles? The rise of English as a *lingua franca* may undermine the status of French in Quebec, Ontario, and the federal government by exerting pressure for English to once again become the default language. Canada's Constitution recognizes that French and English are equal and represent fundamental aspects of Canadian society. However, interest in bringing francophones and anglophones closer together in Canada has waned lately. Ontario is no longer playing a leading role on the constitutional front, as it did in from the 1960s to the 1980s. In other words, we have not seen greater collaboration and more openness between the two language groups. Instead, French and English have become rivals. They seem more related by what divides them than by what unites them.

BIBLIOGRAPHY

Arzoz, X. (2000). "Language Rights as Legal Norms." *European Public Law*, vol. 15, no. 4: 541–574.

Berger, C. (1970). *The Sense of Power: Studies in the Ideas of Canadian Imperialism, 1867-1914*. Toronto: University of Toronto Press.

Bock, M. and G. Gervais (2004). *L'Ontario français: Des Pays-d'en-Haut à nos jours*. Ottawa: Centre franco-ontarien de ressources pédagogiques.

Canada (2010a). *Constitution Act, 1867*. Available online: <http://laws.justice.gc.ca/eng/Const/page-5.html#anchorbo-ga:s_91-gb:s_93>, retrieved on October 29, 2010.

Canada (2010b). *Official Languages Act*. Available online: <http://lois-laws.justice.gc.ca/eng/acts/O-3.01/index.html>, retrieved on October 29, 2010.

Canadian Encyclopedia (2010). "Quebec Act." Available online: <http://thecanadianencyclopedia.com/index.cfm?PgNm=TCE&Params=A1ARTA0006592>, retrieved on October 29, 2010.

Canadian Heritage (2007). *Intergovernmental Cooperation in the Area of Provincial and Territorial Minority-Language Services Successes and Challenges (2003–2007)*. Ottawa: Her Majesty the Queen in Right of Canada.

Cardinal, L. (2001). *Chroniques d'une vie politique mouvementée. L'Ontario français de 1986-1995*. Ottawa: Le Nordir.

Cardinal, L. (2008). "Bilinguisme et territorialité: les enjeux de l'aménagement linguistique au Canada et au Québec." *Hermès*, vol. 51: 133–139.

Cardinal, L. (2010). "Language Policy-Making and planning in Quebec and in Canada." In J. Rudy, S. Gervais, and C. Kirkey (eds.), *Quebec Questions: Quebec Studies for the Twenty-First Century*. Oxford: Oxford University Press: 186–203.

Cardinal, L. and A.-A. Denault (2007). "Empowering Linguistic Minorities: Neo-liberal Governance and Language Policies in Canada and in Wales." *Regional and Federal Studies*, vol. 17, no. 4: 437–456.

Cardinal, L. and S. Lang (2007). "Les Franco-Ontariens et la pensée constitutionnelle de Roy McMurtry." *Mens, Revue d'histoire intellectuelle de l'Amérique française*, vol. 7, no. 2: 279–311.

Cardinal, L., N. Plante, and A. Sauvé (2010). *Les mécanismes d'offre et de demande des services en français dans le domaine de la justice en Ontario : le point de vue des fonctionnaires et des usagers*. Toronto: Ministère du Procureur général.

Centre de recherche en civilisation canadienne-française (2004). "Le règlement XVII." In *La présence française en Ontario : 1610, passeport pour 2010*. Available online: <http://www.crccf.uottawa.ca/passeport/IV/IVD1a/IVD1a.html>, retrieved on October 29, 2010.

City of Ottawa (2010). *Bilingualism Policy*. Available online: <http://www.ottawa.ca/city_hall/policies/bilingualism_policy/index_en.html>, retrieved on October 29, 2010.

Coakley, J. (2008). "Langage, identité et État moderne." In G. Lachapelle (ed.), *Diversité culturelle, identités et mondialisation*. Quebec City: Les Presses de l'Université Laval: 181–199.

Corbeil, J.-C. (2007). *L'embarras des langues. Origine, conception et évolution de la politique linguistique québécoise*. Montreal: Québec Amérique.

Delisle, J. (2009). "Cinquante ans d'interprétation parlementaire." *Revue parlementaire canadienne*, vol. 32, no. 2: 26–31.

Dobrowolsky, A. and J. Jenson (2004). "Shifting Representations of Citizenship: Canadian Politics of 'Women' and 'Children'." *Social Politics*, vol. 11, no. 2: 154–180.

Fernand, J. (2008). *Le point sur la formation des traducteurs et interprètes dans les 12 derniers pays membres de l'UE : vers une réforme du régime linguistique de l'Europe?* Thèse de doctorat, Université Aix-Marseilles I.

Gervais, G. (1993). "L'Ontario français (1821–1910)." In C. Jaenen (ed.), *Les Franco-Ontariens*. Ottawa: Les Presses de l'Université d'Ottawa.

Grin, F. (2007). "Peut-on faire confiance au modèle '1+>2'? Une évaluation critique des scénarios de communication dans l'Europe multilingue." *Revista de Llengua i Dret*, vol. 45: 217–231.

Gouvernement du Québec (2008). *La langue française au Québec : quelques repères*. Available online: <http://www.spl.gouv.qc.ca/fileadmin/medias/pdf/400ans_quelquesreperes2.pdf>, retrieved on October 29, 2010.

Heller, M. (2002). "Alternative ideologies of la Francophonie." *Journal of Sociolinguistics*, vol. 3, no. 3: 336–359.

Irvine, J. (1989). "When Talk Isn't Cheap: Language and Political Economy." *American Ethnologist*, vol. 16, no. 2: 248–267.

Jenson, J. and S. D. Phillips (1996). "Regime Shift: New Citizenship Practices in Canada." *International Journal of Canadian Studies*, vol. 14: 111–135.

Kroskrity, P. V. (2000). "Regimenting Languages: Language Ideological Perspectives." In P. V. Kroskrity (ed.), *Regimes of Language, Ideologies, Polities, and Identities*. Santa Fe: School of American Research Press: 1–34.

Kymlicka, W. and A. Patten (eds.) (2003). *Language Rights and Political Theory.* Oxford: Oxford University Press.

Labrie, N. (2003). "Aperçu comparatif des politiques linguistiques canadiennes." In Michael A. Morris (ed.), *Les politiques linguistiques canadiennes: approches comparées.* Paris: L'Harmattan: 7–54.

Laitin, D. (2007). *Nations, States, and Violence.* Oxford: Oxford University Press.

Lalonde v. Ontario (Commission de restructuration des services de santé) (2001). Available online: <http://www.ontariocourts.on.ca/decisions/2001/december/lalondeC33807.htm>, retrieved on October 29, 2010.

Laponce, J. (2007). *Loi de Babel et autres régularités des rapports entre langue et politique.* Quebec City: Les Presses de l'Université Laval.

Loughlin, J. (2005). "Les changements de paradigmes de l'État et les politiques publiques envers les minorités linguistiques et culturelles en Europe de l'Ouest." In J.-P. Wallot (ed.), *La gouvernance linguistique: le Canada en perspective.* Ottawa: Les Presses de l'Université d'Ottawa: 19–38.

McRoberts, K. (2002). "La politique de la langue au Canada: un combat contre la territorialisation." In D. Lacorne and T. Judt (eds.), *La politique de Babel: du monolinguisme d'État au pluralisme des peuples.* Paris: Karthala: 155–190.

Migneault, G. (2007). "La progression des droits linguistiques au Nouveau-Brunswick dans une perspective historique globale." *McGill Law Journal,* vol. 52, no. 1: 83–125.

Ministerial Conference on the Canadian Francophonie (2010). *À propos de nous.* Available online: <http://www.cmfc-mccf.ca/fr/about.php>, retrieved on October 29, 2010.

Office of Francophone Affairs (2010a). *Designated Agencies.* Available online: < http://www.ofa.gov.on.ca/en/flsa-agencies.html>, retrieved on October 29, 2010.

Office of Francophone Affairs (2010b). *Portrait of the Francophone Community in Ontario.* Available online: <http://www.ofa.gov.on.ca/en/franco.html>, retrieved on October 29, 2010.

Office of the French Language Services Commissioner of Ontario (2008). *Annual Report 2007-2008: Paving the Way.* Toronto: Queen's Printer for Ontario.

Office of the French Language Services Commissioner of Ontario (2010a). *Annual Report 2009-2010: Open for Solution.* Toronto: Queen's Printer for Ontario.

Office of the Commissioner of Official Languages (2010b). *Roles.* Available online: <http://www.ocol-clo.gc.ca/html/roles_e.php>, retrieved on October 29, 2010.

Office québécois de la langue française (2010). *Mission et rôle.* Available online: <http://www.oqlf.gouv.qc.ca/office/mission.html>, retrieved on October 29, 2010.

Ontario (2010). *French Language Services Act.* Available online: <http://www.e-laws.gov.on.ca/html/statutes/english/elaws_statutes_90f32_e.htm>, retrieved on October 29, 2010.

Quebec (2010). *Charter of the French Language.* Available online: <http://www2.publicationsduquebec.gouv.qc.ca/dynamicSearch/telecharge.php?type=2&file=/C_11/C11_A.html>, retrieved on October 29, 2010.

Secrétariat à la politique linguistique (2010). *Mission et mandats.* Available online: <http://www.spl.gouv.qc.ca/ministreetspl/spl/mission-et-mandats>, retrieved on October 29, 2010.

Seymour, M. (2008). "Les lois linguistiques au Québec ou la longue histoire d'un malentendu." In L. Cardinal (ed.), *Le fédéralisme asymétrique et les minorités linguistiques et nationales.* Sudbury: Prise de parole: 203–227.

Silverstein, M. (1979). "Language Structure and Linguistic Ideology." In P. R. Cline, W. Hanks, and C. Hofbauer (eds.), *The Elements: A Parasession on Linguistic Units and Levels.* Chicago: Chicago Linguistic Society: 193–247.

Sonntag, S. (2010). "La diversité linguistique et la mondialisation: les limites des théories libérales." *Politique et sociétés*, vol. 29, no. 1: 15–45.

Taylor, C. (1992). *Rapprocher les solitudes: écrits sur le fédéralisme et le nationalisme au Canada.* Quebec City: Les Presses de l'Université Laval.

Taylor, C. (1994). *Multiculturalisme. Différence et démocratie.* Paris: Aubier.

Université d'Ottawa (UO), Centre de recherche en civilisation canadienne-française (CRCCF), Fonds Association canadienne-française de l'Ontario (C2), C2/470/18, "Ontario, Ministère du Procureur général, s.d., 1922, 1975–1981 – Mémorandum du Ministère du Procureur général." June 23, 1980.

7. FAMILY POLICY IN ONTARIO AND QUEBEC
Different from Afar or Far from Different?

PETER GRAEFE
and ANGELA ORASCH

On October 22, 2008, Parti Québécois leader Pauline Marois was fêted, of all places, in Toronto. The Ontario Coalition for Better Child Care (OCBCC) decided to honour Ms. Marois for being a champion for child care on the occasion of the tenth anniversary of Quebec's introduction of a universal low-cost child care program. The distinction between Quebec, with its innovative child care program to support early learning and high rates of parental labour force participation, and neighbouring Ontario, where middle-class working parents need to make difficult trade-offs about cost and quality, may seem stark. Even in proximate areas, such as parental leaves and child benefits, meaningful distinctions can be made between the provinces. For instance, Diane-Gabrielle Tremblay (2009) argues that Quebec's family policies provide an interesting model for English Canadian feminists to champion, given the policies' ability to deliver better maternity benefits and to encourage a more egalitarian sharing of infant care between parents.

This chapter has two aims. First, it seeks to compare recent developments in family policies in Ontario and Quebec. While it is tempting to highlight divergences, as we have above, it is easy to overlook convergences between the two provinces, particularly in the social pressures motivating family policy and in the conceptions of policy makers about social risks and social architecture. Indeed, while Quebec exceptionalism has a long pedigree in this area, it is notable how quickly the area of exception can change. In the late 1980s and early 1990s, observers might emphasize the pro-natalist features of Quebec policy, especially in the design of child benefits and birth bonuses, while ignoring commonalities in child care. In giving an award to Marois, the OCBCC was recognizing Quebec's 1997 family policy which greatly stripped out explicit pro-natalist goals, aligned the tax/transfer system closer to the approaches of the federal government, but pushed child care into a qualitatively different place than in the other provinces (Jenson 2002; Dandurand and Saint-Pierre 2000). In other words, while we find divergence in policies, we need to be aware of the fluidity of policy differences, on the one hand, and also of the existence of some convergence in the social forms giving rise to the policies and in the ideational frameworks shaping them. Our second aim is to explain the observed commonalities and differences, particularly using existing secondary accounts. While there are many different conceptual frameworks used to create typologies of family policies, the drive to typologize in itself privileges finding differences across countries, so as to fill out the boxes. We instead employ geographic theories that have been used in an attempt to understand the spatialities and temporalities of neoliberalism, as they seek to hold onto the structural forces driving state policies and strategies in all places, even while accounting for variability and seeking to understand the causes for that variability.

To this end, the chapter begins with a brief discussion of how one might define family policy. Family policy has received a new importance in policy discussions due to the way it interacts with the "new social risks" of post-industrial economies, and thus for how it can become a cornerstone for a new social architecture. As such, similarities and differences in policies can be grasped with a political economy framework that relates child care policies to broader struggles within polities over production and reproduction. This framework is then applied to policy developments in this field in Ontario and Quebec over the past 15–20 years and to a discussion of the policy drivers that account for the different policies. In general, we find that the differences between the provinces are driven by the presence of the women's movement and a family movement in the Quebec case, compared to the dominance of child development experts in Ontario.

I.   DEFINING FAMILY POLICY

Delimitating the field of family policy for this study is difficult for two reasons. First, on an empirical level, Quebec provides a series of programs that it defines as comprising its "family policy" and that gives rise to studies and reports within and outside the government in terms of how family policy is succeeding or failing in its ambitions. There is no parallel construction of a family policy field in Ontario (or elsewhere in North America—see Dandurand and Saint-Pierre 2000), with at best rhetorical claims to specific policies helping "working families." Therefore a purely empirical comparison of what these provincial communities define as constituting "family policy" is not possible. As a result, we must rely on social scientific constructions of what family policy is, but even here there are problems.

Maureen Baker, in her magisterial book *Restructuring Family Policy*, defines family policy as "official decisions to implement certain state-sponsored social programs, services, regulations, and laws relating to families" (2006: 15). This is a problematic place to start because the grounds for excluding policies are very weak. Everything from the level of minimum wages to immigration provisions affecting the organization of transnational care chains can be seen as affecting the manner in which families at different points on the income distribution organize their work and caring activities. In practice, work on family policy tends to focus on policies at the interface of the labour market and child bearing/rearing. The usual suspects include child benefits, parental leaves, and child care policies. This reflects an early definition of the field around the problematic of women's increased labour force participation and how this put pressure on "two of the most central institutions in society: the family and the workplace" (Kamerman and Kahn 1981). A second strand of family policy research, about how policies promote particular "model" families in terms of sexuality and parentage, intersects with this first one, particularly in developing multidimensional typologies.

In this chapter, we will adopt this narrow view of family policy, defined by policies immediately conceived around this nexus, albeit while admitting that it is very problematic to call this "family policy" *tout court*. For while it certainly considers how public policies affect the relationships between parents and the labour market, and can sometimes touch on aspects of gender relations in the family related to care work and income sharing, it ignores how many other policies shape families and the possibilities available to those within families. Thus, when we write about family policy, we are conscious of not touching on the whole realm of policies affecting women's autonomy to freely choose familial attachments, such as spouse-in-the-house rules in social assistance or the panoply of measures relating to familial violence. This tendency to take a partial view of women in families (see Brush 2002) no doubt owes something to the emphasis on children, an emphasis that also hides care pressures on families related to the care for elderly relatives.

1.1. Family Policy: International Frameworks

Numerous classificatory typologies exist for comparing family policies across the Western welfare democracies. Existing typologies tend to place Canada in a liberal/market category with low levels of investment and a fairly laissez-faire approach to normative family forms (providing no sustained support to either traditional family forms or to time-strapped dual earner families) (Ferrarini 2006), although some argue that Quebec's more generous parental leaves and its universal child care program push it towards a Scandinavian model of higher investment and greater support for dual-earner families (and by extension working women) (Tremblay 2009). There are nevertheless a number of reasons why this chapter does not simply place Ontario and Quebec within one (or a few) of these typologies, and instead applies a different set of theoretical lenses to organize the comparison.

First, while the cultural importance of notions of the family should make for relatively stable distinctions between countries over the long term, especially given the durability of the broader welfare state and production regime frames within which they are embedded, the multiplication of taxonomies and the lack of consensus around a smaller number of them suggests otherwise. Part of the explanation resides in the difficulty of assembling data across jurisdictions: the service intensity of some family policy makes it hard to quantify; the decentralization of provision makes it hard to get reliable aggregate totals (Ferrarini 2006: 4–6); relatively specific aspects of policy design can have strong implications about ideal family forms; and individual policies may have slightly different aims and goals (see Jenson 2002's discussion of Quebec's family policy), which can either lead to conflicting placements in typologies or the need to consider the overall package of policies when determining a country's placement (see also Baker 2006 for the potential and limits of existing typologies).

An additional problem with comparative typologies is that they are comparing a moving target given substantial recent innovations and investments across the Western post-industrial countries. This raises twin dangers, that typological analysis is insufficiently diachronic, on the one hand, and too prone to emphasize differences between political units at the expense of considering areas where they converge or at least undergo parallel developments. The discourse of international organizations, including the Organization for Economic Co-operation and Development (OECD), tilts strongly towards investing in child-focused family policies. Within this discourse community, it is worth noting, Canada outside Quebec (including Ontario) is seen as a laggard, especially in terms of child care. There are a variety of rationales for investment coming from different actors. These include effects on human capital formation, the potential for lifelong learning, the prevention of future social problems, and encouraging greater gender equity (Mahon 2009).

The most widely known take on child and family policy across the post-industrial economies nevertheless remains the one focused on the "new social risks" of the modern knowledge-based economy. Drawing heavily on the work of Gosta Esping-Andersen (2002), this view argues that the family is at the centre of viable and competitive welfare states for a variety of interacting reasons. First, the two-earner household is central to reducing the risk of poverty, especially child poverty, and so needs to be supported with transfers and services in order to be able to combine paid work with child rearing. This support has a spinoff effect of creating new service jobs, thus contributing to the achievement of full employment. However, given what epistemic communities in child brain science have been saying about the importance of the early years, it is not enough to warehouse children while their parents work—instead, children need access to forms of education and early learning as part of their care if they are to fully develop their capacities for lifelong learning. For similar reasons, child poverty needs to be combated given its demonstrated impact over the life course in terms of imposing higher costs on the state, which again favours policies supporting low-income parents, be they supportive services or income transfers. Variations on this story have been taken up by social policy advocates in Canada (e.g., Jenson 2004; Maxwell 2003) in discussions of new social risks and of the necessary social architecture to manage them, and are certainly visible and discernable in the political speak of the Ontario and Quebec governments.

If we abstract from the language of policy practitioners, though, we can see that the language of "new social risks" points to the inadequation between existing social policies and emerging economic practices, leading to problems of social reproduction. In other words, the forms of neoliberal capitalism practised in the Western countries have squeezed the time and resources that families have to provide or purchase care, which opens a debate about appropriate public policy responses to close the gap. The work on new social risks is strongly conditioned by the realization that the neoliberal policy paradigm either lacks compelling answers to the new social risks or provides answers that are ineffective and inefficient in building competitive post-industrial economies. Phrased in a more critical view, it speaks to a crisis of social reproduction, in the sense that current forms of economic competition are reliant on extra-economic inputs that are consumed faster than they are reproduced (Jessop 2000; Vosko 2006), including the caring capacity of families, social cohesion, and skilling. The response in the more liberal market economies like Canada has been to attempt to re-embed the economic in the social in an effort to realize the gains of neoliberalism while dampening instabilities around social reproduction. This can be seen in a fairly pure Polanyian sense as a re-embedding moment of "inclusive neoliberalism" (Craig and Cotterell 2007),or as a more complicated debate between varieties of liberalism, wherein a more social or egalitarian strain of liberalism has successfully challenged aspects of neoliberalism, leading to an "inclusive liberalism" with a slightly thicker sense of ensuring equality of opportunity to individuals in developing their capacities (Mahon 2008).

In considering family policies in this perspective, one means of distinguishing between them is based not on the dimensions of existing typologies (although these retain their interest and value), but on how family policies are reinvented within the new policy context, and the broader context of economic change. If we are in a new period of social policy making where the child and the family take on more importance as objects of policy, then one angle of comparison is to understand how this perspective is taken up and implemented in different contexts. Following Klodawsky (2009) we can consider three ideal-typical responses: one where family policies are *rolled out* in the goal of extending market metrics deeper into the life world; a second where family policies act as *flanking mechanisms* by ameliorating the worst damages of neoliberalism without challenging the core of the neoliberal project; and a third where they act as *countervailing measures*, opening possibilities beyond neoliberalism. While the level of abstraction involved in such analysis means that policies could relate to more than one response (e.g., a universal child care program could both encourage the greater commodification of parental labour, even as its universality reflected a countervailing break with neoliberalism), this three-pronged distinction allows us to distinguish neoliberal policies from inclusive liberal ones, and indeed to consider policies that push beyond inclusive liberalism towards social democracy. In placing Ontario and Quebec policies against this backdrop, we will also give some consideration to the forces that account for their placement: much work on new social risks gives pride of place to the experts in epistemic communities who identify the risks and solutions to them, but work on inclusive liberalism (e.g., Craig and Cotterell 2007) also suggests that political parties, particularly those trying to appeal to middle-class female voters, have an important role to play in developing such policy responses. Finally, more historical-institutionalist readings suggest we need also look at a broader range of social movement actors in accounting for policy shifts in the area (e.g., Jenson 2002). Thus, if we observe differences, we will attempt to understand these in terms of the agency of actors.

2.   ONTARIO

Ontario has never had a defined family policy, but in the child care sector it was for some time a leader among the provinces. As Mahon has demonstrated in a series of articles (e.g., 2010), child care activism has long been vibrant in Toronto, starting with municipal efforts to retain nonparental child care facilities after the Second World War and extended in the 1970s and 1980s with organizing by second wave feminists seeking an affordable and high quality system. The political organization of this sector has remained a little unusual, however, in being based around the Toronto municipal government and seeking to scale up its model through supportive policies at the provincial and federal levels. Through to the late 1980s, the narrative around this advocacy would be one of provincial success and federal failure. While child care policy proposed by the federal Conservative government in 1988 was roundly deemed insufficient and was then jettisoned, the Liberal provincial government of David Peterson announced its willingness to push forward in the late 1980s with the expansion of junior kindergarten, income-tested (rather than needs-tested) child care subsidies, and direct operating grants to child care centres, although it backed off when federal support was not forthcoming (Mahon 2010).

If we move outside child care to child benefits and parental leaves, however, Ontario has traditionally been reliant on federal initiatives, with parental leaves being delivered through the unemployment insurance system, and child benefits through federal family allowances. The possibility of an Ontario child benefit nevertheless did crop up during the Peterson government, specifically in the *Transitions* report of the

Social Assistance Review Committee. Here it figured as a means of equalizing the treatment of social assistance recipients (who received benefits for their children) and the working poor (who did not), so as to aid transitions from social assistance to work.

2.1. Madly Off in Two Directions

The election of an NDP majority government in 1990 promised to see a further development of family policies, especially as it tried to accelerate the reformism of the Peterson government in a period where some of the new social risk talk was making progress, especially around measures to activate social assistance recipients and to promote healthy child development in the early years. The NDP government planned to introduce universal child care in Ontario by February 1994. The government planned to grant funds to daycare centres directly, organize funding regionally, and set a maximum fee level (White, 1997). However, in 1994, responding to a deep recession of Ontario's economy in the early 1990s, the NDP deferred its longer-term strategy for a universal system, including the conversion of private operations to nonprofit status and the development of preschool for 3- to 5-year-olds. It instead moved to creating new subsidized child care spaces (with supporting funds for capital expenses) to support its activation policies (Mahon 2010), and even here the signals around social assistance reform, such as the 1993 *Turning Point* proposals, pointed to the creation of child benefits as the main line of attack, rather than developing child care services. In its longer-term strategizing, the government nevertheless brought together a coalition of child care advocates with a strong rooting in the women's movement, along with child development experts focused on early learning and prevention, to sketch out an early childhood education system that responded to a wide range of agendas. This would be swept off the table with the 1995–2003 Conservative government, and would come back with much of the feminist content shorn off.

The Conservative party that won the 1995 election nevertheless remained unconvinced by such long-term strategies and tried to roll back NDP initiatives such as pay equity in the child care sector, capital and start-up funds, funding for junior kindergarten, funds for child care in new schools, and privileging nonprofit providers (Mahon 2010). In total, during the Conservative reign, expenditures for child care fell from roughly $600 million in 1994–95 to $516.4 million in 2001 (Cleveland 2003).

The story of child policy is nevertheless a bit more complicated than a simple rolling back of preceding initiatives. It could not escape the influence of thinking around the early years, at least as this was channelled through federal-provincial processes such as the creation of the National Child Benefit (NCB) Supplement. Because this benefit was treated as income, the province was allowed to claw back an equivalent amount from social assistance recipients provided it invested it elsewhere. In 1998, though Ontario introduced its own Child Care Supplement for Working Families to help offset the clawback for low-income working families with nonregulated child care expenses, there nevertheless was no mechanism to ensure it was spent on child care, let along regulated child care. The impetus of federal government interest in early childhood policies again pushed the provincial government to action in 2000, when Ontario signed an Early Childhood Development Agreement (ECDA) with the federal government. Initiated in 2001 and inspired by the National Children's Agenda, the agreement entailed four key programs targeting pregnancy, birth and infancy; parental training and supports; community supports; and early childhood learning, development, and care. The premise of the Plan was to encourage and support the health and intellectual development of the child up to age 6. To this end, Early Years Centres were created across the province to serve as a clearinghouse for parents, communities, and, eventually, child care providers. Services included lending libraries, breastfeeding support, child behavioural counselling, literacy and outreach services, and child-centred activities.

The Early Years Centres were Ontario's main means of channelling new federal funds, but their origins looked back to the Margaret McCain and Fraser Mustard *Early Years Study*, submitted to the provincial government in 1999. The report synthesized much of the neuroscience behind the inclusive liberal case for investments in children, namely that the full development of individuals is greatly related to healthy brain development at a young age. It recommended the creation of early childhood development and parenting centres, with an educational focus and the provision of nonparental care. Yet the implementation of the report, mirroring the provincial response to new federal early childhood programming, was to steer clear of supporting nonparental child care and to instead fund a series of drop-in and resource centres across the province. Indifference to the changing structure of families and social diversity along with the lack of concentrated funding, some argue, resulted in the Early Years Plan "failing to support high-quality, accessible, regulated child care" (Vosko 2006). The result of the Early Years Plan in general and the Early Years Centres in particular was to exacerbate inequalities and escalate tensions in social reproduction because of the ideology of individualization, privatization, and familialization underpinning the Plan. As Mahon (2010) notes more broadly of the ECDA, the Ontario government received $844 million from the federal government without creating (or being obliged to create) a single child care space.

This set of policies was not greatly attuned with new social risks. The Role of Government Panel commissioned by Premier Harris in his last days in office underlined that Ontario's policies were out of touch with social changes such as very high rates (70%+) of labour market participation by women with preschool children, reduced economic security for workers, and increased rates of in-work poverty. As Judith Maxwell's (2003) big picture overview underlined, families and individuals were being asked to carry more risk on their shoulders without the development of new supports to reconcile work and care, to mitigate risks, or to aid moves out of low pay. The thrust of the argument was that neoliberalism had led to an efficiency drive, but one that simply tightened postwar programs rather than retool them for a changed society. More specifically, the failure to deal with new social risks could be observed in several areas. As of 2008, for instance, Ontario had regulated child care spaces for only 13.6% of children aged 0–12 (and 19.6% for 0–5) versus 36% in Quebec (25% for 0–5 in Quebec) (Mahon 2010). Similarly, income inequality in Ontario for families raising children, which used to be more closely clustered than in other provinces, increased dramatically faster over the 1990s, at least when measured in terms of the ratio of the top and bottom deciles. The bottom 40% of families saw their incomes stall since the 1970s despite increasing their annual number of weeks of work (Yalnizyan 2007).

The Liberal victory in the 2003 election hinted at possible changes, in that McGuinty promised to reinvest in child care by making early learning a priority. The federal Liberals were equally on board and promised to tackle the issue comprehensively based on the quality, universal accessibility, and development (QUAD) principles. However, before this initiative could adequately take root, the Harper Conservatives won the federal election of 2006 and, with this victory, announced plans to withdraw from federal funding arrangements. Instead, the Conservatives would launch their own so-called universal child care benefit—a taxable benefit of $100 a month for each child under the age of six that families were not required to spend on child care. In spite of the Harper plan, the McGuinty government chose to go ahead and spend $105.7 million to help municipalities sustain child care centres and $24.8 million to fund an average wage increase of 3% for child care workers (Mahon 2010).

The recession of 2008 compelled the McGuinty government to focus on poverty-reduction strategies, of which reducing child poverty became the most critical. In 2009 Ontario commissioned the Pascal report, which recommended a "seamless day" (full day) for children aged 4–5 and, eventually, after-school care for 6–12-year-olds. The government's policy, which would be rolled out gradually, allocated $200 million to achieve the "seamless day" for 4–5-year-olds and earmarked another $700 million for 2011. This came on the heels of the Pascal report, which was heavily steeped in the worldview that early learning is an economic and social imperative in knowledge-based economies, as well as the development of a poverty-reduction strategy that likewise supported early interventions as a form of prevention. Allocating $63.5 million to replace the federal QUAD funds, the McGuinty government continued to support child care spaces abandoned by the federal government, allowing some 1,000 child care workers to keep their jobs ("Ontario" 2010). Moreover, the province has been working with local government to provide capital funding for centres and increase the number of subsidized spaces (Mahon 2010). On this front, then, we see the renewal of initiatives to ramp up public funding and universal access, especially for 4- and 5-year-olds, but framed largely in terms of child development and prevention, with little in the way of policy design or rhetoric to respond to feminist agendas of gender equality and of job quality for the child care workforce.

While Ontario is ever so slowly closing the gap with Quebec in terms of early childhood education, it was slightly more aggressive in closing the gap with the launch of the Ontario Child Benefit (OCB) in 2007. In 2010, it provides $1,100 per child per year in excess of federal child benefits to low-income parents. The adoption of the OCB places Ontario in the pack of other provinces that have used National Child Benefit Supplement monies clawed back from social assistance recipients to launch a provincial child benefit and, in the process, will wind up the provincial child care subsidy for working parents. This sort of child benefit for low-income Ontarians has a long pedigree, having been raised as part of the *Transitions* review of social assistance in the late 1980s (under the rubric of "taking children off welfare") and again by the NDP government in 1993–1994, although it was abandoned at that point due to the cost and the lack of federal government cooperation. It resurfaced in the progressive social policy community after the 2003 provincial election (e.g., Stapleton 2004) and received additional credibility when put forward by the business-led Toronto City Summit Alliance as part of their report on Modernizing Income Support for Working-Aged Adults. By adding the OCB to federal child benefits and to various small tax credits, low-income parents now receive approximately $6,000 a year for a first child. While the OCB closes the gap with Quebec in terms of support for low-income families, the phase-out point of benefits only reaches partway into the middle class and there is no transfer or tax credit with quasi-universal application like that found in Quebec. It seems almost entirely justified for its ability to break down the welfare wall, as do several other small changes related to extending social assistance health and dental benefits to other low-income earners.

In sum, family policies in Ontario are being introduced largely as flanking mechanisms. On the child care side, there is a nod to universality in plans for full-day junior kindergarten, but within a broader context of underinvestment in child care and education and weak supports for working parents of young children. Likewise, while child benefits do help close the gap between stagnant wages and family needs, their emphasis on the welfare wall means that they remain targeted and stingy and not a transformative game changer for time-strapped middle-income families.

3.   QUEBEC

3.1. Background

Unlike in Ontario, family policy as an explicit area of public policy does have a pedigree in Quebec, which is usually dated from the creation of the ministère de la Famille et du Bien-être in 1961, the creation of the advisory Conseil supérieur de la famille in 1964, and the development of a separate system of family allowances in 1967 (Conseil de la famille et de l'enfance 2008: 10). Both the Ministère and the Conseil were closed as part of the integration of social policy functions into the ministère des Affaires sociales in the early 1970s, but the Conseil had succeeded in developing both a set of ideas about family policy and a supportive network of nonstate organizations in the policy area such that the policy area did not entirely fall off the agenda in the shuffle. From the beginning, ideas about family policy were contested, with the emphasis on vertical redistribution ensuring the well-being of individuals and families having the upper hand, but not entirely displacing an interest in supporting natalism (Jenson 1998: 204). The balance shifted towards natalism (but again, with alternative understandings remaining strong enough to contest the shift) under the Parti québécois in the late 1970s, particularly in the context of developing demographic projections of the population needed to support the province's new industrial strategy, *Bâtir le Québec* (Jenson 1998; Conseil de la famille et de l'enfance 2008). This fed into the Liberals' pro-natalist 1988 family policy, which included the famous "baby bonuses" which were set up to encourage families to have three or more children, as was an additional unpaid parental leave (Baker 1990). There was more to this period than natalism, however, including a further development of concertation between state and nonstate actors: the latter had called for state action in the early 1980s and engaged in a long consultative process which somewhat tempered the focus on birth rates. And in the aftermath of the 1988 strategy, state and nonstate actors worked closely on three action plans, with the final one including commitments by both sets of actors. The re-creation of a Conseil de la famille and the creation of a Secrétariat à la famille in 1988 provided a renewed state capacity for such efforts (Conseil de la famille et de l'enfance 2008). The 1988 policy also reworked taxes and transfers, putting Quebec ahead of the other provinces in delivering supports through the tax system.

Thus, while Baker (1990) emphasized natalism as what set Quebec's policies apart in this period, the two more significant differences with Ontario leading into the current period of welfare state reform was the development of provincial tax-transfer policies (as compared to largely relying on federal efforts as in Ontario), and the structure of interests in the field with the development of a family policy network. While Ontario child-care activists might look to Quebec for inspiration in 2008, it had not been the object of any family policy attention by the mid-1990s and indeed was similarly developed or even less developed than Ontario's system if looked at in terms of spaces, profit/not-for-profit mix, or number of fee subsidies (CRRU 1997).

3.2. Context for Recent Changes

Family policy making from the 1990s onward obviously built on this previous foundation, but also reflected a changed and changing environment. Consistent with other advanced industrial countries, Quebec faced a period of budgetary austerity that encouraged the rationalization of existing programs and the shift of responsibility away from the state and towards families and the third sector (Dandurand and Saint-Pierre 2000). Neoliberal ideas were also present in several important policy discourses, most notably in the area of activation or workfare for social assistance recipients (Jenson 2002), but it is also noteworthy that discourses of prevention were also well embedded in specialist discourses.

Family policy also had to respond to continued changes in the family, including the maturation of the trend to the dual-earner family and increased time-stress, as the increased paid work time supplied by families did not give rise to improved standard of living. The labour force participation rate for Quebec women increased from 41% in 1976 to 61% in 2008 and the employment rate for women aged 25 to 44 increased from 48.4% in 1978 to 79.2% in 2008, outstripping the increase in Ontario from 63% to 77.8% over the same period. Despite this change in labour force participation, incomes have been largely stagnant, with family market incomes falling from $53,900 in 1976 to $51,900 in 2006 (in 2007 dollars) and post-tax and transfer median family incomes trending up from $50,600 to $54,500 in the same time period. At the median, then, the main move has been a shift in the tax and transfer system, making the median family a net beneficiary. The strength of the Quebec tax and transfer system can also be seen in its ability to reduce inequalities between families, reducing the Gini coefficient (a common measure of income inequality) by 0.143 versus 0.109 in Ontario. Child benefits are no doubt part of the story here and, indeed, transfers as a total account for 66% of the reduction in the Gini in Quebec, versus 61% in Ontario (Godbout and Joanis 2009). Despite this difference with Ontario, an equally important point is that labour markets absorbed the increase in women's paid labour supply, but failed to translate the per-capita GDP and productivity growth over the past quarter century into increased well-being, leaving it up to the state to do the heavy lifting.

3.3. The 1997 Family Policy Earthquake and After

In Quebec, the big shift came with the 1997 family policy. The sources of this change are varied. Jenson (2002) emphasizes how the three elements of the family policy (discussed below) worked together as a package that could likewise stitch together a broad range of supporting constituencies. It brought together the emerging expert emphasis on prevention and child development with long-standing demands of the women's and family movements, and wedded a government concern with activating social assistance recipients (for a slightly different interpretation, see Dandurand and Saint-Pierre 2000). The ability to create this consensus owed something to the pre-existing family policy networks and the presence of these networks explains why a policy crafted in a period of budgetary austerity and with a focus on activation nevertheless has a strong flavour of equal opportunity, equity, and solidarity (Jenson 2002).

A first part of the family policy involved integrating three family allowances, including the famous baby bonuses, as well as child benefits within the social assistance system and packaging them into a single family allowance. These family allowances, which decreased with income, were coupled with the maintenance of a nonrefundable family tax credit, the only such credit for families with children in Canada (Jenson 2002; Conseil de la famille et de l'enfance 2008). The second and best-known part of the family policy was the development of a low-cost, universal child care program, to be delivered by Centres de la petite enfance (CPE). These are nonprofit centres set up under the program, which were responsible for offering care as well as supervising family day cares. This prong of the family policy thus encouraged the creation of nonprofit and responsive community organizations with an emphasis on quality and the subsidization of the spaces they created in order to keep the parental contribution to $5 per day (Jenson 2002). The final part of the 1997 strategy to be implemented was the parental leave policy, which required negotiations with the federal government as well as an ultimately unsuccessful challenge of federal jurisdiction in the area. The policy went into effect in 2006 and has proved more popular than anticipated. The program stands apart from the federal one in three ways: first, it offers better replacement rates; second, it hives off some time (3–5 weeks) that can only be used by the father; and third, it is based on earned income rather than employment insurance eligibility, thereby opening access to parents with little work income or who earn their income in atypical jobs that lack employment insurance protection (Chaussard *et al.* 2008; Tremblay 2009).

While the 1997–2003 period was marked by the implementation of the policy and especially the difficult work of developing a large number of new regulated spaces in the face of parental expectations, namely, that they had a right to a space in the system, the post-2003 period has witnessed some changes in the policy that have changed its meaning. Early in their first mandate, the Liberals indicated a preference for raising rates, especially for families with higher incomes, but were pushed back by popular organizations and instead only increased fees to $7 per day. The more important changes were subtler and less evident. First, the Liberals showed a marked preference for providing access to state subsidies tied to the $7-per-day program for for-profit centres, ostensibly because their lack of democratic boards of directors meant they could bring new spaces on line more quickly. The result has been to favour for-profit providers and to increase the dosage of a daycare philosophy over one centred on quality early childhood education (Jenson 2009). Second, the governance of the system was changed to narrow the scope of authority of the Centres de la petite enfance, with their community boards and emphasis on educational quality, in favour of larger coordinating agencies. This trend has been accentuated with the 2010 provincial budget, which increased the tax credit for child-care expenses rather than investing in creating new spaces in the public system (Roy and Robitaille 2010).

At the same time, the Liberal government in 2005 consolidated and enriched child benefits, consolidating existing tax credits and allowances into the refundable Soutien aux enfants tax credit. Couples with children are guaranteed $611 per year for a first child, while single parents receive no less than $916. However, income-tested benefits bring those sums to $2,176 for couples earning under $44,788 and $2,938 for single parents with an income below $32,856, which is roughly two to three times the rate of the Ontario Child Benefit but still $1,000–$2,000 below the rates in many other countries (Conseil de la famille et de l'enfance 2008). At the same time, the government set up another refundable tax credit, the Prime au travail, to replace the existing wage supplement for working parents.

In sum, while the universality and public sector emphasis of the 1997 policy, coupled with its empowerment of community-based organizations (the CPEs) seemingly looked beyond neoliberalism, the treatment of public-sector funding as a means to subsidize private-sector daycare operations points to the further roll-out of neoliberalism, as does the capacity of private operators to resell day care licenses acquired at $157 for a million dollars (at least according to public day-care advocates like Roy and Robitaille 2010) and the relative impunity with which they can charge illegal supplementary fees. The point here is not that the Quebec child care policy has become a "commons" to be privatized as a new profit centre as neoliberalism is rolled out, but to note this countertrend. It still seems safe to present it as part of a flanking strategy, concerned with enabling high labour market participation and with nipping long-term problems in the bud during the early years, that verges on serving as a countervailing strategy in its universalism, its interest in quality, its language around women's equality, and its grounding in community. Nevertheless, changes under the post-2003 Liberal government have shifted the balance between flanking and countervailing elements towards the former.

4.   DISCUSSION AND CONCLUSION

If we were to place the provinces in terms of the categories discussed in section 3 above, we could see them both as experimenting with flanking mechanisms, but where Quebec practice to date has opened doors towards countervailing alternatives. This can be seen most clearly in the choice of a universal, developmental model of early childhood education and its possibilities for higher quality work in the care sector. It can also be seen in a system of parental leaves with higher replacement rates and with incentives for fathers to share in the care.

While the account of this chapter is consistent with the idea of Quebec's difference, it remains that the context of increased labour force participation and stagnant incomes has led both Ontario and Quebec families to respond by increasing hours worked. In this context, then, and despite evidence that family policies are working to change gender roles in a more egalitarian direction in Quebec more quickly than in the rest of Canada (Tremblay 2008), Quebec families are still under a great deal of stress in trying to reconcile caring and paid work responsibilities (Tézli and Gauthier 2009). Moreover, with Ontario's move to full-day junior kindergarten and the adoption of an Ontario Child Benefit, some of the distance between the two provinces on the income and child care fronts is being narrowed, without much evidence that Quebec is going to take a qualitative step that would distance itself anew from Ontario. As such, while there is good reason to portray Quebec policies as a significant policy departure from the Canadian model (which Ontario exemplifies well), it remains a flanking mechanism for neoliberalism as much as a window into a non-neoliberal alternative.

Nevertheless, while the family policies largely sit in the same box, the placement of the provinces in these boxes varies. Consistent with Craig and Cotterell (2007), political parties do matter. Inclusive liberal departures are related to the presence of parties of social reform, be it the PQ in Quebec or the Ontario Liberals, while the progress of inclusive liberalism largely stalls under the right-of-centre Quebec Liberals or is turned back under the right-of-centre Ontario Conservatives. Such an account is nevertheless not entirely satisfactory. It works better for Ontario, where the Harris Conservative government mobilized an angry working and middle-class male constituency, and where the Liberals were elected in 2003 on promises to clean up the dislocation and inequality created by the Conservatives. Even here, though, the Liberals only half fit the script, not filling the mould of the social democratic party.

An additional explanation comes from the study of social movements interacting with the state. As we have seen, family policy in Quebec has been elaborated in an ongoing discussion with actors outside the state, including a family movement and the women's movement. The reasons for the greater porosity of the Quebec state to organized interests, also observed in other policy domains (Hamel and Jouve 2006), remains to be fully explained, but no doubt owes something both to the strength and organization of advocacy groups in Quebec (Laforest 2007) and to nationalism's tendency to attempt to foster the appearance of inclusion (Béland and Lecours 2008). By contrast, the Ontario state was slower to develop mechanisms to represent and engage such groups and quicker to disband such mechanisms in the neoliberal nineties. This brings us back to the role of political parties, but also leads us back to recognizing how institutions as congealments of power limit the freedom of parties, as the announced intent of the post-2003 Liberal party to strip such "corporatism" out of the state encountered significant resistance and has been only partially and stealthily implemented.

This difference in porosity therefore led to differences in who could be part of the inner circle of policy participation in the two cases. While similar ideas about the role of family policy in dealing with new social risks were in the air in both Ontario and Quebec (Mahon 2010), different sets of actors were closely involved in policy discussions, leading to different policy outcomes. Of particular importance were the women's movement and the family movement in Quebec. These actors took a discussion centred around new social risks and broadened the options to include additional values, including vertical and horizontal redistribution in support of families and the value of universal child care as part of a woman-friendly development model.

These actors were not nearly as central to Ontario policy making. The women's movement in Ontario was much weakened under the Harris Conservative government and there was never anything like a family movement. As a result, when the policy community came around to the question of new social risks, there were no voices pushing either a social democratic agenda for child care or a combination of universal and income-tested family benefits. As a result, the actors pushing family policies onto the agenda under the post-2003 Liberal government were much more tied to discourses on prevention in the Early Years and to the importance of child benefits as a means of breaking down a purported welfare wall.

In the bigger picture of thinking about Ontario and Quebec, the case of family policy demonstrates the salience of some well entrenched differences around the porosity of the state and the strength of different social actors (such as the women's and community movements). However, differences also flowed from electoral choices between parties, giving more fluidity over time to the extent and sources of difference. Finally, the temptation when comparing the provinces is to look for differences, but, at least in this policy area, commonalities arising from international policy thinking, the working of contemporary political economies, and broad philosophies about economics and politics mean those differences are inscribed within important similarities that are also worth sounding out.

BIBLIOGRAPHY

Abrahamson, P., T. P. Boje, and B. Greve (2005). *Welfare and Families in Europe.* Aldershot: Ashgate.

Baker, M. (1990). *Family Policy in Québec.* Ottawa: Library of Parliament.

Baker, M. (1995). *Canadian Family Policies: Cross-National Comparisons.* Toronto: University of Toronto Press.

Baker, M. (2006). *Restructuring Family Policies: Convergences, Divergences.* Toronto: University of Toronto Press.

Béland, D. and A. Lecours (2008). *Nationalism and Social Policy.* Toronto: Oxford University Press.

Brush, L. D. (2002). "Changing the Subject: Gender and Welfare Regime Studies." *Social Politics,* vol. 9: 161–186.

Chaussard, M., M. Gerecke, and J. Heymann (2008). *The Work Equity Index: Where the Provinces and Territories Stand.* Montreal: Institut des politiques sociales et de la santé.

Cleveland, G. S. C. (2003). *The Future of Government in Supporting Early Childhood Education and Care in Ontario.* Report for the Panel on the Role of Government, June 1.

Conseil de la famille et de l'enfance (2008). *La politique familiale au Québec: visée, portée, durée et rayonnement.* Quebec City: Conseil de la famille et de l'enfance.

Craig, D. and G. Cotterell (2007). "Periodising Neoliberalism?" *Policy and Politics,* vol. 35: 497–514.

Childcare Resource and Research Unit (CRRU) (1997). *Child Care in Canada: Provinces and Territories.* Toronto: CRRU.

Dandurand, R.-B. and M.-H. Saint-Pierre (2000). "Les nouvelles dispositions de la politique familiale québécoise. Un retournement ou une évolution prévisible?" In M. Simard and J. Alary (eds.), *Comprendre la famille. Actes du 5ᵉ Symposium québécois de recherche sur la famille.* Quebec City: Presses de l'Université du Québec: 59–80.

Esping-Andersen, G. (ed.) (2002). *Why We Need a New Welfare State.* Oxford: Oxford University Press.

Ferrarini, T. (2006). *Families, States, and Labour Markets.* Cheltenham: Edward Elgar.

Godbout, L. and M. Joanis (2009). " Mise en contexte: voir au-delà de la récession." In M. Joanis and L. Godbout (eds.), *Le Québec économique 2009-2010.* Quebec City: Les Presses de l'Université Laval: 5–10.

Hamel, P. and B. Jouve (2006). *Un modèle québécois? Gouvernance et participation dans la gestion publique.* Montreal: Les Presses de l'Université de Montréal.

Jenson, J. (1998). "Les réformes des services de garde pour jeunes enfants en France et au Québec: une analyse historico-institutionaliste." *Politique et sociétés,* vol. 17: 183–216.

Jenson, J. (2002). "Against the Current: Child Care and Family Policy in Quebec." In S. Michel and R. Mahon (eds.), *Child Care Policy at the Crossroads.* New York: Routledge: 309–332.

Jenson, J. (2009). "Rolling Out or Backtracking on Quebec's Child Care System? Ideology Matters." In M. Griffin Cohen and J. Pulkingham (eds.), *Public Policy for Women: The State, Income Security, and Labour Market Issues.* Toronto: University of Toronto Press: 50–70.

Jenson, J. (2009). "Changing the Paradigm: Family Responsibility or Investing in Children," *The Canadian Journal of Sociology,* vol. 29, no. 2: 169–192.

Jessop, B. (2000). "The Crisis of the National Spatio-Temporal Fix and the Tendential Ecological Dominance of Globalizing Capitalism." *International Journal of Urban and Regional Research,* vol. 24: 323–360.

Kamerman, S. B. and A. J. Kahn (1981). *Child Care, Family Benefits, and Working Parents: A Study in Comparative Policy.* New York: Columbia University Press.

Klodawsky, F. (2009). "Home Spaces and Rights to the City: Thinking Social Justice for Chronically Homeless Women." *Urban Geography,* vol. 30: 591–610.

Laforest, R. (2007). "The Politics of State/Civil Society Relations in Québec." In M. Murphy (ed.), *Canada: The State of the Federation 2005.* Kingston: Relations School of Policy Studies: 179–198.

Mahon, R. (2008). "Varieties of Liberalism: Canadian Social Policy from the 'Golden Age' to the Present." *Social Policy and Administration,* vol. 42: 342–361.

Mahon, R. (2009). "Transnationalising (Child) Care Policy: The OECD and the World Bank." Paper prepared for the RC19 Conference of the International Sociological Association, Montreal, August.

Mahon, R. (2010). "Gender and the New Politics of Redistribution: Child Care Policy in Ontario." Paper prepared for The New Politics of Redistribution workshop, University of Toronto, May.

Maxwell, J. (2003). "The Great Social Transformation: Implications for the Social Role of Government in Ontario." Report for the Panel on the Role of Government. Ottawa: Canadian Policy Research Networks.

"Ontario Pumps Billions into Education" (2010). *Toronto Star,* March 25.

Roy, S. and J. Robitaille (2010). "Profits et services de garde ne font pas bon ménage." *Le Devoir*, July 5.

Stapleton, J. (2004). *Transitions Revisited: Implementing the Vision.* Ottawa: Caledon Institute of Social Policy.

Tézli, A. and A. H. Gauthier (2009). "Balancing Work and Family in Canada: An Empirical Examination of Conceptualizations and Measurements." *Canadian Journal of Sociology*, vol. 34: 433–462.

Tremblay, D.-G. (2009). "Québec's Policies for Work–Family Balance: A Model for Canada?" In M. Griffin Cohen and J. Pulkingham (eds.), *Public Policy for Women: The State, Income Security, and Labour Market Issues.* Toronto: University of Toronto Press: 271–290.

Vosko, L. (2006). "Crisis Tendencies in Social Reproduction: The Case of Ontario's Early Years Plan." In K. Bezanson and M. Luxton (eds.), *Social Reproduction.* Montreal and Kingston: McGill-Queen's University Press: 145–172.

White, L. (1997). "Partisanship or Politics of Austerity: Child Care Policy Development in Ontario and Alberta, 1980 to 1996." *Journal of Family Issues*, vol. 18: 7–29.

Yalnizyan, A. (2007). *Ontario's Growing Gap: Time for Leadership.* Ottawa: Canadian Centre for Policy Alternatives.

8. DO THEY WALK LIKE THEY TALK?
Speeches from the Throne and Budget Deficits in Ontario and Quebec

LOUIS M. IMBEAU

Why should we pay attention to what policy makers say? My short answer to this important question is: because they spend most of their time and energy "discoursing," that is, giving speeches, writing memos, discussing issues, sending messages, etc.; they *talk*. As Giandomenico Majone rightly reminded us: "[P]ublic policy is made of language . . . Political parties, the electorate, the legislature, the executive, the courts, the media, interest groups, and independent experts all engage in a continuous process of debate and reciprocal persuasion" (1989: 1). But policy makers also *walk*: they spend, tax, and borrow money; they conceive, adopt, and amend laws, regulations, and international agreements; they create, change, and terminate administrative bodies; they enforce law and wage war; they hold press conferences, dissolve Parliament, send missions abroad, etc. Speech *and* action are the core of policy making and both deserve our attention.

My objective in this chapter is to explore the consonance and dissonance (Imbeau 2009) between policy speech and policy action in the realm of fiscal policy. More precisely, I ask the question whether governments that realize a higher budget balance (or a lower deficit) have a more fiscally conservative stance in their speeches. I address this issue in four parts. First, I discuss the theoretical relationship between speech and action. Second, I broadly describe the bottom-line results of the fiscal policy of the Ontario and Quebec governments over the last 33 years. Third, I describe a method for measuring the provincial premiers' fiscal policy stance and, applying it to their speeches from the throne, I assess their fiscal conservativeness. In the last section I describe the relationship between speech and action and I propose an answer to my starting question.

I.   THE WALK–TALK RELATIONSHIP

I look at the policy process as involving three types of rational actors: policy makers, special interest groups, and voters. When thinking about the role of policy speech in the policy process, I look at the objectives policy makers pursue while "speaking" to special interests and to voters and while "acting" on the budget. This leads me to three conceptions of the walk–talk relationship, each one based on a specific theory and leading to a specific hypothesis (see Table 1).

Table I
Three Conceptions of the Walk–Talk Relationship

Conception	Politician's Objective	Underlying Theory	Hypothesis
Benevolent	To inform economic agents	Ricardo-Barro equivalence theory	Positive
Sophisticated	To convince voters	Median voter theory	Negative
Cynical	To seduce clients	Political entre-preneurship	No relationship

Let's start with a conception that focuses on the relationship between policy makers and special interest groups, the *benevolent conception*, which ensues from Ricardo-Barro's equivalence theorem. It considers a closed economy in which a representative agent consumes, works, and saves. The government is represented by a benevolent planner whose objective is to maximize the welfare of the representative agent. Both the government and the agent have an infinite temporal horizon; therefore, neither intergenerational aspects nor the limited terms of government mandate are taken into account. When public deficits increase public debts, the representative agent knows that, in the future, the government will have to increase taxes in order to pay back the debt. According to the theory of permanent income, the agent determines her consumption level based on her total actualized future revenues. In this case, she concludes that financing public spending through taxes is "equivalent" to financing through borrowing (Barro 1989: 38–39). In this context, the optimal strategy for the benevolent planner is to maintain constant tax rates in order to avoid costs related to unexpected variations in tax rates. To reach this goal, he uses surpluses and deficits as cushions through the application of a tax-smoothing policy: deficits appear when public spending is temporarily high, surpluses when spending is temporarily low (Roubini and Sachs 1989: 910–913).

While applying his tax-smoothing policy, the benevolent planner uses policy speeches to inform the agent of his policy choice so that she makes the right consumption choices, that is, she adjusts her savings to the budget balance: when there is a deficit, the agent saves the money she would have paid in additional tax had the budget been balanced, knowing that futures taxes will have to compensate for the accumulated debt. Thus, when he produces a deficit, the benevolent planner adopts a fiscally liberal speech telling the agent that spending is higher than taxation and, therefore, that she should anticipate higher taxes in the future to reimburse the debt. When the benevolent planner realizes a higher budget balance, he adopts a more conservative stance in his speech, thus informing the economic agent that the government's financial position is improving and, therefore, that she does not have to save now in view of future increased taxes. It follows that the benevolent hypothesis predicts a positive relationship between budget balance and fiscal conservatism.

Now, if we move to a conception focusing on the relationship between policy makers and voters, we get the *sophisticated hypothesis*, which predicts the opposite relationship: fiscal conservatism should be lower when budget balance is higher. Here, the government is represented by a politician who faces re-election in a democratic setting. According to the median voter theorem, the politician realizes a budget that corresponds to the preferences of the median voter. Indeed, if voters can be ordered according to their preferences concerning the budget balance (going from a high deficit to a high surplus) and if we assume that the distribution of voters on this dimension is unimodal (single-peaked preferences) and that people vote according to their preferences (sincere voting), it is easy to see that in a democratic contest on the issue of budget balance, the candidate who can win the support of the median voter wins the election. In its weak version, the median voter theorem states that the median voter always votes for the policy that is adopted. In the strong version of the theorem, the median voter always gets her most preferred policy (Congleton 2002). Therefore, in this context, the realized budget balance corresponds to the budget balance preferred by the median voter.

But the politician also has his own preferences concerning the budget balance because it directly impacts on the quality and quantity of government services, on the one hand, and on his leeway or room to manoeuvre, on the other hand. A deficit means more or better-quality services than the actual level of taxation would provide. But it also means less leeway in the future because of increased debt service expenditures ensuing from additional borrowing. And the opposite is also true. A surplus means more leeway in the future to the extent that it is channelled to debt reimbursement but it also means fewer government services given the taxation level. I assume here that the politician equally values services and leeway. When he becomes aware that the budget balance is going to be lower, he knows that his leeway will deteriorate because of increased debt charges. He then adopts a fiscally conservative speech in an effort to convince voters to change their preferences and to ask for a higher budget balance. When the balance is higher than what the politician wants, his speeches are less fiscally conservative. The sophisticated hypothesis therefore states that the relationship between budget balance and fiscal conservatism is negative (Imbeau 2005).

Both the benevolent and the sophisticated hypotheses are deduced from theories assuming two types of actors, decision makers and special interest groups (the benevolent planner and the economic agent of the benevolent conception) or decision makers and voters (the benevolent politician and the median voter of the sophisticated hypothesis). What happens if we assume a politician facing both special interest groups and voters? We get the cynical conception.

The *cynical conception* of the walk–talk relationship considers a world where a rational maximizing politician tries to seduce his clients, meaning those persons who, he hopes, will buy his services, that is, his policy decisions, against money, promises of future advantages, or electoral support. In this context, the politician is assumed to be a producer of fiscal policy decisions that special interest groups and voters consume. For example, a conservative voter wants a balanced budget or a surplus if there is a debt to reimburse. A liberal voter wants more or better services and therefore is willing to accept a lower balance. Both are willing to exchange their vote for a fiscal policy that corresponds to their preferences. Likewise, a person who does business with the government wants more spending (and therefore a lower balance given the level of taxation) because a part of this spending may end up into her pocket. A person who does not do business with the government wants less spending (and therefore a higher balance given the level of taxation) because she feels that much of this spending flows from her own pocket into someone else's. In its simplest form, this theory holds that this entrepreneur-politician uses his speech to seduce clients in order to make them give up some of their "wealth" in exchange for a given level of budget balance. Knowing that his clients have differing, often contradictory preferences, the entrepreneur-politician speaks in vague and general terms so as to please everybody. Therefore, there should be no systematic relationship between fiscal conservatism in speeches and the budget balance.

To summarize, let's say that we have three different conceptions of the walk–talk relationship, or theories of fiscal policy speech and action, each one yielding a different hypothesis or prediction about what the actual relationship between words and deeds is. Before exposing a method for measuring fiscal conservativeness in speeches, I now turn to assessing fiscal conservatism in action.

2. WALKING THE BUDGET BALANCE IN ONTARIO AND QUEBEC

We have traditionally looked at budget balance (surplus/deficit) as simply resulting from decisions concerning revenue and spending levels. The balance results from the subtraction of spending from revenue. There was not much more to say about it other than to insist on the variety of accounting procedures that could transform a deficit into a surplus (Blejer and Cheasty 1991).

More recently, we have come to consider that budget balance is an important dimension of a government fiscal policy and that it can reveal information about several aspects of a government and its policy. For example, one can see in the budget balance an indication of how a government plans to finance its spending program. Thus a deficit tells one that a government chose not to levy all the taxes that its spending program would require, but rather decided to finance part of its spending through borrowing. A surplus shows that a government renounced to consume as much as it collected either in view of future spending or to pay for past spending. One could also look at budget deficit as an instrument of wealth redistribution from taxpayers to investors and from future to present generations. In 2002, for example, federal, provincial, and local governments in Canada transferred 14% of the money they had levied in taxes to investors as interests paid on their debts. In 1995, this redistribution had reached 22% of public administration revenues in Canada. Public debt is also a way to make future generations of taxpayers pay for present consumption spending, a kind of negative bequest (Cukierman and Meltzer 1989; Tabellini 1991). I adopt here a third conception of a government budget balance. Like many observers of government fiscal policy, I look at budget balance as a diagnosis on the fiscal prudence of fiscal authorities. In that perspective, a higher budget balance indicates that a government is conservative in its management of public funds; a lower one denotes a government that is fiscally liberal with public money.

Figure I
Budget Balances in Canada: 1966–2000
(Percent of Total Spending)

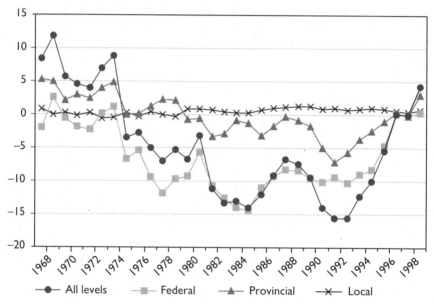

Source: Adapted from the Statistics Canada CANSIM database, <http://cansim2.statcan.ca/>, Table 385-0002.

Data provided by Statistics Canada tell us that, in the aggregate, public administrations in Canada have been fiscally liberal for an important period of time in the last several decades. Figure 1 gives us an overall picture of public budget balances in Canada by level of government. One can clearly see that deficits started to be recurrent in the mid-1970s at the federal level and in the early 1980s at the provincial level. One can also see that Canadian public administrations progressively returned to collectively more fiscally conservative policies in the 1990s. The low balance of 1978 and that of 1985 were due for the most part to the performance of the federal government. However, the drop to the record-low balance of 1992 and 1993 is related to the performance of provincial governments. Their overall budget balance had gone from $681 million (less than 1% of total provincial spending) in 1988 to over $26 billion, or 7.1% of total provincial spending, in 1992.

How do Ontario and Quebec compare? Figure 2 displays the budget balance in Ontario and Quebec, from 1970 to 2003. In the first part of the period, the paths walked by the two provinces were quite different from that of the federal government or of all provincial governments aggregated. Whereas the combined provincial budget balance before 1975 was positive,[1] it was negative in Ontario and in Quebec. Indeed, budget deficits were already important in the seventies in the two provinces, especially in Ontario (–12% of total spending in 1971 and 1977 and –15% in 1975) and continued to be so in the eighties,

Figure 2

Budget Balance in Ontario and Quebec, 1970-2003
(Percent of Total Spending)

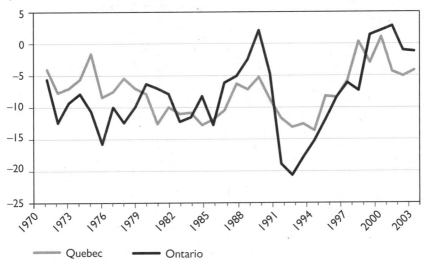

Source: Adapted from the Statistics Canada CANSIM database, <http://cansim2.statcan.ca/>, Table 385-0002.

---

1. The curve is driven up in the positive by the huge surpluses Alberta already had at this time.

though closer to the provincial mean. From 1990 on, the budget balances of the two provinces followed the general pattern. They improved up until 1990, deteriorated until 1992, and then improved again.

Despite these similarities, Ontario and Quebec budget balances differ in important ways. The deficit was higher in Ontario in the 1970s. Ontario had a surplus in 1990, contrary to Quebec which had a negative balance every year before 1998. Ontario's largest deficit (20.5% of total spending in 1992) was much more important than Quebec's (13.3% in 1994).[2]

Within each province, one may separate fiscally liberal premiers from fiscally conservative ones on the basis of the budget balance they realized. Here I assume that premiers who deteriorated the budget balance over the previous year had a fiscally liberal behaviour and those who improved it had a fiscally conservative behaviour. By that standard, Premier Davis was mostly fiscally liberal whereas Premier Harris was mostly conservative, as Table 2 shows for Ontario. In Quebec, Lévesque was mostly liberal and Bourassa equally liberal and conservative in their fiscal policies.

Table 2

Provincial Premiers' Fiscal Policy Action,* in Ontario and Quebec, 1971–2003

	Liberal	**Conservative**
Ontario	– Davis (1974, 1975, 1977, 1980, 1981, 1982, 1983)	– Davis (1972, 1978, 1979, 1984)
	– Rae (1992)	– Peterson (1986)
	– Harris (1998)	– Rae (1993)
	– Eves (2002, 2003)	– Harris (1999, 2000, 2001)
Quebec	– Lévesque (1978, 1979, 1980, 1982, 1983, 1984)	– Bourassa (1973, 1973, 1974, 1986, 1987, 1989, 1993)
	– Bourassa (1971, 1972, 1975, 1976, 1988, 1991, 1992, 1993)	– Lévesque (1977, 1981, 1985)
		– Parizeau (1995)
	– Johnson (1994)	– Bouchard (1997, 1998, 2000)
	– Bouchard (1996, 1999)	– Charest (2003)
	– Landry (2001, 2002)	

* "Liberal": Deterioration of the budget balance (in dollars) over previous year.
"Conservative": Improvement of the budget balance (in dollars) over previous year.

---

2. The most important deficit during this period was realized by the Alberta government in 1986 at 26.8% of total spending.

In summary, the walk of the budget balance in Ontario and Quebec has been a mix of fiscally liberal and fiscally conservative policies over the period without any clear sign of a systematic pattern. One wonders whether the premiers' fiscal talk followed similar patterns.

3. FISCAL TALK: ASSESSING FISCAL CONSERVATIVENESS IN POLICY SPEECHES

We do not have readily available measures of fiscal conservativeness in the speeches given by provincial premiers as we do of their fiscal policy action. To develop such a measure, one has to delineate a conceptual framework and then to choose a measurement method. I now turn to this task.

3.1. Thinking about Actors, Actions, and Discourse: A Conceptual Framework

Social interactions are so complex that we must simplify them through assumptions in order to make sense of what we see. Here I make three assumptions. First, I assume that roles dictate policy positions. In any government, the location of an individual in the organizational structure determines his or her behaviour. When, for example, the premier moves Mr. X from being Minister of Health to being Minister of Education, Mr. X stops defending health programs and starts caring about education programs. For him, education becomes more important than health. His choices or his policy positions change as his role changes. Here is how Graham Allison expressed this idea:

> Where you stand depends on where you sit. Horizontally, the diverse demands upon each player shape his priorities, perceptions, and issues. For large classes of issues, for example, budgets and procurement decisions, the stance of a particular player can be predicted with high reliability from information concerning his seat (1969: 711).

I assume this to apply to any actor in government.

Second, following Wildavsky (1964, 1975, 1988), I assume that there are two roles in the budget process, that of guardians of the treasury and that of advocates of program spending. Any person involved in the making and the realization of a budget plays one of the two roles. Guardians look after the whole budget and the financial health of the government. They do not worry much about government programs, knowing that advocates do. Indeed, advocates care about programs. Therefore, they want to spend money. But it is not their duty to care about the financial position of the government, since they know that guardians look after the whole budget. In the Canadian institutional setting, this implies that actors from the Ministry of Finance and the Treasury Board play the role of guardians, whereas actors from program ministries, such as the Health or Education Ministry, play the role of advocates.[3]

Third, I assume that policy positions are reflected in official speeches, that is, actors' talk corresponds to their roles. This implies that, in any government, there is a typical guardian talk, spoken by guardians, and a typical advocate talk, spoken by advocates. Guardians are fiscally conservative, advocates are fiscally liberal, and so are their speeches. Because of the importance of the Minister of Finance in the Cabinet, I assume that his speeches, more specifically the budget speeches, are fiscally conservative. Because their ministries draw the highest proportion of provincial government spending, I assume that speeches made by ministers of Health or of Education are typical of advocates' speeches in provincial governments.

With this setting, we can characterize the fiscal policy stance of provincial premiers in their speeches from the throne by asking whether they talk more like their ministers of Finance or like their ministers of Health or Education.

3.2. Measuring Provincial Premiers' Policy Positions

To assess a premier's policy position on the conservative–liberal dimension of fiscal policy, we applied the Wordscore technique developed by Laver, Benoit, and Garry (2003). This technique considers texts "not as discourses to be read, understood, and interpreted for meaning— either by a human coder or by a computer program applying a diction- ary—but as collections of word data containing information about the position of the texts' authors on predefined policy dimensions" (Laver, Benoit, and Garry 2003: 312). Here is how Laver, Benoit, and Garry describe their method in nontechnical terms:

> Our approach can be summarized . . . as a way of estimating policy positions by comparing two sets of political texts. On one hand is a set of texts whose policy positions on well-defined *a priori* dimensions are known to the analyst, in the sense that these can be either estimated with confidence from independent sources or assumed uncontroversially. We

---

3. For applications of Wildavsky's model to the budget process at the federal level, see Savoie 1990 and Good 2007; for applications at the provincial level, see Imbeau 2000.

call these "reference" texts. On the other hand is a set of texts whose policy positions we do not know but want to find out. We call these "virgin" texts. All we do know about the virgin texts is the words we find in them, which we compare to the words we have observed in reference texts with "known" policy positions (2003: 313).

Thus throne speeches are compared to two reference texts, each representing an extreme on the liberal–conservative dimension: the budget speech representing the guardians' expression of a fiscally conservative stance (arbitrarily coded +1), and the preliminary remarks by the ministers of Health and of Education at budget hearings representing the spenders' view of a fiscally liberal stance (coded −1). The working of the computer is fairly straightforward. Each word is given a score between −1 and +1, according to the frequency of its occurrence in each reference text. Thus, if the word "deficit" appears 10 times in a 1000-word Education speech and 90 times in a budget speech of equal length, it is scored +0.08 (0.01*−1 +0.09*1). Then, if the same word is found 10 times in a 1000-word throne speech, it is given the loading 0.0008 (+0.08*0.01). Summing up the loading thus found for each individual non-unique word yields the estimated score for the throne speech, our conservatism score. One may think of this example this way: knowing the content of the reference texts, the probability that we are reading the budget speech rather than the preliminary remarks of the Minister of Education while reading the word "deficit" is 0.9 and the probability that we are reading the preliminary remarks of the Minister of Education is 0.1. It is therefore logical to give to the text we are evaluating the loading 0.8 each time we read the word "deficit." Dividing the sum of all these loadings by the total number of words in that text yields a mean that corresponds to the text score. We are all the more justified to do so that:

> we . . . have access to confident assumptions about the position [of the reference texts] on the policy dimension under investigation, [that] the reference texts . . . use the same lexicon, in the same context, as the virgin text", [and that the] policy positions of the reference texts . . . span the dimensions in which we are interested (Laver, Benoit, and Garry 2003: 314–315).

Using this method, we compared the words included in each budget speech and in each "preliminary remark" given by the ministers of Health and of Education in the hearings of the legislative committee reviewing their budget, to the throne speech delivered at the beginning of the legislative session over the period from 1971 to 2003 in Ontario and Quebec. This analysis yielded a conservatism score for 20 years in Ontario and 33 years in Quebec (missing years are due to missing speeches). The scores vary from a minimum of –0.11 (fiscal liberalism) to a maximum of +0.19 (fiscal conservatism), with a value of zero representing a neutral position (see Table 3).[4]

Table 3

Summary Statistics of Conservatism Scores of Speeches from the Throne in Ontario and Quebec, 1971–2003

	Ontario	Quebec
Minimum	–0.03	–0.11
Mean	0.06	0.05
Median	0.05	0.06
Maximum	0.19	0.17
Std Dev	0.060	0.058
Number of cases	20	33

3.3. Comparing Ontario and Quebec Premiers' Fiscal Talk

Ontario and Quebec premiers seem to speak the same language. They are slightly more conservative than liberal in their speeches with mean scores above zero and similar variances. The only noticeable difference is the minimum score in Quebec (–0.11: Bourassa 1971) which suggests that the most fiscally liberal speech in Quebec is much more so than its equivalent in Ontario (–0.03: Harris 1998).

Looking at each premier's fiscal policy position as expressed in the words of his speeches from the throne confirms the first finding that, overall, they are more conservative than liberal, as they tend to concentrate in the "guardian" category (see Table 4). Therefore, provincial premiers in both provinces more often speak like their ministers of Finance rather than like their ministers of Health or Education. Moreover, several premiers seem to be constant in their talk. Rae and Peterson are consistently conservative, as are Bouchard, Parizeau,

---

4. I acknowledge that having only 20 years for Ontario severely limits the validity of any generalization to the entire period. Unfortunately, I was unable to get hold of all the speeches necessary to run the analysis for every year in Ontario.

and Landry. Other premiers play the entire register and sometimes make a conservative speech, sometimes a liberal one, like Davis, Harris, and Eves in Ontario or Bourassa and Lévesque in Quebec. One wonders whether a premier's political longevity is related to his ability to adapt to changing circumstances through being at times liberal and at times conservative in his speeches.

Table 4

Provincial Premiers' Fiscal Policy Position in Throne Speeches in Ontario and Quebec, 1971–2003

	Ontario	Quebec
Guardian (fiscally conservative) (Score > 0*)	– Harris (2000, 2001) – Eves (2002) – Rae (1992, 1993) – Davis (1972, 1975, 1977, 1978, 1979, 1980, 1981, 1984) – Peterson (1986)	– Lévesque (1977, 1978, 1979, 1980, 1983, 1984, 1985) – Bourassa (1973, 1974, 1976, 1988, 1989, 1990, 1991, 1992, 1993) – Bouchard (1996, 1997, 1998, 1999, 2000, 1996) – Johnson (1994) – Parizeau (1995) – Landry (2001, 2002)
Neutral (Score = 0)	– Davis (1974, 1983) – Harris (1999)	– Charest (2003) – Bourassa (1975, 1987) – Lévesque (1981, 1982)
Advocate (fiscally liberal) (Score < 0*)	– Harris (1998) – Eves (2003) – Davis (1982)	– Bourassa (1971, 1972, 1986)

* $p < 0.05$.

But is there a correspondence between speech and action? Do premiers who speak the words of fiscal conservatism also realize conservative budgets, as our benevolent hypothesis would predict? Or do fiscally conservative speeches follow liberal budgets, as our sophisticated hypothesis predicts? Or is the cynical view closer to reality, and should we not find that there is no relationship between fiscal speech and fiscal action?

4.   DO THEY WALK LIKE THEY TALK?

There are two approaches to answering this question. On the one hand, we could follow a common sense approach and focus on the premiers themselves, as we just did, asking ourselves who is benevolent and who is sophisticated or cynical. This is the way we think about politics in everyday life while reading our newspaper or watching the news on television. On the other hand, we could adopt a more scientific approach and detach ourselves from personalities and everyday thinking in order to identify possible patterns of covariation between conservatism scores and budget outcomes.

Let us begin with the first approach and then cross-tabulate the information contained in Tables 2 and 4, namely, fiscal policy position and fiscal policy action. This is what Table 5 does. For each premier, it shows the combination of policy position and policy action. Thus, Davis in 1975 had a guardian speech and a fiscally liberal action. Bourassa in 1986 had an advocate speech and a fiscally conservative action. Following our theoretical discussion, we may say that premiers located in the guardian/liberal or advocate-neutral/conservative cells are sophisticated in their use of speech as they give more conservative speeches when their fiscal policy yields a deteriorated budget balance and they give more liberal speeches when their fiscal policy improves it. Conversely, premiers located in the advocate-neutral/liberal or the guardian/conservative cells are benevolent, as their speeches directly correspond to their actions.

In this table, we see no stable pattern among the Ontarian premiers for whom we have more than one speech: each one is sometimes benevolent and sometimes sophisticated. Davis, for example, shows benevolence in seven speeches and sophistication in four. Harris is benevolent in three speeches and sophisticated in one. Rae and Eves are both benevolent in one speech and sophisticated in the other one. We find similar results among Quebec premiers, except for Landry who is consistently sophisticated in his two speeches. Bourassa, Lévesque, and Bouchard show mixed patterns, as do their Ontarian counterparts. Bourassa shows benevolence in seven speeches and sophistication in seven others. Lévesque is benevolent in three speeches and sophisticated in six. Bouchard is benevolent in three speeches and sophisticated in two others. As we have only one speech by Peterson, Johnson, Parizeau, or Charest, it is impossible to assess their consistency.

Table 5

Provincial Premiers' Fiscal Policy Position by Fiscal Policy Action, in Ontario and Quebec, 1971–2003

Fiscal Policy Position	Fiscal Policy Action**	
	Liberal	Conservative
Ontario		
Guardian (conservative) (Score > 0*)	– Davis (1975, 1977, 1980, 1981) – Rae (1992) – Eves (2002)	– Davis (1972, 1978, 1979, 1984) – Peterson (1986) – Rae (1993) – Harris (2000, 2001)
Neutral (Score = 0)	– Davis (1974, 1983)	– Harris (1999)
Advocate (liberal) (Score < 0*)	– Harris (1998) – Eves (2003) – Davis (1982)	
Quebec		
Guardian (conservative) (Score > 0*)	– Lévesque (1978, 1979, 1980, 1983, 1984) – Bourassa (1976, 1988, 1990, 1991, 1992) – Johnson (1994) – Bouchard (1996, 1999) – Landry (2001, 2002)	– Bourassa (1973, 1974, 1989, 1993) – Lévesque (1977, 1985) – Parizeau (1995) – Bouchard (1997, 1998, 2000)
Neutral (Score = 0)	– Bourassa (1975) – Lévesque (1982)	– Lévesque (1981) – Bourassa (1987) – Charest (2003)
Advocate (liberal) (Score < 0*)	– Bourassa (1971, 1972)	– Bourassa (1986)

* p < 0.05.
** "Liberal": Deterioration of the budget balance (in dollars) over previous year.
   "Conservative": improvement of the budget balance (in dollars) over previous year.

I attempted to detect whether there was some sort of periodical pattern. I found only one with Bourassa who tended to be benevolent in his first political life in the seventies and sophisticated after his return in 1985.

The conclusion to which this common sense approach leads us is that provincial premiers in Ontario and Quebec generally showed a cynical attitude. Sometimes their fiscal speeches accorded with their fiscal actions. Sometimes they did not. While deteriorating the budget balance, they sometimes spoke like advocates of program spending (i.e., they spoke as though they were benevolent) and sometimes they spoke like guardians of the treasury (i.e., they spoke as though they were sophisticated). It is only in Quebec that we find a stable sophisticated attitude in premiers' walk–talk relationship. Indeed, three Quebec premiers showed sophistication (Johnson, Landry, and Charest) but none did among the premiers from Ontario. In addition, there are two provincial premiers who showed a stable benevolent attitude in their walk–talk relationship: Peterson and Parizeau. These conclusions must be qualified by the fact that one third of the budget speeches in Ontario are missing from the analysis and that all the premiers deemed benevolent or sophisticated were evaluated on a single speech, except for Landry for whom we had two speeches.

Now, what does the scientific approach tell us? The scientific approach consists in structuring the problem into a "dependent variable," the effect, and several "independent variables," the causes. The aim of the analysis is to establish the presence of covariation, often through statistical techniques. The intensity and the direction of the relationship can be assessed and, when relevant, hypothesis testing allows one to come to a probabilistic conclusion.

This approach has several advantages over the common sense approach. First, it frees the analyst from personalities and idiosyncrasies as he or she looks for a generalization and a probabilistic conclusion. We are no longer interested in Bourassa or Davis, for example, but with the covariation between fiscal policy positions in speeches from the throne and government financial outcomes. The issue is no longer about who is benevolent and who is sophisticated, but about what the walk–talk relationship is in a given setting. Once one reaches a conclusion, one can replicate the analysis in another setting to assess whether it holds elsewhere. As evidence builds up in one direction or another, we have more confidence in the knowledge thus created.

What we lose in specificity going from the common sense approach to the scientific approach, we gain in generalizability. Second, focusing on covariation allows the analyst to control for the unwanted impact of other variables through a multivariate analysis. This is important because what appears to be an important explanatory factor in a mono-causal explanation often disappears in a multicausal explanation (spurious effect). Likewise, what appears to be an unimportant factor in monocausality may prove to be an important factor in multicausality (suppressor effect). In other words, a multivariate analysis can prove a significant bivariate relationship to be fallacious (spurious effect) or it can reveal as very significant an otherwise insignificant bivariate relationship (suppressor effect). One could think of several possible control variables: economic cycles (Keynesianism, for example, would prescribe a liberal discourse in order to stimulate economic recovery when the economy is slowing down) or electoral cycles (communication specialists would prescribe a more liberal discourse right before an election and a more conservative discourse after the election in order to increase the probability for the incumbent government to be re-elected), or partisan cycles (as parties of the left support more social programs, leftist premiers should have a more liberal discourse), or government vulnerability (a premier leading a minority government should have a more liberal discourse). Third, when it uses the tools provided by statistics, the scientific approach takes into account all the possible values a variable may take, rather than simplifying the distributions into a few categories as we did in Table 5. Variables measured on an interval/ratio scale provide more information and allow more subtle analyses than do simple dichotomies, therefore let us observe the results of a multivariate analysis of the walk–talk relationship. They are displayed in Table 6.

For each province, I ran two regressions of the conservatism score described in Table 3 above, the dependent variable, on change in budget balance (ΔBalance), the independent variable. The first reports bivariate results, the second controls for economic and political variables which are often related to fiscal policy: economic growth (ΔGDP), change in unemployment rate (ΔUnemp), strength of the left (NDP/PQ seats), post-election year, and minority government. The benevolent hypothesis predicts that the regression coefficient will be positive and significant, the sophisticated hypothesis, negative and significant, while the cynical hypothesis predicts that the regression coefficient will be insignificant.

Table 6

Regression Estimates for the Relationship between Fiscal Policy Position and Fiscal Policy Action in Ontario and Quebec, 1971–2003

(Standard errors in parentheses; dependent: Conservatism score)

	Ontario		Quebec	
Constant	0.0634*** (0.0213)	0.0327 (0.0213)	0.04561* (0.01466)	0.007 (0.0223)
ΔBalance	0.0000015 (0.0000071)	—	− 0.000008 (0.0000066)	− 0.000016** (0.000006)
ΔGDP	—	—	—	—
ΔUnemp	—	—	—	−0.002** (0.0008)
Post-election year	—	0.0686*** (0.02005)	—	—
NDP/PQ seats	—	—	—	0.001** (0.0005)
Minority gov.	—	0.0839** (0.03038)	—	—
Rho			0.39 (0.168)	0.34 (0.178)
Durbin-Watson	1.30	1.17	1.43	1.63
R-squared	0.018	0.467	0.047	0.293
N	20	20	33	33

* $p < 0.10$; ** $p < 0.05$; *** $p < 0.01$.

Estimation methods: For Quebec: Prais-Winsten; for Ontario: exact maximum-likelihood with OLS's R^2 and Durbin-Watson.
Results generated with SPSS.

With R-squares almost equal to zero, bivariate results confirm the conclusion of our common sense analysis. There is no relationship between change in budget balance and conservatism score as the regression coefficients for ΔBalance are insignificant in both provinces. The bivariate analysis confirms the cynical hypothesis. There is no congruence between Ontario or Quebec premiers' words and deeds. But multivariate results tell a different story. There is a significant negative relationship between change in budget balance and conservatism score in Quebec. *Ceteris paribus*, that is, taking into account economic and political cycles, the more their fiscal policy deteriorates the budget balance, the more Quebec premiers speak like their ministers of Finance. In Ontario, there is no significant relationship between change in budget balance and conservatism. Quebec premiers have a sophisticated attitude in their walk–talk relationship whereas Ontario premiers are cynical.

In addition, the multivariate results show that the way premiers speak varies with economic and political cycles. In Quebec, speeches are more conservative when the unemployment rate decreases, which is consistent with a counter-cyclical policy: in the upward part of the economic cycle, when employment improves, premiers speak more like guardians of the Treasury than advocates of program spending. A conservative discourse may be viewed as an instrument used to control economic cycles, in the same way as does a restrictive fiscal policy. But there is no significant relationship between economic cycle variables and conservatism score in Ontario. Moreover, we find evidence of a political cycle in both provinces, a partisan cycle in Quebec where the strength of the PQ in the National Assembly is related to higher conservatism in speeches, and an electoral cycle in Ontario where speeches are more conservative in post-election years.[5] This last result is consistent with the electoral cycle theory, which holds that governments tend to spend more prior to elections and to postpone program restrictions until after the election. It is logical to think that the same reasoning holds for conservatism in speeches from the throne. Finally, the presence of a minority government in Ontario coincides with higher conservatism scores. This last finding is counterintuitive, as we would have expected more vulnerable premiers to speak more liberally rather than more conservatively, everything else being equal, all the more in that it is only in the 1990s that the conservative anti-deficit rhetoric has gained more appeal among voters in Ontario, whereas minority governments in Ontario were those of Davis in 1976–80 and Peterson in 1985–86.

CONCLUSION

Which of our three walk–talk conceptions seems to have prevailed in Ontario and Quebec in the last decades? A common sense approach tells us that only one provincial premier has been consistently sophisticated: PQ's leader Bernard Landry. All other provincial premiers for

---

5. Pre-election and election years yielded no significant coefficient.

whom we have more than one speech have been cynical in both provinces. The scientific approach leads us to a different conclusion: the fiscal policy walk–talk relationship in Ontario corresponds to a cynical conception, whereas the sophisticated conception seems to better represent the use of fiscal speech in Quebec. Therefore, which of these two conclusions should we believe? It depends on how we wish to use them. If we seek an answer to the walk–talk question in order to guide our voting decisions, for example, or any other applied decision, I would suggest that we keep to the common sense approach and that we consider that there is no systematic relationship between premiers' policy speeches and their fiscal action. However, if our aim is to foster new knowledge about fiscal policy, the scientific approach should be preferred, as it is the only way to know whether the common sense conclusion suffers from spurious or suppressor effects. The analytical tools applied here allow one to replicate the experiment in various settings so as to assess the validity and the robustness of the conclusion. Only scientific results that have survived serious validity tests should become guides to action. Unsubstantiated science is ideology. Common sense and intuition are always better policy guides than preliminary scientific evidence but, once validated, scientific evidence is a much more reliable guide to action.

BIBLIOGRAPHY

Allison, G. T. (1969). "Conceptual Models and the Cuban Missile Crisis." *American Political Science Review*, vol. 63, no. 3: 689–718.

Barro, R. J. (1989). "The Ricardian Approach to Budget Deficits." *The Journal of Economic Perspectives*, vol. 3, no. 2: 37–54.

Blejer, M. I. and A. Cheasty (1991). "The Measurement of Fiscal Deficits: Analytical and Methodological Issues." *Journal of Economic Literature*, vol. 29, no. 4: 1644–1678.

Congleton, R. D. (2002). *The Median Voter Model.* <http://rdc1.net/forthcoming/medianvt.pdf>, accessed on 20 May 2005.

Cukierman, A. and A. H. Meltzer (1989). "A Political Theory of Government Debt and Deficits in a Neo-Ricardian Framework."*American Economic Review*, vol. 79, no. 4: 713–732.

Good, David A. *The Politics of Public Money.* Toronto: University of Toronto Press, 2007.

Imbeau, L. M. (2000). "Guardians and Advocates in Deficit Elimination: Government Intervention in the Budgetary Process in Three Canadian Provinces." In J. Kleist and S. Huffman (eds.), *Canada Observed: Perspectives from Abroad and from Within.* New York: Peter Lang: 145–156.

Imbeau, L. M. (2005). *Policy Discourse, Fiscal Rules, and Budget Deficit: A Median Voter Model.* Durham: European Public Choice Society.

Imbeau, L. M. (ed.) (2009). *Do They Walk Like They Talk? Speech and Action in Policy Processes. Studies in Public Choice.* Dordrecht: Springer.

Laver, M., K. Benoit, and J. Garry (2003). "Extracting Policy Positions from Political Texts Using Words as Data." *American Political Science Review,* vol. 97, no. 2: 311–331.

Majone, G. (1989). *Evidence, Argument, and Persuasion.* New Haven: Yale University Press.

Roubini, N. and J. Sachs (1989). "Political and Economic Determinants of Budget Deficits in the Industrial Democracies." *European Economic Review,* vol. 33, no. 5: 903–938.

Savoie, D. J. (1990). *The Politics of Public Spending in Canada.* Toronto: University of Toronto Press.

Tabellini, G. (1991). "The Politics of Intergenerational Redistribution." *Journal of Political Economy,* vol. 99.

Wildavsky, A. (1964). *The Politics of the Budgetary Process.* Toronto: Little, Brown.

Wildavsky, A. (1975). *Budgeting: A Comparative Theory of Budgetary Processes.* Boston and Toronto: Little, Brown.

Wildavsky, A. (1988). *The New Politics of the Budgetary Process.* New York: Harper Collins.

9. QUEBEC, ONTARIO, AND THE 2008 ECONOMIC CRISIS
From Generous Counter-Cyclical Policies to an Austere Exit Approach

MOKTAR LAMARI
and LOUIS CÔTÉ

As I look at what passes for responsible economic policy these days, there's an analogy that keeps passing through my mind. I know it's over the top, but here it is anyway: the policy elite—central bankers, finance ministers, politicians who pose as defenders of fiscal virtue—are acting like the priests of some ancient cult, demanding that we engage in human sacrifices to appease the anger of invisible gods.

PAUL KRUGMAN
(Nobel Prize in Economics recipient, 2008)
in the *New York Times*, May 22, 2009

Triggered in the loftiest spheres of the U.S. finance world, the recent economic and financial crisis spread almost instantaneously to the Canadian economy, forcing provincial governments to act quickly and often with little forethought. These spur-of-the-moment decisions did not all have the same effect on controlling the crisis. The particularities of each province's economic fabric and political culture were compounded by political contingencies, ruling-party ideologies, legislative deadlines, etc. This chapter provides a specific comparative analysis of the actions taken by the Quebec and Ontario governments to counter the crisis. Both provinces stand out from their peers for the weight they carry within the Canadian economy;

together, they supply three-quarters of Canada's manufacturing output and are home to two-thirds of the country's active population. They also share extensive economic and financial ties with the U.S. economy and ship the majority of their exports to the American market (72% for Quebec and 84% for Ontario), putting them on the front lines every time a crisis rocks the U.S. economy. Our analytical interest in the two provinces extends beyond their economies' strong ties to that of their southern neighbour. Quebec and Ontario are also representative of the diverse socioeconomic and politico-cultural contexts present across Canada. In addition to possessing different industrial structures, both provinces champion relatively different models for economic development.

This chapter will examine three complementary topics: 1) the impact of the recent crisis on each of the provinces, 2) government response and public policy instruments employed, and 3) the challenges and issues faced by each province as it emerges from the crisis. To investigate these issues, we will employ chronological and comparative analysis tools and draw on three sources of data. The first consists of statistical data on financial variables and economic aggregates describing the progression of the crisis (growth, unemployment, exportation, debt, investment, etc.). The second is made up of government documents on the crisis: arrival of the crisis, government reactions, perspectives on issues related to exiting the crisis. The third consists of analyses produced by the media, stakeholders, and researchers.

I.   SIGNS OF THE CRISIS

To begin, we must return to the origins of the crisis and its spread into Canada. A product of a number of latent and interdependent factors, the recent crisis was essentially a financial crisis caused by insufficiently regulated financial actors. Its origins stretch back to the start of the decade, when it rode in on the heels of the storied dot-com bubble (2001–2003) at a time when declining long-term interest rates in the U.S. became the norm. The rate of return on 10-year U.S. Treasury bonds followed the trend, sliding progressively from 7% to 4%. Far from being the result of a deliberate monetary policy issued by the U.S. Federal Reserve, this downward trend followed the flooding of the American market with lendable funds from developing and oil-exporting countries, which reached previously unheard-of heights. The U.S. market had become the darling of investors seeking high returns and who were willing to assume high levels of risk, attracted by high levels of deregulation uncommon in other developed countries and designed to generate returns at any cost, leading to the creation of questionable and risky finance innovations. Seduced by a dizzying range of loan options at a time when real incomes had stagnated for years, American households turned increasingly to credit—credit granted freely and without a true evaluation of risk. The bubble at the immediate source of the crisis originated in the real estate sector, where risk taking had, reached unimaginable proportions. This worked insofar and for so long as interest rates remained particularly low and profitable investment opportunities were present. Consumers dove into a game of speculation, throwing caution to the wind: they bought, built, renovated, and resold real estate assets with endlessly increasing capital gains. To boost lending opportunities and unload risk related to carelessly granted loans, banks turned to financial engineering to transform dangerous credit into financial products—an operation known in the finance vernacular as securitization.[1] A culture of speculation similar in many ways to gambling slowly became an investing norm, with credit rating agencies doling out generous assessments of the new financial products.

Housing prices soared to dizzying heights. For a typical house of good quality, the average price increase reached upwards of 80% between 1989 and 2006. The volume of housing starts also rose rapidly. In the midst of this real estate boom, banks multiplied their load of high-risk mortgages, leading to a large number of risky securitized assets being traded. Offered by a new generation of investment banks, bank holdings, and hedge funds, these new financial products combined parcels of mortgage loans carrying varying types and levels of risk. This worked so well that a new class of banks, called parallel or shadow banks, was born, making these products their niche of choice. Buoyed by the prevailing market conditions, the banks rode the wave created by the real estate bubble, raking in colossal benefits. These parallel banks were subject to less scrutiny and fewer monitoring rules than conventional banks, they were not required to hold a minimum of liquid reserves nor to contribute to creditor insurance policies, and they did not maintain strong ties with the U.S. Federal Reserve. However, as offer gradually caught up with and then exceeded demand, the first signs of strain began to show in the speculative real estate bubble. Around the

---

1. According to the *Vernimmen* glossary, "[l]*a titrisation est un montage financier qui permet à une société d'améliorer la liquidité de son bilan. Techniquement, des actifs sélectionnés en fonction de la qualité de leurs garanties sont regroupés dans une société ad hoc qui en fait l'acquisition en se finançant par l'émission de titres souscrits par des investisseurs. L'entité ainsi créée perçoit les flux d'intérêts et de remboursement sur les créances qu'elle a achetées aux banques et les reverse aux investisseurs via le paiement d'intérêts et le remboursement de leurs titres*" (<http://www.vernimmen.net>).

same time, interest rates began to climb, following key rate increases by the Federal Reserve and other central banks. Numerous Americans, up to their necks in debt, could no longer keep up with their mortgages and declared bankruptcy, forcing banks to repossess a growing number of houses and properties with plummeting values. This spurred a dom-ino effect, sending prices into a downward spiral as everyone rushed to unload their newly undesirable assets. This deeply affected U.S. banks and their partners around the world, who sustained losses to the tune of hundreds of billions of dollars. The crisis spread quickly to the real economy, shaking consumer confidence and driving down aggregate demand for goods and services.

It was not long before the crisis spread to the Canadian econ-omy, despite the fact Canadian financial markets had not experienced the problems that led to the American financial crisis. Unlike the U.S. under the Clinton administration, the Canadian federal government had not significantly loosened its banking regulations. Even had the Conservative government in power since 2006—a party in favour of market self-regulation—wanted to do so at the start of its term, its minority status would have impeded its success. However, although unaffected by a self-generating crisis, the Canadian financial markets still suffered the effects of their neighbour's misfortune. Major fallout included the asset-backed commercial paper (ABCP) crisis. Figure 1 illustrates the decrease in ABCP values following their ascent from 2004 to 2007.

Figure 1
ABCP Crisis in the U.S. and Canada

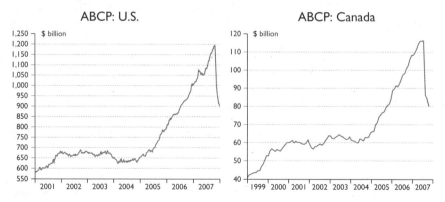

Source: National Bank of Canada (2009).

Beginning in August 2007, nearly $32 billion of the total $117 billion ABCPs circulating in Canada turned toxic and irrecoverable. Compared with Quebec, Ontario was relatively unscathed by the collapse, despite the size of its financial services industry. In terms of absolute value, Ontario's financial sector is more than twice the size of Quebec's. Its finance, insurance, and realty services industry is worth nearly $110 billion, or about 23% of GDP, while the same industry in Quebec tops out at $47 billion, which accounts for 17% of Quebec's GDP. What's more Toronto, the Ontario capital, is North America's third biggest financial hub after New York and Chicago, with nearly 289,000 jobs related in some shape or form to the finance sector. It appears that financial actors from Toronto played a key role in the dissemination of ABCPs to the rest of the Canadian economy. Toronto firm Coventree was behind the sale of nearly 50% of ABCPs held by Canadians, institutional investors, banks, etc. When the Ontario Securities Commission intervened on Coventree to staunch the rush, the harm had already been done. Over 2,000 investors, 100 businesses, and 1,900 individuals saw their investments vanish in the blink of an eye. Coventree sold ABCPs to investors through financial establishments including National Bank, Scotiabank, CIBC, Royal Bank, Deutsche Bank, and BNP Paribas. In Canada, the largest investors duped by Coventree were in Quebec, where over half the losses were sustained: Caisse de dépôt et placement du Quebec, National Bank, and the Desjardins Group alone lost $17 million.

Although less affected by the ABCP collapse than their Quebec counterparts, a number of businesses from the Ontario financial services industry were also swept up in the financial crisis. The Ontario Municipal Employees Retirement System (OMERS) posted a negative total return of 15.3% in 2008 (versus a positive return of 8.7% in 2007), following a net loss estimated at $8 billion caused by the collapse of the global financial markets. The Ontario Teachers Pension Plan posted losses totalling nearly 18% of its portfolio in 2008. The University of Toronto was also affected, and its pension and endowment funds registered a loss of $1.3 billion in 2008, with a negative return of 30%.

The financial crisis spread rapidly to the real economy, particularly the real estate and manufacturing sectors. In Ontario, housing sales tumbled nearly 30% and housing prices decreased on average by 6% per year. Housing starts were also sent reeling, as much in Quebec as in Ontario. In Quebec, the decrease measured nearly 17%, falling from 48,000 new constructions in 2007 to 40,000 in 2009. During the same period, Ontario experienced a 30% decrease, with new constructions tumbling from 75,000 to 51,000. Construction permit values followed the same downward trend—particularly in 2009—to an equal extent in both provinces. The crisis also affected exports in both provinces. Ontario saw its exports drop from $356 billion in early 2007 to $282 billion in 2009, a decrease of nearly 20%. In Quebec, the drop was less pronounced, though exports still fell by 16% over the same period. The recession also fanned the flames of the structural crisis blazing in the forestry sector, which had been suffering from dwindling pulp and paper demand for a number of years already. Faltering demand for timber was yet another nail in the coffin for a sector already struggling to restructure. Of course, Quebec's forestry sector and its structural issues were not the only victims of the crisis—the Ontario automobile industry was also hit hard.

The crisis dealt a staggering blow to the Canadian automobile industry—concentrated in Ontario—where big U.S. multinationals such as GM, Chrysler, and Ford had set up shop. In Ontario, the automobile sector suffered a 30% production decrease resulting in major factory shutdowns and thousands of layoffs, all within a short period of time. Industrial hubs such as Oshawa, where car manufacturers are some of the largest employers, were hit hard. With over 70,000 jobs slashed in a single month, November 2008 will remain etched in the collective conscience as the low point in a period where 175,000 people lost their jobs between October, 2008 and March, 2009. Windsor registered the country's highest unemployment rate (for a large city), topping out at 13.7%. Ontario therefore experienced a highly abrupt change in its unemployment rate. Until the recession, unemployment rates had typically been higher in Quebec than in Ontario. Between 2007 and 2009, however, the annual rate of unemployment in Ontario jumped from under 6% to over 9%. Figure 2 illustrates the "seesaw pattern" of the two provinces' unemployment rates over a number of successive quarters in 2007 and 2008.

While the Quebec unemployment rate registered a downward trend throughout all of 2007 and the end of 2008, Ontario rates soared over the same period. These variations can be explained by the structure of the economy. Compared with Ontario, Quebec possesses a more diverse industrial fabric consisting primarily of SMEs. Quebec also benefited from innovation and research and development investments made between 1996 and 2003, which led to the implementation of a number of highly technological aerospace, pharmaceutical, IT, and communications sectors, among others. These cutting-edge technological sectors seem to have helped the Quebec economy better weather the shock of the crisis and cushioned it from the brunt of the social fallout.

Figure 2
Changes in Monthly Unemployment Rates, 2005–2009

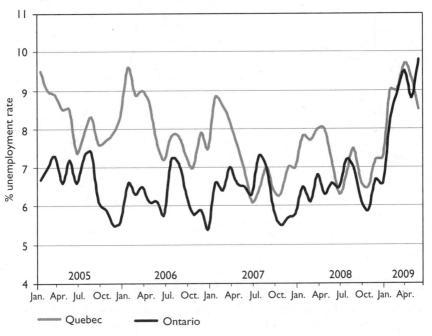

Due to layoffs, pay cuts—as was the case for some 10,000 Chrysler Canada employees who accepted an agreement in principle to help the company save nearly $240 million per year—,and, more generally speaking, decreased consumer confidence, demand fell. Combined with declining exports and plummeting investments, this drop in demand slowed economic growth. Both provinces saw their numbers fall before sinking into the red for three successive quarters. And although the Ontario economy was the first affected, posting a negative growth rate for the first time in over 30 years, the Quebec economy fell harder and for a slightly longer period of time.

Figure 3

Ontario and Quebec Quarterly Growth Rates, 2005–2009

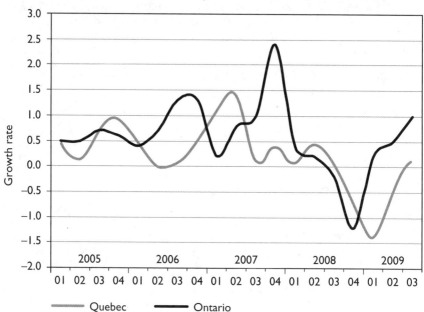

2. GOVERNMENT RESPONSE TO THE CRISIS

The scope of the fallout from the crisis prompted governments from a variety of G20 countries to act quickly, first to protect their financial institutions and then to stabilize their economies and stimulate demand. After weathering two decades of criticism and suspicion, Keynesian and post-Keynesian policies were widely applied. In this section we will examine the Quebec and Ontario governments' reactions to the crisis and analyse their responses from monetary and financial, economic, and social perspectives. But to fully comprehend all of the above, we must first recall the prevailing political climate in each province in the run-up to the crisis.

2.1. Political Climates

In summer 2008, when the two economies encountered the financial crisis, the Quebec and Ontario governments were in somewhat different positions. In Ontario, Dalton McGuinty and his Liberal party had just been elected to a second term in October 2007. The party's house majority made it well positioned to steer the province out of the crisis. In Quebec, the Jean Charest Liberals had also been elected to a second term in March 2007. However, theirs was a minority government hampered by a staunch opposition determined to block a number of initiatives including the adoption of the provincial budget, at the risk of toppling the government at any moment. Another major difference between the two political contexts resides in the fact that the Quebec government was constrained by an antideficit law during its time in power. Adopted in 1996, the law greatly reduced government leeway to adopt measures involving public spending. On the other hand, in 2004 Ontario adopted the *Fiscal Transparency and Accountability Act*, which obliges it only to keep citizens abreast of the state of public finances and to plan its actions from a perspective of overall economic growth and factors influencing growth over the short, medium, and long terms.

In the summer of 2008 the Quebec government quietly engaged in a strategy that would enable it to survive and even regain majority status. It was necessary to act quickly before the crisis spread in order to limit its scope. The Charest government decided to call an early election, positioning itself as the government of choice to combat the emerging crisis. It focused on the province's positive economic results from preceding years (sustained growth and a downward trend in unemployment rates), vaunting the managerial know-how to tackle the challenges of crisis-related risks and issues. In a series of equally ambiguous and controversial public announcements, Charest declared that Quebec would not run up a budgetary deficit, and filtered—if not suppressed—hot-button economic and financial information in order to preserve voter confidence. As a result, the historic losses posted by Caisse de dépôt et placement du Québec ($40 billion) and shrinking tax revenues were kept quiet until after the votes had been counted.

Voters elected Charest into office. Strengthened by its majority, his government quickly changed its tune, bringing to light the province's economic struggles, including the Caisse de dépôt et placement du Québec losses and a major projected budgetary deficit. In the winter of 2009 the government forced the adoption of a law repealing the antideficit law in order to push through its stimulus plans.

2.2. Monetary and Financial Responses

As federated states, Quebec and Ontario do not possess all available monetary instruments for countering an economic crisis and stimulating recovery. Here, the Bank of Canada plays the leading role. Given the scope of the crisis and spurred by other central banks, the Bank of

Canada lowered its key interest rate a number of times, dropping all the way to 0.25%—the lowest observed rate since the 1930s. In just two years (January 2007–December 2008), the rate sank from 4.25% to 0.25%, making it negative in real terms as it dipped below inflation, which hovered between 1% and 2% during the same period. The disappointing results achieved through the use of monetary instruments sowed seeds of doubt among expert macroeconomists who, until then, saw monetary instruments as a sort of silver bullet against economic crisis. Having exhausted its conventional defense of adjusting the key interest rate, the Bank of Canada decided to act in the form of direct loans to certain large businesses, injecting them with additional liquidity.

The Quebec and Ontario governments intervened on a different level. In addition to the communication campaigns launched to boost investor confidence in the quality of the Canadian banking system, they were also responsible for managing the ABCP crisis. As a result, the Ontario Securities Commission and Autorité des marchés financiers du Québec caught wind of irregularities surrounding ABCPs, leading to penalties of some $140 million being brought down on the main banks involved in selling ABCPs. The Quebec government's reaction was particularly strong, with the goal of limiting damages resulting from the ABCP crisis. Conscious of the threat looming over Quebec's three largest financial institutions—Caisse de dépôt et placement, Desjardins Group, and National Bank were Canada's three largest ABCP holders—the government worked to find a way to freeze the value of the ABCPs held by Canadian financial actors in order to delay and limit their potential losses. A committee chaired by business lawyer Purdy Crawford drew up a plan for the short-term conversion of the ABCPs into long-term notes. Adopted as part of the Montreal Accord, the Crawford plan enjoyed the support not only of the major financial institutions involved and the Quebec government, but also of the Ontario and Alberta governments, as well as the Federal Government and the Bank of Canada, which supplied several billion dollars of collateral to implement the plan.

2.3. Economic Responses

While the financial and monetary stabilization efforts of the Quebec and Ontario governments were limited by their jurisdictions, the same cannot be said of their economic efforts, where heavy spending was used to target public infrastructure and support for business.

In both provinces, government response to the crisis consisted mainly of investment in infrastructure. In Quebec, over $42 billion were earmarked for programming over a span of five years. However, these amounts had already been decided upon well before the crisis reached Quebec. In fact, it all began with the announcement of the Quebec Infrastructure Plan in 2007, a year before symptoms of the crisis first manifested in the Quebec economy. The infrastructure projects represented real and pressing needs. The overall state of infrastructure was deplorable: built for the most part in the 1960s and 70s during the province's shift toward modernization, its upkeep had been continuously sacrificed in favour of the public deficit for 20 years. In fact, it took a terrible and arresting accident and a commission of inquiry to draw the government's attention to the serious risk posed to users of the province's roadways and public buildings. The accident occurred in September 2006: around 12:30 p.m., an overpass collapsed on an urban boulevard, instantly killing five people. The commission of inquiry, led by former Quebec premier Pierre-Marc Johnson, recommended a "*virage rapide et énergique qui permettra non seulement de stabiliser la situation, mais aussi de redonner à la population du Québec des infrastructures de premier ordre.*" The Quebec Infrastructure Plan (Commission d'enquête sur l'effondrement du viaduc de la Concorde 2007) was launched in response to this recommendation, with the goal to "*faire en sorte que les réseaux routiers, hospitaliers et scolaires québécois, rendus vétustes par des années de laxisme et de sous-financement, soient en aussi bon état que ceux de nos voisins canadiens et américains d'ici 15 ans*" (Radio-Canada 2009).

The investments granted by the province spread out over five years and apply primarily to the following sectors: transport (roads, bridges, etc.), health, and municipal infrastructure. The education, justice, and public security sectors rank lower on the list of priorities identified for investment. As we will see later on, the infrastructure investments announced in Ontario must be carried out within a shorter period of time and do not address the same priorities. Although Quebec's immediate financing was for a lesser amount, the province found itself better positioned to inject the allocated amounts at the best time. In fact, as the crisis ballooned and the factory closures began—particularly in the forestry sector—the technical stages of design and planning for the infrastructure work (e.g., diagnostics, priority analysis, technical reports, financing packages, etc.) had already reached an advanced stage within Quebec's government organizations. This coincidence was very fortuitous for Quebec's economy. The government had calls for tender ready to launch in order to embark on a number of major heavy infrastructure projects within the sectors of transport (bridges, roads, etc.), education (schools), and health (hospitals, home care centers, etc.). Furthermore, licensed labour—particularly within the forestry sector—could be quickly and easily recovered and employed within the infrastructure projects. These workers did not require training to be hired on construction sites, which use production processes similar to those the workers were already familiar with. The crisis was later used to justify the major increase in debt associated with the plan. Finance minister Raymond Bachand explained the situation to Parliament in the following terms:

> Parce qu'au fond, la dette ce n'est pas compliqué, vous investissez en infrastructures, vous empruntez. Ce qui est important, c'est d'être capable de le rembourser. Vous soutenez l'économie en temps de récession, vous avez un déficit. Ce qui est important, c'est d'être capable de revenir à l'équilibre budgétaire (National Assembly of Quebec 2009).

In Ontario, $32.5 billion were allocated to infrastructure work, but within a plan spread out over only two years. These investments were intended to retain or create 300,000 jobs over the period in question. The main sectors tapped for investment were 1) transport (road and urban transport), at nearly $9 billion; 2) health, at over $7 billion; and 3) education, at $3.7 billion. The balance of the budgetary envelope—some $12 billion—was earmarked for the municipal, justice, and waterworks and environmental preservation sectors.

Both governments also devoted a major portion of spending to supporting business. The liquidity shortages experienced by a number of companies—particularly those in the manufacturing sector—created a sense of urgency that spurred the governments to intervene quickly to prevent bankruptcies and layoffs. A great effort was made to relaunch private investment. In Ontario, the automotive industry received a great deal of government support, to the extent that some questioned the validity of using such large amounts of public funding to prop up not just private businesses, but also multinational and non-Canadian corporations. Suffering from a contracting credit market, the automotive industry (Chrysler, GM, etc.) received support to the tune of $10 billion from two levels of government: $4 billion from the provincial government and $6 billion from the federal government. The government was not nearly so generous with other sectors of the Ontario economy. However, the following measures are also worth noting: the granting of nearly $130 million over three years to the agricultural, mining, and forestry product sectors; over $300 million in 2009–2010 and 2010–2011 to support the entertainment and arts and innovation sectors; a $250-million investment in the new Emerging Technologies Fund; a $50-million investment over five years to encourage the implementation of a smart electricity network; and a $300-million/six-year investment in research infrastructure.

The Ontario government also took advantage of the crisis to court multinational corporations, inviting them to settle in the province in return for generous public subsidies. A number of multinationals present in Canada and abroad were approached. The most visible success was Samsung, which announced mid-crisis that it would invest $7 billion in Ontario to produce 2,500 megawatts of clean energy, creating over 16,000 jobs. In return, the Ontario government hastened to reward the company with nearly $450 million. This discretionary policy was criticized by a number of observers, political parties, and lobbies in Ontario.

In Quebec, support for the manufacturing sector was less controversial. Announced in November 2008, a working capital and investment fund geared toward business stabilization and recovery called the Renfort program received government funding totalling $2 billion over two years. Managed by Investissement Quebec, it allowed for direct business loans and supplied loan guarantees. A second initiative took the form of a government capital contribution to Société générale de financement in the amount of $1.25 billion paid over two years (2009 and 2010), enabling this other public corporation to grant loans and acquire an interest in small and medium businesses (equity, quasi-equity, etc.). Government intervention in the forestry sector was somewhat limited. In its 2009–2010 budget, the government announced two measures totalling $100 million. The first measure accounted for two-thirds of the amount and was dedicated to silvicultural development work (plant production, reforestation, etc.). The second measure was a social one aimed at assisting workers from the sector who had been laid off, particularly those whose retirement funds were affected by the bankrupting of their employers. The modesty of the two measures would seem to indicate that the government had adopted a laissez-faire approach, allowing the sector to purge its own dead weight. As a result, rather than supporting businesses condemned to failure, the government was able to concentrate its efforts on those the market could sustain. It appears that many employees from the sector understand the stakes and are ready to forego wage hikes in order to reduce production costs and remain employed. A different measure specifically targeting homeowners was launched in 2009 to encourage home renovations through the creation of a temporary (one-year) refundable tax credit equal to 20% of eligible expenses. Its cost to the budget was estimated at $250 million and it should benefit over 170,000 Quebec homes. In Quebec, the returns from this measure and a complementary program initiated by the federal government are estimated at some $3 billion in renovations and 2,000 new jobs. However, though the credits have generally met with approval, some observers have noted that, because they coincided with construction starts on a variety of infrastructures, the home renovation support programs have overheated the construction market, leading to price increases of up to 20%, or the same amount as the credit granted.

2.4. Social Responses

In both provinces, the most influential social actions targeted the workforce. In Quebec, the actions were carried out as part of the Employment Pact. As its name suggests, the Pact was negotiated by actors from Commission des partenaires du marché du travail du Québec, a provincial commission made up of representatives for employers, unions, the education sector, community organizations, and public employment services. The Employment Pact was launched before the crisis in order to mitigate labour shortages faced by the province as a result of its demographic stagnation and aging population, as well as to increase business productivity. In the beginning, the Pact called for $987 million in investment over three years, to be paid both by business ($439 million) and the government ($548 million). The financed initiatives targeted the following four areas: helping the unemployed and social assistance recipients with regard to finding employment and workforce integration, promoting employment (for instance by increasing the minimum wage), offering a greater variety of training programs in outlying regions, and recognizing competencies, particularly given the province's immigration boom (many workers have received training outside of Canada). In March 2009, in the thick of the recession, the initial measures were enhanced as part of the Employment Pact Plus: "*Ensemble vers la relance.*" Financed by the federal and provincial governments to the tune of $460 million, this addition increased the effectiveness of the measures, which benefited some 16,000 businesses and 400,000 unemployed workers. The Pact appears to have softened the crisis's blow to unemployment. It is worth noting, however, that the crisis did not hit Quebec as hard as other Canadian provinces and the U.S. thanks to the province's efficient economic and social models and, in particular, the automatic stabilizing role played by the policies that set Quebec apart form the rest of North America in terms of redistribution, family support, and the fight against poverty. Thanks to existing programs and services, families affected by the crisis were able to sidestep poverty and social exclusion, and laid-off workers benefited from training programs and direct support to help them re-enter the job market and mitigate the insecurity and inactivity of unemployment.

In Ontario nearly $700 million were earmarked over a two-year period for a group of measures designed to produce or reinforce occupational training and literacy initiatives in order to help workers cultivate the skills necessary for the jobs of tomorrow. Summer youth employment programs also grew by nearly 60% (100,000 participants in 2009) thanks to an addition of about $90 million. Populations hard-hit by unemployment saw an increase in their living and housing allowances. Families with children were specifically targeted through an increase in the children's benefit thanks to an investment of over $400 million over three years. Low- and medium-income families thus received a nearly 100% increase in the benefit, the per-child ceiling for which rose from $600 to $1,100 per year in July 2009.

2.5. Conclusions

Analysing the measures implemented by the Quebec and Ontario governments makes it possible to identify certain commonalities. These measures can be broken down into the following seven types, which are typical of the economic stimulation policies born out of the recession:

- timely measures, which injected the required investments at a time when the economy needed them most. The speed at which the measures were implemented was necessary for them to achieve the desired effect;
- targeted and direct measures, which lent support to the hardest-hit segments of the population and economic sectors in order to keep them afloat and recover as soon as possible. Direct support through grants and loans is preferable to indirect support, such as through tax credits;
- automatic stabilizer measures, which support the consumption of laid-off workers and other vulnerable people such as single-parent families, children, the elderly, etc.;
- strong leverage measures, which have a direct, speedy impact on other sectors of the economy;
- interim measures, which do not appear to extend beyond the crisis period. Here, it is essential to take the economic cycle into account: once recovery picks up, temporary measures must be ended in favour of regular initiatives and mechanisms;
- prudent measures, which are founded on financial realism and a sense of responsibility to rebalance the budgets as quickly as possible to ease the burden of debt; and

Quebec–Ontario Relations – A Shared Destiny?

- infrastructure measures, which prepare for recovery through investment in research and development, innovation, higher education, public transit, social housing, the green economy, and more.

3. EXIT CHALLENGES

Following considerable government intervention to counter the crisis, Quebec and Ontario both came to terms with budgetary deficits once again. Since 2008 the Quebec government has declared an annual deficit of $4.5 billion, equivalent to nearly 1.5% of the province's GDP. During the same period, Ontario ran up a deficit of some $25 billion, or 2.4% of its GDP. As figure 4 shows, this led to an increase in debt. While Ontario's debt ballooned progressively to $184 billion or 26% of the province's GDP, in the coming years Quebec's is expected to reach some $130 billion, or 42% of GDP. While this number is below the IMF's acceptable symbolic ceiling of 60% (IMF 2010), it is still much higher than its Ontario equivalent. This difference in the amount of debt doubtlessly played a role in the decisions made to spur economic recovery, slash deficits, and reduce the burden of the debt.

Figure 4

Net Debt to GDP in Quebec and Ontario between 2000 and 2009

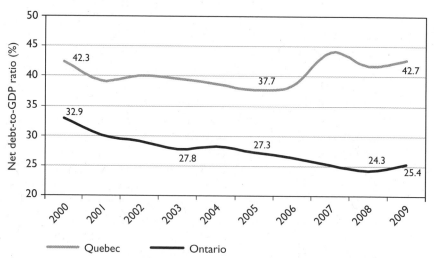

In the spring of 2010 the governments of both provinces announced plans for rebalancing their budgets. Each took a different approach. The Quebec government chose a much shorter deadline for eliminating the deficit—in 2013—while the Ontario government has set its sights on 2018, with an interim target of halving the deficit by 2015. The measures adopted for cutting public spending and increasing revenue by raising taxes and/or implementing fees for public services also differ.

3.1. Cutting Costs

In Quebec, the government has already implemented a strict program cost-monitoring process (reducing the number of public agencies, replacing only one in two positions vacated for retirement) and wishes to limit cost increases to 2.8% annually beginning in 2011–2012 and until the budget is rebalanced. This program could harm a number of government programs and commitments since, in recent years, program cost increases have totalled between 4% and 6%, depending on the ministry. This reduction in expense growth will total roughly $5.8 billion and be shouldered by both ministries and organizations. To reach its goal, the government will employ a number of cost-cutting measures, beginning with the ones that carry the most symbolic weight. It has therefore promised to freeze minister and deputy salaries for two years in addition to incentive pay for public-sector managers and senior staff. A similar measure was requested of government corporations whose incentive pay is determined by their own boards. The government also shored up its public administration employee attrition measure by extending the rule for replacing only one in two retired workers—which previously applied only to civil servants—to cover administrative staff (including managers) in the health and education networks. It is worth noting that in 2004 the Charest government set a target of decreasing public service staff by 20% within 10 years, but that the constant effort made during the first six years resulted in a decrease of only 5%.

In its latest budget (2010–2011), the Quebec government also announced a comprehensive payroll freeze for its ministers until 2013–2014, a gradual 10% reduction of administrative operating expenditures by 2013–2014, and a 25% decrease in training, travel, and marketing costs. An act (Bill no. 100) was passed (60 votes to 39) on June 12, 2010, to constitutionalize a return to a balanced budget and formalize the announced budget cuts. The government also undertook a review of its programs and decided to end the automatic renewal of expiring programs. A program performance evaluation and assessment tool inspired by the U.S. Program Assessment Rating Tool (PART) is to be designed in collaboration with a team of researchers from École nationale d'administration publique in order to assess the performance of all government programs. Long sheltered from budget cuts, health and education also began feeling the effects of specific budget-tightening measures. As a result, the health and social services network was tasked with implementing a budgetary framework to review its processes in order to increase productivity and progressively eliminate annual operating deficits. Finally, the government announced the merger or abolition of some 30 public funds and bodies.

The Ontario government also plans to limit spending growth to 2% overall and to 3% in the healthcare sector through steep drops in medication costs, requiring a major change in the way Canada's pharmaceutical companies are regulated. However, this measure is not slated to take effect until 2012–2013, until—according to the government—economic recovery is off to a solid start or—according to other sources—the next elections have passed. The Ontario government's cutback program resembles the one in Quebec, but is not as aggressive. It has also pledged to reduce the size and costs of its administration by decreasing its number of civil servants by 5% over 3 years. It announced a two-year pay freeze for ministerial and Legislative Assembly staff, as well as for parapublic and public-sector employees excluded from collective agreement negotiations. It has said it wishes to freeze civil servants' wages for two years as well, but after the negotiations for the next collective agreements (in 2014), many observers feel this is a rather unlikely scenario. The government would also like to modernize its services to improve its customer service and increase its efficiency.

3.2. Increasing Revenue

While the Quebec government is determined to alleviate the deficit for the most part by cutting costs, it has also created measures that should enable it to increase its revenues. These measures include consumption taxes and price-setting for public services. Not only will taxes not be increased, but the government still plans to meet its objective of eliminating the capital tax charged to corporations, which represents a loss of nearly a billion dollars in revenue per year. The province is also granting additional credits to Revenu Québec in order to finance increased tax recovery efforts and to fight tax avoidance in hopes that it will recover over $1.2 billion per year. To generate new income, the province has turned to two consecutive increases in its sales tax, raising it from 7.5% to 8.5% in January 2011 and then to 9.5% in January 2012, filling nearly all the vacant space left by the Harper government's cuts to the federal goods and services tax. Each of these two Quebec sales tax increases will boost revenues by $1.6 billion. An increase in the Road Tax of one cent per litre is also planned for April of each year from 2010 to 2013. Relatively limited rate increases will also affect the previously protected sectors of healthcare and education. In its 2010–2011 budget, the government announced a progressive unfreezing of and rise in university tuition fees beginning in 2012. As for healthcare, the government made the surprising and even shocking decision to implement a user fee for health services, which would have led to an annual health contribution for each adult costing $25 in 2010, $100 in 2011, and $200 as of 2012. This decision was repealed in September 2010. Additionally, heritage block electricity rates will be gradually unfrozen beginning in 2014: the heritage rate will increase by one cent per kilowatt-hour between 2014 and 2018 and be adjusted according to inflation thereafter.

Although dissimilar in terms of initial positioning (among other reasons), the Ontario government made choices that are in some ways similar to those made in Quebec. In addition to not raising taxes, the Ontario government has pledged to provide household tax relief to the tune of $11.8 billion over a period of three years. This commitment will result in income tax breaks for 93% of taxpayers, and over 90,000 low-income taxfilers will not be required to pay any Ontario income tax. Although the systematic tax breaks will widen the chasm between the two provinces' tax rates, Ontario's move to exempt low income earners from paying tax reflects a commonality, since Quebec's various tax credits and non-taxable children's benefit mean that at least 50% of Quebecers do not actually pay a cent of tax. Where consumption taxes are concerned, the Ontario government decided to replace its retail sales tax with a more modern value-added tax, which was combined with the federal goods and service tax (GST) to create a harmonized sales tax (HST) that took effect on July 1, 2010. Equivalent to the old retail sales tax, the provincial component of the HST is set at 8%, which is lower than Quebec's sales tax rate. This sales tax harmonization fits into a larger framework of a policy to update Ontario's taxation to increase efficiency and improve the province's productivity and competitiveness compared with its neighbours. A transitional measure totalling $4.2 billion was created to help Ontarians adapt to the harmonized sales tax.

In June 2010 premier Dalton McGuinty also announced that his battle to reduce the deficit would not exclude the sale of a certain proportion of energy-related government corporations such as Hydro One and Ontario Power Generation, as well as others including Ontario Lottery and Gaming Corporation (OLGC) and the Liquor Control Board of Ontario (LCBO). These statements appear to suggest that the short-term quest for liquidity may be used to justify the privatization of highly profitable public corporations that contribute significantly to the province's budget revenues.

3.3. A Return to Growth

The return to growth of the Quebec and Ontario economies, which are both very open, hinges on exports. In this respect, the value of the Canadian dollar plays a crucial role. For a few years now, Quebec and Ontario have suffered the effects of a dollar that has climbed alongside oil prices due to strong oil exports from three Canadian provinces (primarily Alberta). This obstacle, called the "Dutch disease,"[2] causes the appreciation of the Canadian dollar to inflate the price of Quebec and Ontario exports. In fact, it appears that the accumulation of wealth by oil-exporting provinces is damaging to provinces that export manufactured goods. Protectionist measures implemented in the U.S. as part of the *Buy American Act* put additional pressure on exports. For Quebec and Ontario exporters, winning back lost markets will likely be difficult, and new export markets will have to be conquered. As a result, it is imperative that the manufacturing sector increase its productivity in order to become more competitive. Compared to Ontario, Quebec is lagging behind in productivity by 10%. This productivity gap widens even further when compared with the U.S., where it reaches nearly 15%. Training and innovation are key tools for boosting productivity and maintaining or developing an economy's comparative advantages. Unfortunately, when it comes to government action in research and development (R&D), Quebec appears to be progressively losing its comparative advantages over its neighbours, who have not only made considerable investments, but have also consolidated their institutions by forming ministries or organizations dedicated to this strategic sector in order to exit the crisis and pursue new technologies. For example, the three grant funds for university research have largely dried up after being merged into a single fund with budget perspectives actually declining. Conseil de la science et de la technologie was simply axed.

---

2. This term appeared in the 1960s when, following a sizable increase in income resulting from the discovery and mining of natural gas in the North Sea, the Dutch currency appreciated sharply while the Netherlands' exports lost their competitivity.

CONCLUSION: ISSUES AND DEBATE

The relatively vigorous counter-cyclical interventions enacted by the Quebec and Ontario governments in response to the crisis did not engender any significant debate. The fact that the governments' approaches were essentially Keynesian in nature may have been the source of some surprise, since in Quebec, Ontario, and other Western societies, the monetarist approach had already proved its worth. The governments appear to have favoured a rather pragmatic approach, but the Charest government's trajectory suggests that the opposite may in fact be true. It is important to remember that, when it came into power in 2003, the Liberal government—convinced the Quebec model was not only ineffective, but harmful to the province's development—promised a true break with tradition, with decreased government presence and a planned top-to-bottom review of the government's structure and programs. However, beyond revising efforts in support of economic development and placing a number of forums for and types of joint action on the backburner, its approach to governance did not change significantly. At first, due to the pressure of public opinion and then the arrival of new ministers more open to these perspectives, the government gradually rediscovered the virtues of interventionism and joint action. Cast aside for a time after being judged as excessive, inefficient, and even useless in a modern liberal economy based on the free market, government corporations such as Investissement Québec and Société générale de financement regained their popularity. The Employment Pact is another instance of this "rediscovery," as in 2003 the Liberals had considered axing Commission des partenaires du marché du travail or at least restricting its prerogatives rather than utilizing it. The crisis appears to have accelerated this discovery, with the government aligning itself once more with a traditional approach to the Quebec model of socioeconomic development (Bourque 2000; Côté, Lévesque, and Morneau 2007).

While the adopted approaches for confronting the challenges of exiting the crisis sparked a great deal of debate and opposition within Quebec, the same cannot be said for Ontario. Debate about debt has remained heated throughout Quebec since the fall of 2009. Talk centres around the relationship between good debt (tied to investment) and bad debt (running expenses). Ministère des Finances[3] and certain lobbies are exaggerating the situation, while still others insist that it is not

---

3. In the fall of 2009 the Quebec finance minister formed an advisory committee on the economy and public finance made up of four economists. From December 2009 to February 2010, it produced three reports that fanned the flames of the debate.

so black and white. The former are zeroing in on gross debt—with a 94% GDP ratio, Quebec ranks 5th among OECD member countries—while the latter believe that net debt is key, placing Quebec in 11th place with a 43% GDP ratio.[4] Furthermore, a number of civil society actors have contested the government's decision to eliminate the deficit over such a short period of time. Disagreements have also emerged over the issues of downsizing public expenditures, the risk of a decrease in the quality of public services, and the government's activities in general. Some believe that downsizing, coupled with equally drastic cuts to the ministries' budgets, are not possible without penalizing users of public services. Key sectors such as education, health, and social services, as well as families may suffer as a result, jeopardizing gains made over the past five decades. The same goes for the regulation and monitoring functions performed by government agencies. Government choices concerning taxation were also criticized, with debate centring among other things on the respective virtues of income and consumption taxes as relates to their economic impact and distributive justice. Some socio-economic actors against the household tax cuts implemented before the crisis, capital tax cuts, and increased sales tax are calling for a more progressive approach to taxation. The pricing of public services has also met with similar opposition. Challengers argue that pricing often leads to a decrease in service use, particularly among the poor, which may cause them to forego things such as preventive care and suffer major problems as a result. They also believe that replacing universal measures with specific ones can lead to the stigmatization of those who use the latter—a well known effect of social assistance—,eventually leading to a weakened sense of solidarity (e.g., social, intergenerational, etc.).

In Ontario, government decisions provoked far less debate. The government showed less haste to return to a balanced budget. It chose to wait for recovery to begin before proceeding with more drastic cut-backs to public spending and reasserted on numerous occasions its desire to assist the disadvantaged and to base its actions and cutbacks on the population's level of affluence. It is important to note that Ontario enjoys favourable structural conditions both where debt and demographics are concerned: while Quebec's population growth hovers around 0.8% per year, Ontario's is nearly 1.3%. With two-thirds of this growth due to immigration, it provides Ontario with available

---

4. It is worth noting that the increase in net debt observed in the 2006 and 2007 data can be largely explained by an accounting reform implemented in 2007. The 2007 accounting reform incorporated into the government's reporting entity new entities whose cumulative deficits were henceforth added to the government's. The recognition of these deficits led to an increase in the debt attributed to the cumulated deficit of $6 billion on March 31, 2007.

and qualified labour and offsets the aging of its population, giving its public services more breathing room. Quebec is not however without its own strengths. Over the past half century, it has built a development model based on institutional devices and an array of services unparalleled anywhere in North America. Combining the pursuance of individual interests and solidarity, competition and joint action, this model has proven itself through the creation of a diversified and dynamic economy. It not only allowed for significant economic recovery in the 1960s, but also supported considerable social and cultural development. Furthermore, some would like to see the return to a balanced budget strengthen government intervention rather than weaken it, and public services—designed as investments rather than just expenses—reformed as collective instruments rather than reduced to a question of individual consumption.

BIBLIOGRAPHY

Bourque, G.-L. (2000). *Le modèle québécois de développement: de l'émergence au renouvellement*. Quebec City: Presses de l'Université du Québec, Collection Pratiques et politiques sociales.

Commission d'enquête sur l'effondrement du viaduc de la Concorde (2007). *Rapport final*. Available online: <http://www.cevc.gouv.qc.ca/Rapport/index.html>, retrieved on November 3, 2009.

Côté, L., B. Lévesque, and G. Morneau (2007). "L'évolution du modèle québécois de gouvernance: le point de vue des acteurs." *Politique et sociétés*, vol. 26, no. 1: 3–26.

Government of Quebec (2009). *Plan québécois des infrastructures 2008-2013*. Available online: <http://www.aqesss.qc.ca/docs/PLanquébécois d'infrastructures %202008-2013.pdf>, retrieved on November 9, 2009.

Krugman, P. (2008). *Appeasing the Bond Gods*. Available online: <http://www.nytimes.com/2010/08/20/opinion/20krugman.html>, retrieved on November 9, 2009.

National Assembly of Quebec (2009). *Travaux parlementaires, vendredi 6 novembre 2009*.

Radio-Canada (2009). *Québec se lance dans la rénovation*. Available online: <http://www.radio-canada.ca/nouvelles/Politique/2007/10/11/001-Infrastructures-quebec.shtml>, retrieved on November 4, 2009.

Vernimmen (2009). *Definition of "Titrisation."* Available online: <http://www.vernimmen.net/html/glossaire/definition_titrisation.html>, retrieved on November 4, 2009.

10. PARALLEL POLICIES
Convergence and Divergence in Forestry Management and Governance in Ontario and Quebec

GUY CHIASSON, ÉDITH LECLERC,
and CATALINA GONZALEZ HILARION

The forestry industry has long been an important driver of economic development in Ontario and Quebec, as in the rest of Canada (Drushka 2003; Howlett 2001; Thorpe and Sandberg 2007). Yet despite the historic importance of forestry in Canada, relatively few studies have examined forestry policy in these two provinces. Moreover, the issue of interprovincial relations as related to forestry —and particularly Ontario–Quebec relations—is absent from the literature. This chapter aims to take some first steps to rectify this situation. Recent changes in federal and provincial jurisdictions have had a noticeable influence on modes of forestry governance in Canada (Chiasson, Blais, and Boucher 2006), raising the issue of how these changes affect interprovincial relations.

Forestry management in Canada is largely decentralized; control over forests has been vested overwhelmingly with the provinces ever since it was enshrined as a provincial jurisdiction in the Canadian constitution. The federal government's role has historically been a small one, limited primarily to research support and international trade (Tree Canada 2010; Howlett and Rayner 2005). The provinces thus benefit from ownership of the vast majority of public forest lands and thus hold the critical power to allocate timber quotas. In Ontario and Quebec nearly 80% of forests are under direct provincial control, compared to less than 1% under federal control (Ontario 2009; Quebec 2010). Of course, federal initiatives are not always limited in scope to federal land, but the provinces remain much more powerful than Ottawa with respect to forest issues. Yet as Michael Howlett has noted, despite this decentralization, the provinces have followed strikingly similar forestry policy paths:

> As befits a national policy regime characterized by provincial jurisdiction and variations in regional and local forest resources, there are differences between jurisdictions in terms of both the length of time each policy regime was left in place and the specific point in time at which a new regime was instituted. Different governments in the various jurisdictions adopted similar forestry policies, usually in the same order of sequence, but not at the same times (2001: 29).

In other words, the Canadian provinces have historically opted for convergent forestry management models. This convergence is rather surprising given the near-total absence of readily apparent or formalized mechanisms. Thus, we propose the term *policy parallelism* for this unplanned and uncoordinated convergence between the provinces.

This chapter will focus on present-day Ontario–Quebec interprovincial relations. Several forestry governance researchers have noted that the 1990s were a time of key forestry policy changes in Canada (Blais and Chiasson 2005; Hayter 2003). The end of the 20th century, then, could mark the end of postwar forestry policy and the beginning of a shift to a new forestry regime (Blais and Boucher 2008; Howlett 2001). These changes have largely taken the form of a shift in forestry policy objectives. Scholars such as Luc Bouthilier (2001) argue that regimes focused on timber management—which aim to maximize timber supply to the forestry industry—are gradually giving way to regimes based on sustainable forestry management (SFM). Other scholars contend that this change in public forest use reflects the declining importance of natural resource extraction as part of Canada's transition to a post-staples economy (Hayter 2000; Thorpe and Sandberg 2007).[1]

----

1. Harold Innis developed the "staples" thesis in the 1930s to describe an economy dependent on massive exports. Innis's work (1930) showed how regional Canadian economies were based around the extraction of natural resources. More recent work (Thorpe and Sandberg 2007) has used the term "post-staples" to describe the transition away from a resource-based economy and new ways to use the natural environment for economic development.

Either way, this shift in forestry objectives has been accompanied by major changes in decision-making mechanisms. Whereas decision making in a supply management paradigm was essentially confined to the government and major industry players (Howlett and Rayner 2001, 2005, 2006), new stakeholders have since been invited to the table (Appelstrand 2002; Chiasson, Andrew, and Perron 2006; Hayter 2003). What is more, since 1990 sustainable forestry management has become a prominent concern of the international community, which increasingly demands that sustainable development practices be followed. This concern has been formalized in a number of international forums such as the United Nations Forum on Forests (UNFF), the United Nations Conference on Environment and Development (UNCED, also known as the Rio Summit), the UN Commission on Sustainable Development (CSD), and the Intergovernmental Panel on Forests (IPF) (Gareau 2005; Howlett 2001; Pülzl and Rametsteiner 2002). The notion of sustainable forestry management is also gaining ground in the forestry products market through certification and other initiatives (Burton *et al.* 2006; Cashore *et al.* 2007). In addition to ensuring that SFM practices are followed, this focus on sustainability has driven decision makers to increasingly adopt a logic of *governance*; i.e., to increasingly share decision-making authority among public institutions and other civil society actors, including those based outside of the province in question and even outside of Canada (Hayter 2003; Parkins 2006).

This chapter will compare Quebec and Ontario forestry policy against the backdrop of a radically changing industry. How does the governance ethos play out in relations between the two provinces? The discourse around forestry governance adopted by these two provinces stresses the need to break down borders between the public and private sectors in order to meet new international forestry standards and requirements (Chiasson and Labelle 2009). Does the same principle apply to borders between provinces? Do the Ontario and Quebec governments feel the need to develop consultation and cooperation mechanisms? Or has the *policy parallelism* of previous regimes simply carried over into the 21st century?

The chapter first looks at what is arguably the main Ontario–Quebec cooperation mechanism, the Canadian Council of Forest Ministers (CCFM), whose mission is to implement common provincial policy orientations in sustainable forestry management. Then it turns to the Ontario and Quebec governments' public forest land management reforms of the 1990s. This background will allow us to question where "parallel" forestry policy fits in to current reforms.

I. THE CANADIAN COUNCIL OF FOREST MINISTERS: MULTILATERALISM IN CANADIAN FORESTRY

The CCFM is the most obvious instance of forestry cooperation between Ontario and Quebec, as well as Canada's other provinces and territories. The organization, founded in 1985, brings together provincial and territorial forestry ministers (and senior civil servants) from across the country. The federal minister of natural resources attends, and Ontario sends two ministers—the Minister of Northern Development, Mines, and Forestry and the Minister of Natural Resources—bringing the total number sitting on the council to 14. The federal minister always acts as secretary while a different provincial or territorial minister presides each year. To clearly understand the position and role of the CCFM in Canadian forestry, it is worthwhile to briefly situate the organization with respect to recent international developments.

Forestry has been a hot international issue at least since the 1992 Rio Summit. In the post-Rio period, adoption of SFM practices at the sovereign state level has come to be widely viewed as an essential component of sustainable development on a global scale. Concern over SFM has been institutionalized, as mentioned, in a number of international UN forums. Processes to secure the support of countries present at international meetings and subsequent discussions to define concrete SFM practices have obliged states to identify measures needed to implement sustainable forestry management. The Canadian government is among those who have signed on. While the CCFM predates Rio, the organization did not write SFM into its core mandate until after the summit. Closely following Rio, it adopted the following definition of SFM: "management that maintains and enhances the long-term health of forest ecosystems for the benefit of all living things while providing environmental, economic, social and cultural opportunities for present and future generations" (CCFM 2010a). Canada has since participated in further international initiatives, notably the Montreal Process,[2] where it and eleven other countries set criteria and indicators for sustainable forestry practices in boreal and temperate zones. Once the criteria had been defined and Canada had endorsed them, the CCFM officially adopted the six sustainable forestry management criteria. These criteria and the indicators derived from them have been used since 1999 as a forestry management framework throughout Canada. On its website the CCFM defines itself as "[g]overnments working in partnership to

---

2. See <http://www.rinya.maff.go.jp/mpci/>.

ensure Canada remains a world leader in Sustainable Forest Management and supports a competitive forest sector" (2010a). This statement suggests that SFM is a rallying point for interprovincial cooperation.

A survey of CCFM initiatives (2010b) confirms that developing SFM is a central concern. Several policy papers on key CCFM areas of interest testify to the organization's commitment to SFM, including *Canadian Wildland Fire Strategy, Forest Sector Innovation Framework,* and *A Vision for Canada's Forests: 2008 and Beyond,* whose stated aim is to "achieve sustainable forestry in Canada." However, the council has recently broadened its mandate and begun work on a new policy on adapting forests to climate change.

The CCFM focuses primarily on developing research, innovation, and sustainable forestry management guidelines for forestry stakeholders, including industry players and provincial governments. The council's mandate complements traditional provincial forestry management responsibilities (regulating cutting rights and access to forest lands) and also extends into areas that overlap with federal jurisdiction (forestry research and international cooperation), but does not necessarily stop there. CCFM policy papers are unquestionably useful guides for provincial forestry managers seeking to update their practices. However, the frameworks developed by the council are not legally binding and adoption of CCFM policy directions has been uneven across provinces.

In short, the CCFM is a forum for multilateral cooperation among all Canadian provinces and the federal government that focuses primarily on SFM and Canada's desire to develop new practices to meet its international commitments. Ontario and Quebec play an active role in this multilateral body, as evidenced by the presence of two Ontario ministers. The CCFM is a forum where ministers and senior civil servants from Ontario and Quebec can meet, talk, and catch up on each province's new directions in forestry. However, formal Ontario–Quebec collaboration stops there. Despite their common border and contiguous forests, the two provinces have never developed a forum, at least not a formal one, for bilateral cooperation on forestry issues.

Nonetheless, Ontario and Quebec are involved in certain specific targeted bilateral and multilateral initiatives. However, these are generally orchestrated by civil society actors, even if provincial forestry managers participate. One such example is a project initiated by FSC Canada[3] to develop a forestry standard "that will apply in the forests of southern Ontario and Quebec, which will complete a set of accredited

---

3. FSC is the Canadian branch of the Forest Stewardship Council, the leading certification body for forestry products.

voluntary standards applicable across Canada" (FSC 2010). The working group for the Great Lakes/St. Lawrence region was successful in developing voluntary standards recommended for Ontario and Quebec, first in 1999 and again in 2005. Even though the standard was not drafted by the provinces directly but rather by an FSC member group, there still appears to have been some kind of conciliation to apply similar standards in Ontario and Quebec. Like the CCFM, these other forms of bilateral coordination provide innovative ways to collaborate, particularly when compared to traditional policy parallelism. Before these coordination mechanisms were established, formal cooperation in forestry was rare; now the provinces appear to recognize its value. It remains to be seen to what extent this multilateral collaboration will translate into convergent practices in Ontario and Quebec. In the next section, we will critically re-examine the reforms in the Ontario and Quebec forestry management systems since the 1990s to see whether convergence is an observable trend.

2.   MAJOR FORESTRY REFORMS IN ONTARIO AND QUEBEC

Forestry policy in most of Canada moves in similar directions and is shaped by similar forces. Gaudreau (1999) speaks of a *"trame commune,"* or "shared storyline," that has historically produced forestry policy convergence. In recent years international developments have profoundly influenced the shape of provincial forestry policy, which would suggest that recent reforms should also result in policy convergence. But do similar conditions actually lead the provinces to think about and react to forestry issues in the same way? A close examination of current Ontario and Quebec forestry policy—elements of continuity and breaks with tradition, changes and reforms—will explore the notion of *policy parallelism* and test its limits as an explanatory framework.

2.1. Convergence toward SFM and Heterarchical Governance

Major international forums have grown in scale in recent years, mobilizing a multitude of stakeholders to implement initiatives and action plans. Pülzl and Rametsteiner (2002) argue that these forums promote a decision-making model based on heterarchical governance. In recent years, they write, international discussion forums have come to mirror the complex, intertwined relationships between state and non-government actors by seeking to foster participation, inclusiveness, and, ultimately, consensus. Initiatives and concrete actions agreed upon at these forums focus on problems such as deforestation, forest degradation, and especially the path to follow in implementing SFM. SFM becomes a principle guiding forestry resource use toward practices respectful of economic, social, and cultural societal values—while at the same time fostering forest health and diversity (CCFM 2010a). Canada's forest strategies are drafted within this international context, which in turn influences provincial forestry policy. For example, we have seen how after the 1992 Rio Summit Canada committed to "green" forestry principles. Following Pülzl and Rametsteiner (2002), who suggest studying heterarchichal governance as it relates to EU states' decision-making mechanisms, our initial observations confirm that heterarchical governance is widespread in Canada's national forestry management programs. Our study also suggests that the provinces tend to adopt SFM principles at the same time as Canada. We hope to identify elements of provincial forestry policy in Ontario and Quebec that reflect and illustrate this "shared storyline."

Ontario and Quebec's respective forestry policies are based on multi-use principles and the forests' natural production capacities—principles closely tied to SFM. In Quebec SFM figures prominently in the 1986 forestry policy that recognizes the dynamic relationship between the forest and the communities who live there (Bouthillier 2001). Ontario's 1994 forestry policy is also based on SFM principles such as preserving forest ecosystems through conservation and diversity and mimicking natural disturbances (Lawson, Levi, and Sandberg 2001). In both cases, forestry policy had to be rewritten repeatedly to bring concepts into line with new international definitions. Quebec's 1986 forestry policy has been reviewed and revised several times to ensure proper emphasis was placed on SFM principles. In 1987, for example, in addition to changes respecting the restoration of wildlife habitat and reductions in cutblock size, Quebec implemented a standards guide (regulation respecting standards of forest management for forests in the domain of the State, or RSFM) based on biodiversity preservation and shared forest use (Bouthillier 2001). Both this review and Ontario's *Crown Forest Sustainability Act* (CFSA) coincided with the 1992 Rio Summit. In the years that followed, Quebec forestry policy was reviewed several times, notably in 2001 and 2003, to better reflect SFM aims. A complete forestry policy overhaul, to be discussed later, came in 2010.

In Ontario, meanwhile, a number of environmental reforms, which will also be discussed later, bolstered SFM. While many of these addressed SFM principles and related actions, concrete changes were also made to the decision-making process.

Some of these environmental reforms brought changes to provincial forestry policy and highlighted the shift toward heterarchical governance. In 1993, for example, forestry policy was made subject to Ontario's *Environmental Bill of Rights* (EBR) and the province created an agency to give citizens a role in provincial forestry management: the Environmental Commissioner of Ontario. This public interest watchdog on environmental matters can order a voluntary investigation or audit of any project touching on Ontario's natural resources. A survey of documents available on the site of Ontario's Environmental Registry[4] shows increasing participation of environmental non-governmental organizations (ENGOs) in the negotiation process. While the Rio Summit is not directly responsible for the creation of Ontario's EBR, this development remains an excellent example of heterarchical government. Moreover, the principles set out in summit documents are based on SFM. The 1997–99 Land for Life consultation process is an even clearer example of heterarchical governance. This public participation initiative, Ontario's largest ever, involved a broad dialogue and debate on integrating alternative forest uses into forestry planning—another linchpin of SFM. Public discussions primarily attracted representatives of First Nations and environmental groups as well as tourism and recreation stakeholders. The discussion's most significant outcome was a new coalition of three major Ontario ENGOs—the World Wildlife Foundation, the Federation of Ontario Naturalists, and the Wildlands League—called the Partnership for Public Lands. This coalition, which also represents the public, has stepped forward as a leader in forestry planning negotiations and consultations. The Land for Life process, which coincided with the emergence of major international forestry forums and successfully integrated stakeholders traditionally excluded from forestry planning, reveals the shift to heterarchical governance in Ontario forestry management.

In Quebec, the first guidelines for heterarchical governance were implemented in 1986 and later reinforced. Under the Forest Act, businesses holding timber supply and forestry management agreements (TSFMs)[5] were entitled to harvest timber, but were also responsible for managing a certain percentage of the forest under their agreement. In heory, the 1986 Act required public support for forest management plans to ensure shared use under SFM principles. Forest management plans drafted by forestry companies had to be submitted to other

---

4. In this regard, see Ontario's Environmental Registry's web site, <http://www.ebr.gov.on.ca/ERS-WEB-External/index.jsp>.

5. The Quebec government issues timber supply and forestry management agreements to private companies. TSFMs guarantee the company's right to harvest a defined volume of timber in a specific area in exchange for payment.

forestry stakeholders, but only for information purposes. In practice, however, there were few if any remedies available to contest decisions, and the complaint process was onerous (Bouthillier 2001). One of the first amendments to the act made public consultation on forestry management plans mandatory, implementing a more participatory model. And since 2001, the direction taken by Quebec's Ministère des Ressources naturelles has been to bring together stakeholders to draft plans. This consultation model is based on consensus-building among all forestry stakeholders (Quebec's regional county municipalities, or RCMs, aboriginal groups, wildlife reserve managers, industry). Private businesses were now required to share the fundamentals of their forest management plans and come to agreement with other stakeholders on the specifics of management planning. As the Quebec Chief Forester's *Report on Sustainable Forest Management 2000–2008* (Quebec 2010) makes clear, SFM implementation is constantly evolving, but is proceeding in a satisfactory manner in Quebec. Gradually opening forestry practice to input from new stakeholders is an example of heterarchical governance primarily being practised on a local scale at the community level.

The dual logic of SFM and heterarchical governance is also apparent in more recent reforms—the 2007 reform and the latest version of the Forest Act, adopted in 2010 and coming into force in 2013. With the new Sustainable Forest Development Act, ecosystem-based development—based on mimicking natural disturbances—makes the Quebec government responsible for forest development. This trend toward ecosystem-based management is in line with SFM principles. The new law also requires each of Quebec's administrative regions to create regional commissions responsible for developing public land and natural resources. These commissions have become the preferred consultation mechanism for producing land and resource use plans for regional development. The regions thus develop a framework and set objectives, especially for forest use. Under these mechanisms, regional partners make choices based on their priorities in accordance with provincial government guidelines. In short, the regions represent their populations, driving forestry policy forward at the community level through a regional body that brings together new stakeholders. There is a larger role for local political bodies than in the 1986 Act. For example, municipalities are more involved in consultations, which is fitting as they depend on industrial development and forestry resources to thrive (Houde and Sandberg 2003). Regional bodies thus become a locus for consultation and community participation in natural resource planning, a shining example of both heterarchical governance in action and SFM implementation.

In both cases, international pressure can be felt driving the shift from hierarchical to heterarchical governance, which translates into a larger role for stakeholders traditionally excluded from forestry management. Forestry policy has increasingly found innovative ways to integrate environmental concerns into forestry practices and acknowledge both the limits of nature and potential economic impacts. Here a degree of convergence is apparent in forestry policy and SFM principles. Reforms have been implemented simultaneously in both Quebec and Ontario and have essentially coincided with Canada's endorsement of international principles. Provincial discourse has similarly converged around SFM principles, despite the absence of bilateral mechanisms. This convergence cannot be directly ascribed to the major international negotiations or the endorsement of Canadian guidelines, but the provinces are nonetheless highly supportive of the ideas from international forums and Canada's endorsement of the same.

2.2. Territorialization of Forest Management versus Reconstruction of Provincial Governance

Although forestry policy in Quebec and Ontario has followed the same trajectory toward heterarchical governance and incorporation of SFM principles, forestry governance practices differ in the two provinces. Ontario's SFM-based forestry policy tends to separate uses geographically, drawing forestry region borders in such a manner as to conceal less appealing activities (logging) behind a screen of picturesque woodlands set aside for tourism and recreation activities. Quebec has adopted a different strategy. Since 1986, and even more during the period 2007–2013, it has sought to strike a balance between existing and potential uses within a given area. This pronounced difference between the two provinces bears investigation. We have already outlined the distinct paths taken by Quebec and Ontario in the area of forestry management reform (Chiasson, Gonzalez, and Leclerc, forthcoming), despite government openness to heterarchical governance. We have also described Ontario's path as *reconstruction* of provincial governance, as opposed to Quebec's policy of the *territorialization* of governance. We will now outline these two paths.

In Ontario, heterarchical governance has meant increased integration of ENGOs and environmental discourse province-wide. Environmental groups in Quebec have seen no such integration. Since its inception, Ontario's Ministry of the Environment has put in place a number of public participation mechanisms, mostly at the provincial level but also more locally. According to interviews conducted for this study, however, local and regional processes remain marginal in Ontario as loci of forestry management and debate. Forestry governance is mainly consolidated at the provincial government level.

The Lands for Life process put in place by the Ontario Government demonstrates the increasingly central position of major ENGOs in forest decision making. This has led to significant victories for environmentalists, like the large increase in the number of forested areas protected from logging. But Lands for Life also reveals the extent to which forestry negotiations in Ontario have been carried out at provincial forums from which local stakeholders have been largely excluded. In Quebec the opposite is true.

Quebec's far-reaching 2007 reforms gave rise to new legislation in 2010 which clarifies points sketched out in earlier versions. The Sustainable Forest Development Act provides for three different levels of public participation—local, regional, and provincial—and two levels of discussion: first, at the local level for forestry operations planning, with businesses required to submit their forest management plans to local participative processes, and then at a higher level, where broad policy outlines are determined. What is more, the new Act introduces a regional level of participation between the provincial and local with the creation of regional land and natural resource commissions. These new commissions are designed to serve as a bridge between the two other levels by providing regional land use plans, slated for completion by late 2010. These various participation mechanisms bring together stakeholders from all sectors with interest in the forest: recreation and tourism (hunting, fishing, and trapping), business (industry, resource extraction and processing companies), government, First Nations, forest users (ornithologists, mycologists), and environmental conservation and management groups (ENGOs, watershed management). These various actors are given a role to play at the local, regional, and national levels. Forestry has come to be closely associated with local and regional development, with the province serving as a "referee" in territorial forums. In-depth analysis of both provinces' forestry policies shows them both attempting to adapt to basic SFM principles and heterarchical forestry governance but following very different paths to get there. This divergence demonstrates the institutional particularities of each province.

CONCLUSION

This chapter has demonstrated that Ontario and Quebec's forestry policies have evolved along similar lines, with a "shared storyline." This storyline has developed in response to international currents and the forums Canada has joined. To coordinate their efforts, the provinces have created a multilateral mechanism that has had some degree of influence over sustainable forestry development in the two provinces. However, the chief finding of our analysis is to confirm the presence of a certain "parallelism" in forestry policy, suggesting that changes to provincial forestry policy come as a response to larger international movements that result in actions being implemented on both sides of the Ontario–Quebec border. The same can be said for the shift toward SFM and the participative, or heterarchical, governance described by Pülzl and Rametsteiner (2002) in an EU context. In both Canadian and European examples, this shift has followed in the wake of new international forestry priorities. In the past, parallel forestry policy in Ontario and Quebec developed in the near total absence of interprovincial consultation and cooperation. Now the CCFM has emerged as an important forum for multilateral dialogue. While the CCFM may not have the means to enforce the application of its guidelines, it still tackles issues of crucial importance in Ontario and Quebec forest management. To properly understand interprovincial relations requires close examination of the CCFM.

The importance of policy parallelism must not, however, overshadow the specificity of the paths taken by Ontario and Quebec. We have illustrated the development of two provincial strategies, each distinct despite a shared commitment to SFM. Whereas Quebec has developed a territorialized form of governance, forestry governance in Ontario remains centralized at the provincial level, yet ready to reconstruct policy in response to international trends. These two distinct paths seem to reflect the influence of institutional traditions in the two provinces. The path of territorialization clearly shows the historic importance of regions in the Quebec state apparatus (Morin 2006), as does the closer integration of forestry management and regional development. Ontario's reforms, on the other hand, effectively demonstrate the public policy influence of southern Ontario's urban stakeholders (Paquet 2006). These institutional traditions provide the backdrop against which contemporary policy parallelism has emerged.

BIBLIOGRAPHY

Appelstrand, M. (2002). "Participation and Societal Values: The Challenge for Lawmakers and Policy Practitioners." *Forest Policy and Economics*, vol. 4, no. 4: 281–290.

Blais, R. and J. L. Boucher (2008). "Les régimes forestiers québécois. Régimes d'accumulation, structures d'acteurs et modèles de développement." *Cahiers du Centre de recherche sur les innovations sociales* (ET0836).

Blais, R. and G. Chiasson (2005). "L'écoumène forestier canadien: état, techniques et communautés. Évolution d'un certain savoir-faire." *Revue canadienne des sciences régionales*, vol. 28, no. 3: 487–512.

Bouthillier, L. (2001). "Québec: Consolidation and the Movement towards Sustainability." In D. Howlett (ed.), *Canadian Forest Policy: Adapting to Change*. Toronto: University of Toronto Press: 237–278.

Burton, P. J., C. Messier, W. L. Adamowicz, and T. Kuuluvainen (2006). "Sustainable Management of Canada's Boreal Forests: Progress and Prospects." *Ecoscience*, vol. 13, no. 2: 234–248.

Cashore, B., G. Auld, J. Lawson, and D. Newsom (2007). "The Future of Non-State Authority on Canadian Staples Industries: Assessing the Emergence of Forest Certification." *Policy and Society*, vol. 26, no. 1: 71–91.

CCFM (2010a). *Conseil canadien des ministres des forêts*. <http://www.ccfm.org/francais/index.asp>. Accessed on September 9, 2010.

CCFM (2010b). *Conseil canadien des ministres des forêts – initiatives du CCMF*. <http://www.ccfm.org/francais/coreproducts.asp>. Retrieved on September 9, 2010.

Chiasson, G., C. Andrew, and J. Perron (2006). "Développement territorial et forêts : la création de nouveaux territoires forestiers en Abitibi et en Outaouais." *Recherches sociographiques*, vol. 47, no. 3: 555–572.

Chiasson, G., R. Blais, and J. L. Boucher (2006). "La forêt publique québécoise à l'épreuve de la gouvernance : le cas de l'Outaouais." *Géocarrefour*, vol. 81, no. 2: 113–120.

Chiasson, G., C. Gonzalez, and É. Leclerc (forthcoming). "La gouvernance participative des forêts publiques : l'Ontario et le Québec, des chemins parallèles?" *Territoires en mouvement*.

Chiasson, G. and A. Labelle (2009). "Décentralisation et consultation dans le régime forestier au Québec: une analyse du discours des municipalités." *Économie et solidarités*, vol. 38, no. 2: 43–58.

Drushka, K. (2003). *Canada's Forests: A History*. Montreal and Kingston: McGill-Queen's University Press.

FSC (2010). *Forest Stewardship Council*. <http://www.fsccanada.org/francais.htm>. Retrieved on September 20, 2010.

Gareau, P. (2005). "Approches de gestion durable et démocratique des forêts dans le monde." *VertigO*, vol. 6, no. 2.

Gaudreau, G. (1999). *Les récoltes des forêts publiques au Québec et en Ontario, 1840-1900*. Montreal and Kingston: McGill-Queen's University Press.

Hayter, R. (2000). *Flexible Crossroads: The Restructuring of British Columbia's Forest Economy*. Vancouver: University of British Columbia Press.

Hayter, R. (2003). "The War in the Woods: Post-Fordist Restructuring, Globalization, and the Contested Remapping of British Columbia's Forest Economy." *Annals of the Association of American Geographers*, vol. 93, no. 3: 706–729.

Houde, N. and L. A. Sandberg (2003). "'To Have Your Cake and Eat It Too?' Utility, Ecology, Equity, and Québec's New Forest Act, 2001." *Cahiers de géographie du Québec*, vol. 47, no. 132: 413–432.

Howlett, M. (2001). *Canadian Forest Policy: Adapting to Change.* Toronto: University of Toronto Press.

Howlett, M. and J. Rayner (2001). "The Business and Government Nexus: Principal Elements and Dynamics of the Canadian Forest Policy Regime." In M. Howlett (ed.), *Canadian Forest Policy: Adapting to Change.* Toronto: University of Toronto Press: 23–62.

Howlett, M. and J. Rayner (2005). "Policy Divergence as a Response to Weak International Regimes: The Formulation and Implementation of Natural Resource New Governance Arrangements in Europe and Canada." *Policy and Society*, vol. 24, no. 2: 16–45.

Howlett, M. and J. Rayner (2006). "Understanding the Historical Turn in the Policy Sciences: A Critique of Stochastic, Narrative, Path Dependency, and Process-Sequencing Models of Policy-Making over Time." *Policy Sciences*, vol. 39, no. 1: 1–18.

Innis, H. (1930). *The Fur Trade in Canada: An Introduction to Canadian Economic History.* Toronto: University of Toronto Press.

Lawson, J., M. Levi, and A. Sandberg (2001). "Perpetual Revenues and the Delights of the Primitive: Change, Continuity and Forest Policy Regimes in Ontario." In M. Howlett (ed.), *Canadian Forest Policy: Adapting to Change.* Toronto: University of Toronto Press: 279–315.

Morin, R. (2006). *La régionalisation au Québec. Les mécanismes de gestion et de développement des territoires régionaux et locaux, 1960–2006.* Montreal: Albert Saint-Martin.

Ontario (2009). *Les forêts de l'Ontario: faits saillants.* Ministère des Richesses naturelles: <http://www.mnr.gov.on.ca/stdprodconsume/groups/lr/@mnr/@forests/documents/document/243738.pdf>. Retrieved on September 10, 2010.

Paquet, G. (2006). "Ottawa/Gatineau, cité-région transfrontalière: gouvernance baroque et bricolage." In M. Robitaille, G. Chiasson, and J.-F. Simard (eds.), *L'Outaouais au carrefour des modèles de développement.* Gatineau: Centre de recherche en développement territorial et Université du Québec en Outaouais.

Parkins, J. R. (2006). "De-centering Environmental Governance: A Short History and Analysis of Democratic Processes in the Forest Sector of Alberta, Canada." *Policy Sciences*, vol. 39, no. 2: 183–202.

Pülzl, H. and E. Rametsteiner (2002). "Grounding International Modes of Governance into National Forest Programmes." *Forest Policy and Economics*, vol. 4, no. 4: 259–268.

Quebec (2010). *Ressources et industries forestières: Portrait statistique, édition 2010.* <http://www.mrnf.gouv.qc.ca/publications/forets/connaissances/stat_edition_complete/complete2010.pdf>. Retrieved on September 9, 2010.

Quebec (2010). *Report on Sustainable Forest Management in Quebec 2000–2008,* Bureau du Forestier en chef, <http://www.forestierenchef.gouv.qc.ca/report_on_sustainable_forest_management/>.

Thorpe, J. and L. A. Sandberg (2007). "Knotty Tales: Canadian Staples and Post-Staples Forest Policy Narratives in an Era of Transition from Extractive to 'Attractive' Industries." *Canadian Political Science Review,* vol. 1, no. 1: 57–72.

Tree Canada (2010). *La forêt canadienne.* <http://www.treecanada.ca/site/?page=publication_download_canadaforest&lang=fr>. Retrieved on September 15, 2010.

11. QUEBEC AND ONTARIO'S INTERNATIONAL RELATIONS
Explaining the Differences

STÉPHANE PAQUIN

For years now the governments of both Ontario and Quebec have pursued their own foreign policy parallel to that of the federal government, a practice known as paradiplomacy (Paquin 2004; Massart-Piérard 2005; Aldecoa and Keating 1999; Soldatos 1990). In this chapter we argue that paradiplomacy is when a provincial government mandates a party to negotiate directly with other parties abroad. Among the main issues addressed in paradiplomacy are economic and trade policy, foreign investment, efforts to attract decision-making centres, export promotion, science and technology, energy, the environment, education, immigration, labour force mobility, multilateral relations, international development, and human rights. Paradiplomacy is also increasingly concerned with security issues, especially border security. A distinction must be drawn between paradiplomacy, which is the work of actors duly mandated by a government, and internationalization. Internationalization refers to the establishment of international treaties and standards that increasingly impact areas of government jurisdiction. Internationalism thus affects the modern state in virtually every field of jurisdiction (Paquin 2004; Slaughter 2004).

Paradiplomacy is neither new nor a recent phenomenon. The government of Quebec first established an international presence in the 19th century: in 1816 Lower Canada (modern-day Quebec) opened a foreign office to represent its special interests within the

British Empire (Paquin 2006). Ontario posted an immigration officer in Great Britain as early as 1869, but did not open its own international delegation in London until 1908 (Dyment 2001, 56, 62).

Today, Quebec and Ontario's respective international relations agendas are a study in contrast: while Ontario engages in low-intensity paradiplomacy, Quebec favours high-intensity "identity paradiplomacy" whose fundamental aim is to construct and reinforce Quebec's national identity. Identity paradiplomacy is distinct from protodiplomacy in that it does not aim for political independence (Paquin 2005, 2002). The twofold purpose of Quebec's international relations strategy is to galvanize Quebec's development as a nation and to achieve international recognition as a nation. The distinction is important as Quebec also tends to be very institutionalized in its international activities—the province seeks to imitate the degree of institutionalization of sovereign states, but on a smaller scale. In contrast, Ontario's strategy is very low-key and lacks a true centre of gravity.

Quebec is part of a small, select group of non-sovereign federated states active in international relations (Criekemans 2010). In 2010 Quebec's Ministère des Relations internationales (MRI) had a budget of C\$124 million and employed 549 civil servants, with some 259 posted abroad (MRI 2010: 58). An accurate count would also include employees of other ministries who work on such international matters as economic affairs (promoting exports, attracting foreign investment, addressing free trade issues), border security (growing in importance since September 11, 2011), immigration policy, environmental issues, education, and culture. MRI (2006: 13) estimates total Quebec government expenditures on international affairs at \$350 million. This is the highest figure of any federated state in the world (Criekemans 2010).

In 2010 Quebec had 28 offices in 17 foreign countries, including a Paris office whose status approaches that of an embassy.[1] In fact Quebec has more foreign offices than many sovereign states have embassies: three more than New Zealand, the same number as Finland, and only seven fewer than Israel.

Since 1965 Quebec has signed around 550 international agreements or "*ententes*" with sovereign or federated states in close to 80 different countries. Over 300 of these agreements remain in force. Some involve sovereign countries such as France or Belgium. The most

---

1. Seven general delegations, five delegations, ten bureaus, four trade branches, and two areas of representation in multilateral affairs—UNESCO and the International Organization of La Francophonie (MRI 2009: 4).

important concern labour force mobility, education, social security, telecommunications, and the environment. In 2009 the Quebec government carried out 53 missions, an average of 4.5 per month (MRI 2009: 2).

Ontario's international relations are much less institutionalized. Without a government ministry dedicated to international relations, Ontario's international activities are dispersed among several different ministries and thus lack a centre of gravity. According to David Dyment, Ontario's offices abroad have historically focused largely on trade. Cultural matters and identity claims are clearly absent from Ontario's international relations agenda; so is immigration, a key concern for Quebec. One reason for Ontario's lack of involvement in these areas is that, even without an immigration policy or major programs, it already attracts a relatively large share of immigrants to Canada. The Ontario government is happy to leave immigration in the hands of the federal government (Dyment 2001: 56).

Ontario is also notable for the dearth of reliable data on the province's international activities. "Data on personnel and spending is incomplete and difficult to obtain" (*ibid.*: 58). What data exists is scattered and more suitable for ad hoc use. It is known that in 1988 Ontario had 15 international offices and 171 civil servants assigned to international issues. Operating costs for these offices totaled $21 million. Dyment (*ibid.*), based on an analysis of the Ontario government phone directory, reports that by 1990 the number of people working on international matters had risen to between 400 and 600. This number includes approximately 200 people, or 40% of the total, working abroad—50 Ontario civil servants and 150 local hires—while the remaining 60% worked in Ontario. Shortly thereafter, the Ontario government closed all foreign offices. In 2011 Ontario no longer independently operated a single foreign office. Only ten "Ontario Marketing Centres" located within Canadian diplomatic missions represent the province abroad.[2]

How to explain these differences? How to explain that two provinces with so much in common have adopted such different international relations strategies?

---

2. Ontario Marketing Centres are located in Beijing, London, Los Angeles, Mexico D.F., Munich, New Delhi, New York, Paris, Shanghai, and Tokyo (<http://www. ontarioexports.com>).

Four major variables account for the development of paradiplomatic activity (Paquin 2002, 2004). The first relates to the global or international system, while the other three are domestic factors. The variables affecting the governments of Ontario and Quebec are as follows:

1. Internationalization and globalization
2. Type of state
3. Identity and minority nationalism
4. Personality of decision makers

These fundamental variables may not explain everything, but they represent the underlying forces that account for the worldwide phenomenon of paradiplomacy. In the first two variables, Ontario and Quebec face similar pressures: both are subject to the pressures of internationalization and globalization and both fall into the same "type of state" and thus have a reason to promote their spheres of domestic jurisdiction internationally. The fundamental difference between the provinces is explained by variable 3, related to nationalism and identity, and variable 4, pertaining to the personalities of decision makers in their capacity as policy makers.

Unlike Quebec, Ontario's international relations are not part of a national movement that developed in reaction to the nationalism of the dominant country (Paquin 2004, 2006). Nationalism is a shared trait of the top three decentralized governments most active in international relations—Quebec, Flanders, and Catalonia—suggesting that this "identity variable" (no. 3) is fundamental (Paquin 2005; Lecours and Moreno 2001). In Quebec, Catalonia, and Flanders, nationalism partially explains the intensity of these non-sovereign nations' international activities. This factor has, moreover, been grossly underestimated in the literature on this phenomenon.

Ontario and Quebec also differ substantially in terms of the personalities of decision makers, especially in their roles as policy makers. While some Ontario politicians have shown leadership on international matters, for the most part Ontario's international relations are characterized by ad hoc, reactive, and rather arbitrary decision making. Quebec's approach, however, has been cumulative, with no discernable difference between parties. Both the Quebec Liberal Party (QLP) and Parti Québecois (PQ) favour a strong international role for the Quebec government.

To demonstrate our hypothesis, we will review each of these four variables to systematically compare Ontario and Quebec.

I. INTERNATIONALIZATION AND QUEBEC AND ONTARIO INTERNATIONAL RELATIONS

Internationalization and globalization comprise the first variable because they directly affect federated states within their areas of jurisdiction. Internationalization and the development of international standards and norms impact the sovereignty of federated states, i.e., their ability to formulate and implement policy. It is thus understandable that provinces take an active interest in certain international negotiations, such as the Kyoto Protocol or the Canada–European Union free trade agreement.

Since the creation of the United Nations following the Second World War, every sphere of provincial government activity in Canada has fallen within the purview of at least one, and frequently more than one, international treaty or intergovernmental organization (Karns and Mingst 2004; Smouts 1999). Issues such as education, public health, public procurement, labour force mobility, cultural diversity, the environment, subsidies for business, investor relations, elimination of non-tariff trade barriers, agriculture, services, and more are addressed within international organizations and at themed conferences. Nor is this a marginal phenomenon: some experts estimate that around 40% of federal legislation either establishes or refers to international treaties or standards (De Mestral and Fox-Decent 2008: 578). No study has yet been carried out at the provincial level.

Canadian provinces are therefore increasingly aware that their political power and sovereignty—meaning their ability to set and implement policy—is subject to negotiations at these international forums and bilateral meetings. This has a direct impact on Canada, which, unlike some other federations, lacks the constitutional power to impose the treaties it ratifies on the provinces. The provinces must be brought to the table.

The 1867 *Constitution Act* (formerly the *British North America Act*) scarcely touches on international relations. There is in fact no constitutional basis in Canada for attributing international relations to a particular level of government, which makes sense given that the 1867

Constitution did not make Canada an independent country but rather a dominion within the British Empire. Jurisdiction over international relations thus fell to London, not the Canadian government. The only section of the 1867 *Constitution Act* that touches on international law is section 132, concerning Imperial treaties. This section stipulates that the

> Parliament and Government of Canada shall have all powers necessary or proper for performing the obligations of Canada or of any province thereof, as part of the British Empire, towards foreign countries, arising under treaties between the Empire and such foreign countries.

In other words, the federal government is not empowered to conclude international treaties, but is authorized to implement treaties enacted by the British Empire—even in matters of provincial jurisdiction. Canada did not gain sovereignty over foreign policy until the 1931 Statute of Westminster. The question that soon arose was the following: Does the federal government have the power to force the provinces to implement its treaties even when said treaties pertain to matters of exclusive provincial jurisdiction?

Ontario, not Quebec, was first to raise the question of provincial jurisdiction in international affairs. In 1936 Ontario contested the federal government's right to legislate in areas of provincial jurisdiction when implementing international agreements (Patry 1980: 155), sparked by the issue of employment contracts. Prime Minister R.B. Bennett, elected in 1930, wanted to offer Canadians a Roosevelt-style "New Deal." As this was not an area open to federal intervention, the easiest means to this end was to ratify International Labour Organization agreements rather than amend the Constitution. The federal government thus ratified three different agreements, one on working hours, another on a weekly day of rest, and a third on a minimum wage. By forcing implementation of these agreements, the federal government was in effect interfering in labour, a provincial jurisdiction.

The Ontario prosecutor, A. W. Roebuck, was unafraid to push his argument to its logical conclusion (quoted in Patry 1980: 155):

> There are no grounds whatever for saying that the parties to advise His Majesty in matters relating to the jurisdiction of the Provinces have in some way come to the Dominion Ministers. The Province has the right to advise the Crown in matters where its legislative powers apply. Ontario has a right to enter into an agreement with another part of the British Empire or with a foreign State. So far as the legislative and executive authority are concerned the Governor-General and the Lieutenant-Governors of the Provinces, and the Dominion Parliament and the Provincial Legislatures are equal in status.

In 1937 the British Privy Council's Judicial Committee—still the Canadian justice system's final court of appeal—ruled on the matter. This decision would be of capital importance in defining the respective powers of Canada's federal and provincial governments in international relations. The judges stressed that federalism is the basis of Canada's Constitution and that a sovereign parliament is not required to take legislative measures to implement a treaty signed by the federal executive. This ruling held for provincial legislatures as well. In Canada, then, the power to implement treaties is shared.

There are two basic steps to adoption of treaties in Canada: 1) conclusion, which includes negotiation, signature, and ratification, and 2) implementation. The first step lies solely within the purview of the federal executive. The second step—adopting the necessary legislative measures to enforce the treaty—is shared between federal and provincial legislators. It is thus necessary to incorporate international treaty requirements into domestic law by enacting legislation at the appropriate level. In Canada a treaty does not automatically override existing laws. Judges rule based on the law, not treaties (Paquin 2010).

One example of this principle is the 1958 UN Convention on the Recognition and Enforcement of Foreign Arbitral Awards, concluded by the federal executive (step 1) but implemented (step 2) by both provincial and federal governments. Another is the Hague Convention on the Civil Aspects of International Child Abduction, concluded by the government of Canada but implemented exclusively by the provinces (Paquin 2010).

In 1965 the famous Gérin-Lajoie doctrine emerged in response to Quebec's concerns (shared by Ontario) about the impact of internationalization on areas of provincial jurisdiction. This doctrine promoting the international extension of Quebec's jurisdiction in matters of provincial jurisdiction (Paquin 2006)[3] was articulated in a 1965 speech by Quebec's Deputy Premier and Minister of Education, Paul Gérin-Lajoie:

> Il n'y a, je le répète, aucune raison que le droit d'appliquer une convention internationale soit dissocié du droit de conclure cette convention. Il s'agit des deux étapes essentielles d'une opération unique. Il n'est plus admissible non plus que l'État fédéral puisse exercer une sorte de surveillance et de contrôle d'opportunité sur les relations internationales du Québec.

---

3. In fact, Gérin-Lajoie did not use the historic phrase—"*la doctrine Gérin-Lajoie du prolongement international des compétences internes du Québec*"—until 1967, during debates at Quebec's Natioanl Assembly over the establishment of a ministry of intergovernmental affairs.

Gérin-Lajoie, following in the footsteps of the Ontario prosecutor of the 1930s, was suggesting overturning the old formula to allow Quebec to negotiate and implement its own international treaties in fields of provincial jurisdiction.

The doctrine remains topical today. Quebec's most recent international relations policy (MRI 2006: 14) makes a similar argument to the one Gérin-Lajoie put forward in 1965:

> *L'évolution de la situation internationale au cours des dernières décennies a fait apparaître des enjeux qui touchent presque toutes les compétences relevant du gouvernement du Québec, que ce soit dans le domaine du développement économique, de la santé, de l'éducation, de la culture ou de la sécurité. La plupart des ministères et des institutions publiques sont aujourd'hui interpellés par les questions internationales et l'exercice du mandat du ministère des Relations internationales repose sur une collaboration étroite avec les ministères et les autres partenaires du secteur public, y compris avec le gouvernement fédéral canadien.*

The treaty conclusion process rendered closer cooperation between the federal government and the provinces inevitable. The two levels of government have more and more reason to work together, which has boosted executive federalism. Nevertheless centralizing reflexes have remained strong in Canada (Savoie 2004). For Richard Simeon (2001), federal–provincial relations remain the weak link in Canadian federalism.

To date the provinces have been most interested in bilateral and multilateral international trade negotiations. With the advent of free trade, the federal government created various consultation mechanisms at the request of the provinces. Since the beginning of the Tokyo Round of multilateral trade negotiations in the 1970s, the government of Canada has developed consulting mechanisms with the provinces on federal initiatives in international trade (Kukucha 2008; Bernier 1979). These mechanisms grew necessary because the federal government was beginning to tackle issues that clearly fell within provincial jurisdiction. The provinces had major interests to defend, and their positions were not always in line with Ottawa's. The federal government, for its part, sought to ensure that its bargaining positions reflected provincial interests.

As subsequent rounds of trade talks also touched on issues of provincial jurisdiction, consultation mechanisms remained in place (Whinham 1978–1979). Since 1980 this practice has been formalized through regular federal–provincial consultations on trade policy (Fairley 1988). Consultations stand to become more frequent as international negotiations increasingly apply to domestic policy on subsidies to business or to provincial and local regulations liable to create trade barriers. Natural resource pricing and agricultural subsidies are just two examples of international issues that impact provincial jurisdictions. During the 1980 US–Canada Free Trade Agreement negotiations, and again in the early 1990s during North American Free Trade Agreement (NAFTA) negotiations, the provinces played an active role in debate over these agreements' potential impact on their economies and fields of jurisdiction. When Brian Mulroney's Conservative government began free trade talks in 1985, the provinces were quick to put forward their views, not only at the premiers' conference but also by sending representatives to the preparatory committee set up by Canada's chief negotiator (Doern and Tomlin 1991: 126–151). But when the premiers tried to secure a seat at the bargaining table, the Mulroney government said no (Hart *et al.* 1994: 139).

Ontario and Quebec both retained the services of high-profile lobbyists to make sure their concerns were heard in Ottawa. Ontario hired Bob Latimer, a former senior civil servant with the Ministry of Foreign Affairs and the Ministry of Industry and Trade; Quebec worked with Jake Warren, one of the Canadian negotiators during the Tokyo Round (*ibid.*).

Throughout the free trade negotiations, the premiers strongly voiced their concerns. For example, Ontario premier David Peterson, alarmed by rumours that the 1965 Auto Pact was on the table, travelled to Washington in 1987 to convince American officials to exclude it. Later, as the provinces began to assess the impact of the agreement the federal government had negotiated, the premiers delivered their verdict. In the summer of 1988 every province except Ontario and Prince Edward Island ratified the agreement. The process was essentially the same for NAFTA negotiations in the early 1990s (Abelson and Lusztig 1996).

The federal government later formalized the practice of meeting with the provinces to solicit their views on technical matters and help shape their bargaining strategy. Such an arrangement was inevitable: as we have seen, the federal government does not have the constitutional power to impose treaties in areas of provincial jurisdiction. The same pattern of federal–provincial negotiation spread to numerous forums, including the quarterly "C-Trade Meeting" that brings together federal, provincial, and territorial representatives to share information and set the Canadian position on international trade policy issues, including trade negotiations (Paquin 2010).

Trade is not the only matter of provincial concern. Ontario and Quebec are particularly interested (though for often different reasons) in the United Nations Framework Convention on Climate Change and the Kyoto Protocol. Both these international agreements, if implemented in Canada, would have profound and irreversible impacts on municipal and provincial policy—specifically energy, transportation, and urban planning. Ontario went so far as to criticize the Quebec government's attitude and in particular its regulations on automobile pollution, reflecting the interests the largely Ontario-based auto industry then undergoing restructuring (Bourgault-Côté 2010).

Questions of international public health have also garnered attention in recent years. If another crisis like the Severe Acute Respiratory Syndrome (SARS) scare were to hit Canada, provincial and municipal authorities would be on the front lines managing the crisis. This explains why some provinces, including Ontario and Quebec, wish to hold one or more permanent seats—if not independently, then within the Canadian delegation—at the World Health Organization (WHO), to better monitor policy developments. The federal government's refusal to offer the provinces a seat in international organizations and conferences took an alarming turn in 2005 when Paul Martin initially refused to allow Quebec government delegates to attend an international conference in Montreal to discuss avian flu; Martin eventually bowed to public pressure.

The 2003 SARS outbreak should, however, have served as a valuable lesson. The syndrome infected 438 people, caused 44 deaths, and cost the Ontario economy close to a billion dollars (Wilson 2006). The epidemic also highlighted a serious lack of cooperation and communication among the provinces, the federal government, and the WHO. These communication problems caused Canada to lose the confidence of the WHO, which issued an alert recommending that travellers avoid Toronto specifically and Canada generally.

It is thus apparent that both Ontario and Quebec are deeply affected by internationalization. The decision-making process on international treaties has forced the federal government and the provinces to work in concert on international matters. A recent example was the May 2009 announcement of negotiations for a "new generation" Canada–European Union free trade agreement. As the EU's primary concern is provincial public procurement, it made sure provincial delegates would have a place in the Canadian delegation (Robitaille 2009). The government of Quebec sent former Parti Québécois premier Pierre Marc Johnson as head negotiator. Ontario also sent a large delegation. During the January 2010 Brussels round of talks, the Canadian delegation comprised 50 delegates with 28 representing the provinces.

2. TYPE OF STATE

"Type of state," the second variable, takes into account both a state's system of government (democratic or otherwise) and institutional structure (unitary, decentralized, or federal). For example, paradiplomacy is less common or harder to implement in authoritarian regimes than in democratic systems. Democratization thus made paradiplomacy possible for a number of Mexican states (Schiavon 2010). The type of state variable also factors in the degree of decentralization. The more decentralized a political system, the more fields of jurisdiction federated states have to defend and promote. Federated states with a high number of jurisdictions tend to have greater resources and larger bureaucracies. This variable explains why paradiplomacy first emerged within federal systems (Soldatos 1990).

Within Canada's federal system, the provinces have many constitutional jurisdictions, large civil services, and copious financial resources. Sovereign states generally seek to fully exercise their constitutional jurisdictions. The same applies to federated states, which are, at least in theory, sovereign within their fields of jurisdiction. It is in the interest of provincial governments to protect their fields of jurisdiction against federal interference, and sometimes even to seek greater independence from the central power. Consequently, the provinces are not inclined to yield matters of provincial jurisdiction (the economy, natural resources, labour, health, education, and culture) to the federal government when they extend to the international arena. They generally feel that these matters are their responsibility. There is, of course, substantial asymmetry among provinces: the greater a province's resources, the greater its means to protect its constitutionally enshrined interests. The rest is a question of political will.

In the decades following Confederation, the international interests of the provinces, like those of the Dominion, were essentially limited to attracting immigrants and forging commercial ties (Beaudoin 1977). Since then, however, the scope of the provinces' interests has broadened to the point where today provincial governments are as concerned by free trade and environmental issues as their federal counterpart. The provinces maintain an international presence to protect their interests in a number of fields. We have already examined the constitutional aspect. Other significant interests include 1) business interests, 2) transborder relations, 3) environmental issues, and 4) security (Michaud and Ramet 2004; Stevenson 1982).

2.1. Business Interests

"Business interests" refers notably to provincial strategies to promote exports, attract foreign investment and international events, and build a positive image to spur investment in the province. Protecting and promoting business interests accounts for most Canadian provincial government activity abroad. When provinces maintain delegations abroad, organize trade missions, and establish diplomatic relations, they do so primarily with a view to stimulating economic growth through business, investment, or tourism. The provinces seek to expand foreign markets— especially in manufacturing and natural resource extraction—, develop secondary sectors, and raise new capital. They also work to protect their business interests against commercial manoeuvring by competitors.

This is far from a new phenomenon. Between 1867 and the end of the 19th century, historian Jean Hamelin notes, Quebec was already pursuing foreign capital. In 1881 Quebec premier Adolphe Chapleau spent nearly six months in France, largely to secure loans for the province. He returned to Quebec intent on further developing Quebec–France relations. The following year he appointed a general agent for Quebec in Paris, Senator Hector Fabre, who held the position until 1910. In 1883 the federal government also appointed Fabre as Canada's Paris Commissioner General. His mandate was to attract French immigrants and promote cultural exchanges and trade. Fabre was also a driving force behind the establishment of Montreal's French Chamber of Commerce. Honoré Mercier was another envoy who spent time in Paris to secure loans.

This situation would change at the beginning of the 20th century as American capital came on the scene. Instead of investment, Quebec began looking for new markets. New foreign offices were opened for this purpose. In 1908 the Quebec government enacted a law establishing a foreign office in the United Kingdom, which opened in 1911. In 1914 Quebec posted a general agent in Brussels (Hamelin 1969); the federal government had already done so in 1907. Ontario's U.K. foreign office opened in 1908.

Since the 1970s accelerated economic and financial globalization has meant an increasingly important economic role for the provinces. Policies to attract foreign investment and promote exports were critical, as became clear in the wake of the 1982 economic crisis (Lisée 2006).

The Ontario government (quoted in Grossman 1980) set up Export '80:

> a new program which will launch a revitalized, better financed and more comprehensive trade strategy for Ontario. [And after] an intensive internal assessment of Ontario's activities our review indicates a need to expand and modify [our] activity, particularly in the area of foreign offices.

Quebec, strongly urged by Minister of Foreign Trade Bernard Landry, separated intergovernmental affairs and international relations in 1984. This led Minster of Intergovernmental Affairs Jacques-Yvan Morin to resign while Landry took the helm of the newly created Ministère des Relations internationals (MRI). In 1984 Quebec released its first detailed international relations policy statement. *Québec dans le monde ou le défi de l'interdépendance : énoncé de politique de relations internationales* confirmed Quebec's shift to an international relations strategy focused on trade. But the policy statement was shelved soon after the 1985 election of Robert Bourassa's Liberal government.

The next major MRI policy statement, *Le Québec et l'interdépendance. Le monde pour horizon. Éléments d'une politique d'affaires internationales*, would not come until September 1991. This "white book" focused primarily on economic strategy. The government's overriding concern was to make Quebec competitive internationally by leveraging its "comparative advantages." It recommended fostering technology transfer and attracting foreign investment and proposed targeting selected industrial clusters such as aeronautics, telecommunications, pharmaceuticals, and consulting engineering. The document also stressed Quebec's cultural uniqueness, a product of its shared North American and European heritage. To implement this international business policy Minister John Ciaccia led trade missions to 40 countries. While the United States was Quebec's priority, it also sent missions to Europe, Latin America, the Middle East, and Asia.

Today economic issues remain Ontario and Quebec government priorities. It comes as no surprise that the United States, by far Canada's biggest trading partner, is the primary focus of provincial diplomacy. In the mid-1990s, every Canadian province traded more with bordering U.S. states than with the neighbouring provinces (Courchene 2000, 2003).

The provinces also sought to protect their economic interests abroad. Since the early 1980s the Ontario and Quebec governments have vigorously protected their interests against American softwood lumber producers who lobbied to impose high tariffs on Canadian imports. Provincial premiers also frequently visit major U.S. financial centres such as New York, Chicago, Atlanta, and Los Angeles in pursuit of new markets and capital.

2.2. Transborder Interests

The geographic position of Quebec and Ontario makes it necessary for them to coordinate policies and strategies with their U.S. neighbours and provides an incentive to take part in international relations. Globalization, integrated North American markets, and interdependence have all helped step up relations between the Canadian provinces and U.S. and Mexican states. Federated states within each of the three NAFTA member countries—ten Canadian provinces, 50 U.S. states, and 32 Mexican states—have responded to shared challenges by concluding numerous bilateral and multilateral agreements and implementing substate transnational partnerships. Dramatic growth in trade with U.S. states—especially border states—has forced the provinces to initiate interprovincial consultations and coordinate actions with their U.S. counterparts to address issues of provincial jurisdiction.

Today some 400 agreements are in force between U.S. states and Canadian provinces—over 100 on environmental and natural resource issues alone. Two-thirds of these agreements have been signed in the last 20 years and involve at least 46 U.S. states and every Canadian province (Paquin 2008). The Canadian and U.S. governments are not signatories of about half these agreements (Conklin 1997: 195). There are also more than 20 trade corridors linking Canadian provinces and U.S. states, created after U.S.–Canada trade grew in the wake of the Free Trade Agreement. Quebec and a number of other Canadian provinces also take part in the NASCO summits that bring together U.S. and Mexican states (Parent 2001).

Quebec and Ontario representatives carry out hundreds of missions to the U.S. and Mexico each year. When the provinces suggested creating a lobby group to represent them in Washington, Canada responded by establishing a Provincial/Territorial and Parliamentary Affairs Section of the Advocacy Secretariat at the Canadian Embassy; this also allows Ottawa to keep an eye on provincial activities in Washington. The Alberta government has been represented within this embassy since March 2005. Ontario, which is already represented at the Canadian Consulate in New York, is planning to follow suit in 2011.

Quebec turned down the federal government's invitation, preferring to open its own government office in Washington in addition to those in New York, Atlanta, Boston, Chicago, and Los Angeles. In Mexico,

Quebec has a government office, while Ontario is represented within the Canadian Embassy in Mexico City. A dozen U.S. states are represented in Canada, while some 18 others are represented in Mexico.

The intensification of transnational relations has also given rise to often highly specialized substate transnational organizations, in which Ontario and Quebec often play a role (Chaloux 2009; Government of Canada 2005). These organizations act in a wide range of fields such as healthcare, climate change, shared water resource management (e.g., in the Great Lakes), navigable waters, law enforcement, energy, fighting forest fires, environmental protection, border security, electrical grid management, and bridge and road network administration.

Most substate transnational organizations were created in recent years, many in the wake of the North American Free Trade Agreement. Usually, one or more Canadian provinces join existing American organizations, some of which bring together members of parliament and congresspeople, while others include premiers and governors. For example, since 1995 both Ontario and Quebec have been international members of the Council of State Governments, which has been active since 1933. Quebec, New Brunswick, and Nova Scotia have been members of the Eastern Regional Politics Conference since 1990. Ontario, Manitoba, and Saskatchewan are associate members of the Council of State Governments–Midwest, while Alberta and British Columbia are members of the Council of State Governments–West. The National Conference of State Legislatures, created in 1975 to promote communication among U.S. state legislatures and give them a unified voice in Washington, has included Quebec's National Assembly as an associate member since April 2000. Ontario and Saskatchewan are members of the regional Midwestern Legislative Conference (Chaloux 2009).

The most important coordination mechanism is undoubtedly provided by "mini-summits" like the Conference of New England Governors and Eastern Canadian Premiers, founded in 1973. The Conference brings together six U.S. states—Connecticut, Maine, Massachusetts, New Hampshire, Rhode Island, and Vermont—and five Canadian provinces—Quebec, New Brunswick, Nova Scotia, Prince Edward Island, and Newfoundland (Chaloux 2009; Lubin 1993). The first summit was held in the summer of 1973. It became an annual event in the wake of the oil crisis that occurred later that year in October, driven in part by interest in large Canadian hydroelectricity reserves from U.S. states looking for alternative energy sources. Today the conference focuses primarily on economic matters but issues such as energy, agriculture, transportation, tourism, the environment, and (especially post-9/11) border security are also up for discussion. Since 2000 private-sector actors have also attended.

In the West in 1991, British Columbia, Alberta, and the Yukon joined forces with five U.S. states—Alaska, Idaho, Montana, Oregon, and Washington—to form the Pacific Northwest Economic Region, which aims to promote economic development and trade and leverage regional influence in Ottawa and Washington. The association includes 17 working groups on subjects such as energy, the environment, and high tech, as well as a private sector board. Since the mid-1960s, the Ontario government has played a central role in managing environmental problems in the Great Lakes, a role that includes establishing cooperation mechanisms with bordering U.S. states. The Council of Great Lakes Governors, created in 1983, has eight U.S. member states; Ontario and Quebec signed on as associate members in 1997 (Chaloux 2009; Dyment 2001).

Some Canadian provinces are also members of associations of federated states. Quebec and Bavaria are cofounders of the Conference of Heads of Government of Partner Regions, which also includes Upper Austria, Shandong, Western Cape, São Paulo, and Florida. Quebec also holds an observers' seat at both the Conference of European Regions with Legislative Power, which includes Catalonia and Flanders, and the Assembly of European Regions. Ontario has been an associate member of the "Four Motors of Europe" since 1990.

2.3. Environmental Issues

The Ontario and Quebec governments find themselves increasingly compelled to take action to protect their interests at the international level. In the 1980s Ontario actively cooperated with the federal government to pressure U.S. Congress on the issue of acid rain (Munton and Castle 1992). Ontario also played a very active role in setting environmental standards during NAFTA negotiations in the early 1990s (Abelson 1995).

These examples show a province responding to concerns over environmental threats from abroad. But Ontario and Quebec's environmental practices have also been perceived as a threat, sparking foreign pressure to change these practices. Two examples are forestry practices and the Great Whale hydroelectric project in Quebec. Both foreign environmental groups such as the Rainforest Action Network and transnational groups such as Greenpeace have worked to change provincial policies by organizing boycotts and negative publicity campaigns. In the 1980s Greenpeace led a campaign in Europe calling for a boycott on seal fur. The EU banned seal products in 2009.

In the case of the Great Whale project, aboriginal leaders including Matthew Coon Come, Grand Chief of the Cree, and Ethel Blondin, member of the Déné Nation and Liberal MP for the Western Arctic, went to the U.S. to voice concerns over potential environmental impacts. They were successful: on March 16, 1992, William Hoyt put a moratorium before the New York State Assembly to block the purchase of $13 billion in electricity from Hydro-Quebec while the state conducted its own environmental impact assessments; the Assembly voted overwhelmingly in favour (Forest and Rodon 1995, 35–58).

The moratorium led the Quebec and Canadian governments to work together. They mandated Quebec's delegate general, Léo Paré, and Canada's consul general in New York, Alan Sullivan, to lobby Albany to overturn the moratorium.

2.4. Security Interests

In Canada matters of "international security" and "territorial defence" are generally associated exclusively with the federal government. This association is justified insofar as these activities fall under national defence and border protection, two federal fields of jurisdiction.

But the provinces are also involved in security, which can come under their jurisdiction in two ways. First, under Section 92 of the *Constitution of Canada*, the provinces (and municipalities, which are under provincial jurisdiction) play a central role in protecting the civilian population and enforcing laws through policing. Until very recently, a clear line seemed to separate activities aimed at protecting the territory from foreign threat, a federal matter, and those pertaining to domestic security, a provincial concern.

A number of phenomena have called this separation into question, leading the provinces to take a greater interest in security and defence. In the words of Quebec's Ministère des Relations internationales (2006: 67):

> À l'aube du XXIe siècle, plusieurs menaces à la stabilité internationale découlent de facteurs non militaires qui, à l'exemple du terrorisme, de la criminalité transnationale, des pandémies et de la dégradation de l'environnement, interpellent directement les responsabilités qu'exerce le Québec seul ou conjointement avec le gouvernement fédéral.

Cybercrime is another issue that is soliciting provincial interest.

The growing threat of terrorism in particular has come to the forefront, especially post-9/11. Fighting terrorism demands provincial resources (police, firefighters, healthcare providers) as much as, if not more so than, federal resources (armed forces, information services, Canada Border Services Agency, etc.). Quebec's MRI (2006: 68) again speaks to this issue:

> Le Canada et le Québec ne sont pas à l'abri d'une attaque terroriste. C'est pour-
> quoi le gouvernement du Québec a pris des mesures spéciales visant à accroître la
> sécurité. Il a ainsi apporté des modifications législatives pour sécuriser l'émission
> des actes de l'état civil et pour agir plus efficacement en cas d'infraction à la loi sur
> l'immigration. La Sûreté du Québec et le Service de police de la ville de Montréal,
> en collaboration avec la Gendarmerie royale du Canada, participent à l'équipe
> intégrée de sécurité nationale et de lutte contre le terrorisme. Le ministère de
> la Sécurité publique a créé un groupe de travail portant sur les menaces
> de nature chimique, bactériologique, radiologique et nucléaire. Un plan de
> sécurité civile est en place pour gérer les conséquences de catastrophes
> de diverses natures, incluant celles d'une attaque terroriste.

Given the phenomenal growth of trade with the United States, the provinces' prosperity has come to depend on access to the American market. This has led the provinces to adopt initiatives to discourage U.S. authorities from implementing standards whose stringency might impede trade or hinder the free movement of people. The Quebec government shored up cooperation with bordering U.S. states by con-cluding memoranda of understanding on information sharing with Vermont and New Hampshire, as well as a cooperation agreement on the fight against terror with the State of New York. The governments of both Quebec and Ontario are part of the Northeast Regional Homeland Security Directors Consortium that unites ten U.S. states and three Canadian provinces (MRI 2006: 68). Both also helped implement a range of measures to increase security and efficiency at the Canada–U.S. border. On December 12, 2001, Canada and the United States decided to build a "smart border." A number of related programs require provin-cial cooperation: NEXUS, which accelerates border clearance procedures for U.S. and Canadian citizens; FAST/EXPRESS, which fosters quick and secure shipping; and C-TRAP (Customs Trade Partnership against Terrorism), which aims to expedite the transit of preinspected goods through customs. Transborder organized crime has also spurred the provinces to assume greater control over security policy. Transborder crime includes drug and tobacco smuggling, smuggling of contraband weapons, human trafficking, and money laundering. These are not small-scale concerns: in 2004 the UN Office on Drugs and Crime esti-mated the number of drug users at 200 million, and the total value of the drug trade at US$320 billion (*ibid.*).

Since the SARS outbreak in Ontario, the provinces have also become more involved in the fight against pandemics. In 2004 the UN Secretary General's High-Level Panel on Threats, Challenges, and Change stressed that infectious diseases pose a major threat to international security given the speed with which a pandemic can spread, the number of people potentially affected, and the strain pandemics place on governments (UN 2004). In March 2006 Quebec's Minister of Health and Social Services released an action plan to combat an avian flu pandemic. The plan puts in place epidemiological surveillance and prevention measures, a vaccination campaign, an antiviral drug deployment strategy, a communication plan to inform the public, and measures to control hospital access and keep the healthcare system open and functional—even during a major outbreak (Ministère de la Santé et des Services sociaux 2006).

Some international security activities may also concern Ontario and Quebec. Many are already part of international aid and development programs and will play an increasing role in peace-building and post-conflict reconstruction missions. It is not uncommon to see police officers, election observers, or Hydro-Quebec or Ontario Hydro representatives in international missions led by the UN or similar organizations like the Organization for Security and Cooperation in Europe (OSCE) (Dyment 2001: 63–66). Quebec's MRI, through its Secrétariat à l'aide internationale, operates a financial assistance program that funds numerous international cooperation projects designed to strengthen the fabric of civil society in countries ravaged by war or natural disasters. The secretariat has funded projects in Guatemala, Nicaragua, and the African Great Lakes area. The province's motives in undertaking such projects often mirror those of the federal government, whether seeking to assert its own identity on the international stage, acting out of solidarity and compassion, or appealing to voters from diaspora communities.

3.   IDENTITY AND MINORITY NATIONALISM

The third variable encompasses minority nationalism and identity. When a province or region possesses a distinct identity—ranging from mere regionalism to highly institutionalized nationalism like Quebec's—it fosters the development and boosts the intensity of federated states' international activities. Such conditions also engender identity paradiplomacy. The identity mismatch between the central power and the federated state mobilizes "identity builders" ("*entrepreneurs identitaires*"[4]) and spurs higher-intensity paradiplomacy.

Minority nation identity builders play an active role in international relations because the failure to do so would leave the field open to the central government. In the words of Renaud Dehousse (1989: 284):

> *Accepter les prétentions du pouvoir central au contrôle exclusif des relations internationales équivaudrait pour les autorités régionales à lui permettre d'intervenir par ce biais dans les domaines qui leur sont traditionnellement réservés. Leur réaction face à ce qu'elles perçoivent comme une menace pour leur existence est unanimement négative.*

Identity, one of the main drivers of Quebec's international activities, is not a factor in Ontario.

An unapologetically nationalist discourse emerged in Quebec in the 1960s to justify stepping up international relations. Jean Lesage, in his speech inaugurating the Maison du Québec in Paris, stressed that Quebec is more than just a Canadian province. He presented the "state" of Quebec—not the province—as a lever against the threat of assimilation in North America. For Lesage, the Maison du Québec in Paris "*sera le prolongement de l'action que nous avons entreprise dans le Québec même*" (Bernier 1996: 30).

This is not to suggest that Lesage intended to work clandestinely to achieve Quebec independence. The Quebec Liberal Party's federalist leanings are beyond doubt. For Claude Morin, then a deputy minister in the Quebec government, Quebec's international actions were not the work of politicians or civil servants discreetly laying the groundwork for independence. Rather, the desire to play an active role on the international stage served domestic ends: international policy decisions were "*reliées à des problèmes ou à des besoins concrètement ressentis en ce temps-là*" (Morin 1987: 35). One significant factor, for Morin, was the strong desire felt by politicians and officials for Quebec to have an international presence. By doing so, the new wave of 1960s Quebec

---

4. The term "*entrepreneurs identitaires,*" translated here as "identity builders," was coined by Bertrand Badie. Identity builders are social actors who develop strategies to construct a distinct identity; who make national, religious, or ethnic identity claims; or who question the established political order. In Quebec, identity entrepreneurs work to construct the nation of Quebec rather than Canada. These actors will go abroad in search of the material and symbolic resources they need to strengthen the idea of national identity. See Badie (1995) and Badie and Smouts (1999).

nationalism sought to break with traditional nationalism, particularly the policies of the Union Nationale and the *"Grande Noirceur"* period. Morin (1987, 36) writes that

> [à] *un certain moment de cette période intense, on aurait parfois dit que tout ce qui ne s'était pas encore fait, ou même tout ce qui était interdit ou peu recommandable auparavant, devenait soudainement essentiel, urgent et possible. D'une idéologie faisant du repli sur soi une vertu, de la conservation de l'acquis une vocation et de la suspicion envers les influences étrangères une stratégie, on passa sans trop de discernement, à l'autre extrémité du pendule.*

Even before this period many Quebec intellectuals sincerely wished for stronger ties with foreign countries. The Canadian government, found to discriminate against francophones by the Royal Commission on Bilingualism and Biculturalism, was not a compelling option; Quebecers thus pinned their hopes on the Quebec "state." Naturally, Quebec turned to France, where much of the (generally francophile) Quebec elite already pursued university studies. Quebecers, a vast majority of whom were francophone, would have found it hard to countenance an interest in another country like the U.S. or U.K. Nor would these countries have been as receptive to Quebec's efforts.

In 1960, as Quebec was building its state apparatus, France–Quebec rapprochement was seen as an important "nation-building" tool. Quebec faced difficulties that could be more easily solved with the help of a country such as France. This led to the first international agreements on cooperation and education. The education system had been overhauled since the arrival of Jean Lesage's Liberals, who created the first-ever Quebec ministry of education. Understandably, Quebec's needs were great in this area—particularly in terms of technical expertise. Policies fostering cooperation with France would allow Quebec to more quickly catch up, responding to what were felt to be accrued deficiencies. France had the financial and human resources to lend Quebec the specialists it needed to develop its own system (Morin 1987: 37).

From the early 1960s on Quebec would establish a set of cooperation policies with France and other French-speaking countries to strengthen the status of the French language and bolster the development of Quebec as a nation (Bélanger 1994: 425). These exchanges and imported development models did not stop at cultural matters. For example, the Caisse de dépôt et placement, today one of Canada's largest fund managers, is another product of France–Quebec cooperation. André Marier, an economist influential in the Quiet Revolution, took his inspiration from the Caisse des Dépôts et Consignations de France and worked with French elites to adapt the concept to the realities of 1960s Quebec. The Caisse des Dépôts et Consignations de France, created in 1816, used the deposits and retirement funds of civil servants to secure state loans. In Quebec, the Caisse's role would be to promote a culture of ownership, foster a francophone middle class, and free the Quebec government from its economic dependence on the Montreal financial establishment, which was essentially controlled by Montreal's anglophone elite and had notably refused to finance electricity nationalization, forcing the Quebec government to turn to Wall Street.

In 1965 Paul Gérin-Lajoie, Quebec's Deputy Premier and Minister of Education, would also use nationalist arguments to justify developing an international policy for Quebec: in his view, Quebec was inadequately represented by the federal government and the Canadian foreign services ignored the French-speaking world. Gérin-Lajoie felt it necessary for Quebec to forge closer ties with Francophonie countries because federal diplomacy was not doing the job. Between 1950 and 1964 only 0.4% of Canada's foreign aid budget went to French-speaking countries.

It has often been claimed that Quebec diplomacy emerged to make up for the underrepresentation of francophones in the Canadian diplomatic service. Studies presented during the Royal Commission on Bilingualism and Biculturalism supported this view. The Ministry of Foreign Affairs even attempted to stonewall the work of two Quebec academics (including André Patry, author of the Gérin-Lajoie doctrine) officially mandated by the Commission to study whether Canada's biculturalism was upheld at the Ministry of Foreign Affairs. The other researcher, Gilles Lalande (quoted in Patry 1980: 79) describes the episode:

> *Non sans malveillance, la direction du ministère* [des Affaires étrangères] *nous a donné de nombreuses illustrations de la méfiance qu'elle entretient à l'égard de ceux de l'extérieur, y compris les chercheurs accrédités, qui désirent consulter les dossiers officiels, voire les moins confidentiels, portant sur la politique étrangère du Canada. Au mépris du mandat de la Commission, le ministère nous a refusé l'accès à tous ses dossiers de travail, même quand ils étaient de caractère général, prétextant pour certains qu'ils contenaient des renseignements confidentiels et, pour d'autres, qu'ils renfermaient des documents secrets. C'est de haute lutte que nous avons arraché l'autorisation de parcourir les documents, pourtant essentiels à notre étude, produits par la commission Glassco. Cette concession ne nous fut faite cependant sans qu'on l'assortît des restrictions suivantes: nous ne pouvions avoir accès à ces documents qu'en présence d'un représentant du ministère et il nous était défendu de prendre des notes... Les limites déjà imposées n'étant pas suffisamment embarrassantes, les autorités ont chargé un représentant du ministère de parcourir et d'épurer tous les documents que l'on nous destinait, même ceux qui n'avaient qu'un intérêt historique.*

In his report Lalande found it *"pour le moins étonnant que la loi du nombre n'ait pas permis à un seul agent de carrière de langue française d'être chef de mission dans la très grande majorité des pays où les intérêts canadiens sont jugés les plus importants"* (quoted in Patry 1980: 79). André Patry, author of a second study for the Commission, found that English was always the language of communication in the Ministry of Foreign Affairs and with international organizations—including the Union Postale Universelle whose sole official language was French. The Glassco Commision came to the same conclusion in 1962, finding that "the number of French Canadians holding key positions in the government administration is insignificant" (quoted in Hicks 2006).

If Quebec failed to act on international relations it would be left to the federal government to negotiate international agreements in Quebec's fields of jurisdiction.

Other factors also led Quebec to chart its own international course. International relations are, in theory at least, a matter for sovereign nations. Becoming an international actor able to meet with heads of state was a giant symbolic leap for Quebec—and a highly attractive prospect for identity builders (Lecours and Moreno 2001: 4). Branching out into the international scene can also be a strategy to strengthen identity domestically. Appearing in an international setting raises the Quebec premier's profile and prestige at home. Developing strong bilateral relations with sovereign states like France is also critical. Quebec, a substate entity, has managed to cultivate closer ties with France than Canada, a sovereign nation, has forged with Great Britain. With General Charles de Gaulle recognizing Quebec in his 1967 speech and Quebec taking a seat alongside sovereign nations at international conferences, the psychology of nationhood in Quebec was utterly transformed in the 1960s. As Quebec came to hold a stronger position in the international arena, Quebecers became less inclined to see themselves as destined for subservience, *"porteurs d'eau nés pour un petit pain"* as the traditional saying has it.

Emerging in the 1960s, Quebec's desire to take its place in the world was bolstered by globalization: Quebec nationalism now favoured developing international strategies (Paquin 2001; Keating 1997). For Alain Dieckhoff (2000) Quebec nationalism cannot be reduced to a simple shift in mood or the awakening of a primitive tribal force, but is rather a fundamental manifestation of modernity. Quebec nationalism, once a protectionist, autarkic impulse, today champions free trade and international expansion. Quebec's leaders used nationalism to justify support for regional integration. Pierre Martin explains that *"le Québec n'a pas endossé le libre-échange en dépit de son nationalisme; le Québec a choisi le libre-échange à cause de son nationalisme"* (1995: 2). Nor is Quebec just a passive observer as globalization runs its course: the province actively promotes globalization through the FTA and NAFTA. Quebec was also a major supporter of the UNESCO Convention on the Promotion of the Diversity of Cultural Expressions.

4. PERSONALITY OF DECISION MAKERS

The final factor is the personality of decision makers, especially in their policy-making role. The emergence of foreign policy at the federated state level owes much to the personality of certain politicians (Balme 1996: 29). International relations activity tends to be unequally distributed among regions in a single country. As Richard Balme (*ibid.*) points out in his writings on the role of politicians in regional cooperation,

> [c]es coopérations sont souvent portées sur les fonds baptismaux par de grands leaders régionaux: O. Guichard et avant qu'il devienne premier ministre, J.-P. Raffarin sur la façade atlantique, L. Späth en Bavière, J. Pujol en Catalogne, pour n'en citer que quelques-uns. Le leadership pèse sur les déterminations de l'action collective régionale.

On this matter Ontario and Quebec differ profoundly. For David Dyment, who has written a Ph.D. dissertation on Ontario's international activities, Ontario's international relations are characterized by reactive decision making that has led to a number of inexplicable decisions. Even if some politicians, like Liberal premier David Peterson, have made major contributions to developing Ontario's international relations, the fact remains that Ontario's international policy is marked by a lack of continuity that has prevented lasting institutionalization of international relations in the province.

According to a study by Ontario's Minister of Intergovernmental Affairs (quoted in Dyment 2001: 61),

> Over the years offices have been opened and closed with seeming randomness. More than half the offices opened have been closed, some just years after they were opened, some have subsequently been reopened. There has been no mechanism to make decisions about openings and closings, location and mandate on the basis of long-term strategic considerations. The pattern suggests a deficiency in the decision-making process.

From 1944 to 1961, a period of moderate growth, two new Ontario foreign offices opened (in New York and Chicago), bringing the total to three. Interestingly, in 1965 Ontario had five foreign offices, one more than Quebec (which had recently opened offices in Paris and London, and maintained a delegation in New York).

Between 1962 and 1973, the number of Ontario foreign offices jumped from three to sixteen. This number fell to seven between 1974 and 1979. But this period of decline was followed by one of rapid growth: between 1980 and 1992 the number soared from seven to nineteen, prior to the 1993 closure of all offices by Bob Rae's NDP government. These closures saved a mere $17 million per year; $7 million went elsewhere. During the entire period (1944–1993) the province had opened offices in 25 different cities (Dyment 2001: 56).

The Rae government's decision to close all Ontario foreign offices can be explained by a serious recession accompanied by a large government deficit, the release of a report questioning the usefulness of operating these foreign offices, and a scandal involving the lavish lifestyle and philandering of an Ontario representative in New York.

To cut down on waste from repeated openings and closures, the provincial governments turned to "cohabitation," i.e., renting offices within existing Canadian embassies, consulates, and high commissions. This solution let the provinces maintain offices, save money, and avoid the high cost of opening new offices. Another solution, borrowed from the U.K., was to enlist business leaders to act as part-time trade ambassadors abroad for an honorarium of $1 per year.

Unlike Ontario, Quebec's international relations history is marked by major international players and true innovators including Jean Lesage, Paul Gérin-Lajoie, Daniel Johnson Sr., Claude Morin, Louise Beaudoin, and Jean Charest. The process in Quebec has been one of cumulative expansion, with few of the significant contractions seen in Ontario (Paquin 2006). The only cutbacks in Quebec's international relations since the 1960s were those ordered by Lucien Bouchard in 1996, under his government's zero-deficit policy. A few years later the Parti Québecois changed direction and stepped up international relations. Under Jean Charest's Liberals this trend has continued with the Quebec–France understanding on labour mobility, Quebec's participation in the Western Climate Initiative, and work toward an EU–Canada free trade agreement.

CONCLUSION

A number of conclusions can be drawn from the above. Although Ontario has only developed a low-intensity paradiplomacy, circumstances still often lead the Ontario government to act on the international scene, if only to protect its constitutional interests. Despite Ontario's low degree of institutionalization, the province does carry out significant international activities. Unlike Quebec, Ontario has chosen a low-profile strategy that eschews "brick and mortar" investments.

Quebec is another story. The structure of the Ministère des Relations internationales and the protocol for Quebec premiers' international activities are two examples of how the province seeks to imitate the practices of the Ministry of Foreign Affairs, but on a smaller scale. There is cross-party consensus in Quebec on the importance of protecting the province's interests abroad.

The Quebec–Ontario difference is explained neither by the type of state nor by internationalization but rather by the other two variables: identity and minority nationalism and the personality of decision makers—especially the role of premiers as policy makers.

BIBLIOGRAPHY

Abelson, D. E. (1995). "Environmental Lobbying and Political Posturing: The Role of Environmental Groups in Ontario's Debate over NAFTA." *Canadian Public Administration*, vol. 38: 352–381.

Abelson, D. E. and M. Lusztig (1996). "The Consistency of Inconsistency: Tracing Ontario's Opposition to the NAFTA." *Revue canadienne de science politique*, vol. 29, no. 4: 681–698.

Aldecoa, F. and M. Keating (eds.) (1999). *Paradiplomacy in Action: The Foreign Relations of Subnational Governments*. London: Frank Cass.

Badie, B. (1995). *La fin des territoires*. Paris: Fayard.

Badie, B. and M. C. Smouts (1999). *Le retournement du monde. Sociologie de la scène internationale*, 3rd. ed. Paris: Presses de Sciences Po/Dalloz.

Balme, R. (1996). "Pourquoi le gouvernement change-t-il d'échelle?" In R. Balme (ed.), *Les politiques du néo-régionalisme. Action collective régionale et globalisation*. Paris: Economica.

Beaudoin, L. (1977). "Origines et développement du rôle international du gouvernement du Québec." In P. Painchaud (ed.), *Le Canada sur la scène internationale*. Montreal and Quebec City: Centre québécois de relations internationales et Presses de l'Université du Québec: 441–471.

Bélanger, L. (1994). "La diplomatie culturelle des provinces canadiennes." *Études internationales*, vol. 25, no. 3: 421–452.

Bernier, I. (1979). "La Constitution canadienne et la réglementation des relations économiques internationales au sortir du 'Tokyo Round.'" *Cahiers de droit*, vol. 20: 673–694.

Bernier, L. (1996). *De Paris à Washington. La politique internationale du Québec.* Quebec City: Presses de l'Université du Québec.

Bourgault-Côté, G. (2010). "L'Ontario en colère contre le règlement québécois sur la pollution automobile – L'Ontario était avertie, dit Québec." *Le Devoir*, February 13: A3.

Chaloux, A. (2009). *Fédéralisme, relations transfrontalières et changements climatiques : le cas de la Conférence des gouverneurs de la Nouvelle-Angleterre et premiers ministres de l'Est du Canada.* M.A. thesis, Université de Sherbrooke.

Conklin, D. (1997). "NAFTA: Regional Impacts." In M. Keating and J. Loughlin (eds.), *The Political Economy of Regionalism*. London and Portland: Frank Cass: 195–214.

Courchene, T. J. (2000). "NAFTA, the Information Revolution, and Canada–U.S. Relations: An Ontario Perspective." *The American Review of Canadian Studies*, vol. 30, no. 2: 159–180.

Courchene, T. J. (2003). "FTA at 15, NAFTA at 10: A Canadian Perspective on North American Integration." *North American Journal of Economics and Finance*, vol. 14: 263–285.

Criekemans, D. (2010). "Regional Sub-state Diplomacy from a Comparative Perspective: Quebec, Scotland, Bavaria, Catalonia, Wallonia, and Flanders." *The Hague Journal of Diplomacy*, vol. 5, nos. 1–2: 37–64.

Dehousse, R. (1989). "Fédéralisme, asymétrie et interdépendance: aux origines de l'action internationale des composantes de l'État fédéral." *Études internationales*, vol. 20, no. 2: 283–309.

De Mestral, A. and E. Fox-Decent (2008). "Rethinking the Relationship between International and Domestic Law." *McGill Law Journal*, vol. 53, no. 4: 576.

Dieckhoff, A. (2000). *La nation dans tous ses États. Les identités nationales en mouvement.* Paris: Flammarion.

Doern, B. G. and B. W. Tomlin (1991). *Faith and Fear: The Free Trade Story.* Toronto: Stoddart.

Dyment, D. M. (2001). "The Ontario Government as an International Actor." *Regional and Federal Studies*, vol. 11, no. 1: 55–79.

Fairley, S. H. (1988). "Jurisdictional Limits on National Purpose: Ottawa, the Provinces and Free Trade with the United States." In M. Gold and D. Leyton-Brown (eds.), *Trade-Offs on Free Trade: The Canada–US Free Trade Agreement*. Toronto: Carswell: 107–116.

Forest, P.-G. and T. Rodon (1995). "Les activités internationales des autochtones du Canada." *Études internationales*, vol. 26, no. 1: 35–58.

Gérin-Lajoie, P. (1965). *Texte de l'allocution prononcée par Monsieur Paul Gérin-Lajoie, vice-président du Conseil et ministre de l'Éducation, devant les membres du corps consulaire de Montréal, le 12 avril.*

Government of Canada (2005). *L'émergence de régions transfrontalières. Rapport provisoire.* Ottawa: Projet de recherche sur les politiques.

Grossman, L. (1980). *Ontario Hansard*. Minister of Industry and Tourism, May 13, 1814.

Hamelin, J. (1969). "Québec et le monde extérieur." *Annuaire statistique du Québec, 1968–69*. Quebec City: Gouvernement du Québec: 19–26.

Hart, M., B. Dymond, and C. Robertson (1994). *Decision at Midnight: Inside the Canada–US Free-Trade Negotiations*. Vancouver: University of British Columbia Press.

Hicks, B. M. (2006). "Is 'French Fact' Still Relevant to Liberal Party?" *Toronto Star*, February 22: A17.

Hocking, B. (1995). "Regionalism: An International Relations Perspective." In M. Keating and J. Loughlin (eds.), *The Political Economy of Regionalism*. London: Frank Cass: 90–111.

Karns, M. and K. Mingst (2004). *International Organizations. The Politics and Processes of Global Governance*. Boulder: Lynne Rienner.

Keating, M. (1997). *Les défis du nationalisme moderne. Québec, Catalogne, Écosse*. Montreal: Les Presses de l'Université de Montréal.

Kukucha, C. J. (2008). *The Provinces and Canadian Trade Policy*, Vancouver: UBC Press.

Lecours, A. and L. Moreno (2001). "Paradiplomacy and Stateless Nations: A Reference to the Basque Country." Working Paper 01-06, Unidad de Políticas Comparadas (CSCI).

Lisée, J. F. (2006). "Comment le Québec est devenu une région-État nord-américaine." In S. Paquin (ed.), *Histoire des relations internationales du Québec*. Montreal: VLB.

Lubin, M. (1993). "The Routinization of Cross-Border Interactions: An Overview of the NEG/ECP Structures and Activities." In D. M. Brown and E. H. Fry (eds.), *States and Provinces in the International Economy*. Berkeley: Institute of Government Studies Press.

Martin, P. (1995). "When Nationalism Meets Continentalism: The Politics of Free Trade in Quebec." *Regional and Federal Studies*, vol. 5, no. 1: 1–27.

Massart-Piérard, F. (2005). "Du local à l'international : nouveaux acteurs, nouvelle diplomatie." *Revue internationale de politique comparée*, vol. 12, no. 2: 191–206.

Michaud, N. and I. Ramet (2004). "Québec et politique étrangère : contradiction ou réalité?" *International Journal*, vol. 59, no. 2: 303–324.

Michelmann, H. J. and P. Soldatos (1990). *Federalism and International Relations: The Role of Subnational Units*. Oxford: Clarendon.

Ministère de la Santé et des Services sociaux (2006). *Pandémie d'influenza. Plan québécois de lutte à une pandémie d'influenza – Mission santé*. Quebec City: MSSS.

Ministère des Relations internationales du Québec (2006). *La politique internationale du Québec : la force de l'action concertée*. Quebec City: MRI.

Ministère des Relations internationales du Québec (2009). *Rapport annuel de gestion, 2008–2009*. Quebec City: MRI.

Ministère des Relations internationales du Québec (2010). *Rapport annuel de gestion, 2009–2010*. Quebec City: MRI.

Morin, C. (1987). *L'art de l'impossible. La diplomatie québécoise depuis 1960*. Montreal: Boréal.

Munton, D. and D. Castle (1992). "Reducing Acid Rain, 1980s." In D. Munton and J. Kirton (eds.), *Canadian Foreign Policy: Selected Cases*. Scarborough: Prentice Hall Canada.

Palard, J. (1999). "Les régions européennes sur la scène internationale: condition d'accès et systèmes d'échanges." *Études internationales*, vol. 30, no. 4: 657–678.

Paquin, S. (2001). *La revanche des petites nations. Le Québec, l'Écosse et la Catalogne face à la mondialisation*. Montreal: VLB.

Paquin, S. (2002). *La paradiplomatie identitaire. Le Québec et la Catalogne en relations internationales*. Ph.D. dissertation. Institut d'études politiques de Paris.

Paquin, S. (2004). *Paradiplomatie et relations internationales. Théorie des stratégies internationales des régions face à la mondialisation*. Brussels: Presses interuniversitaires européennes / Peter Lang.

Paquin, S. (2006). "Les relations internationales du Québec avant la Révolution tranquille." In S. Paquin (ed.), *Histoire des relations internationales du Québec*. Montreal: VLB: 13–23.

Paquin, S. (2008). "La paradiplomatie des États américains et la cohérence de la politique étrangère des États-Unis." In F. Massart-Piérard (ed.), *L'action extérieure des entités subétatiques. Approche comparée. Europe – Amérique du Nord*. Leuven: Les Presses de l'Université Louvain-la-Neuve.

Paquin, S. (2010). "Federalism and Compliance with International Agreements: Belgium and Canada Compared." *The Hague Journal of Diplomacy*, vol. 5, nos. 1–2: 173–197.

Parent, R. (2001). "Entente conclue entre le Québec et l'État de New York." *Le Nouvelliste*, December 5: 15.

Patry, A. (1980). *Le Québec dans le monde*. Montreal: Leméac.

Robitaille, A. (2009). "Sommet Canada-UE – Québec compte sur l'appui de Bruxelles." *Le Devoir*, May 7: B1.

Rosenau, J. N. (1990). *Turbulence in World Politics. A Theory of Change and Continuity*. Princeton: Princeton University Press.

Savoie, D. J. (2004). "Power at the Apex: Executive Dominance." In J. Bickerton and A. G. Gagnon (eds.), *Canadian Politics*, 4th ed. New York: Broadview Press: 145–162.

Schiavon, J. A. (2010). "Sub-state Diplomacy in Mexico." *The Hague Journal of Diplomacy*, vol. 5, nos. 1–2: 65–97.

Simeon, R. (2001). "Conclusion." In J. P. Meekison (ed.), *Relations intergouvernementales dans les pays fédérés. Une série d'essais sur la pratique de la gouvernance fédérale*. Ottawa: Forum des fédérations: 105–123.

Slaughter, A. M. (2004). *A New World Order*. Princeton: Princeton University Press.

Smouts, M. C. (1999). "Que reste-t-il de la politique étrangère?" *Pouvoirs*, vol. 88: 11–29.

Soldatos, P. (1990). "An Explanatory Framework for the Study of Federated States as Foreign-Policy Actors." In H. J. Michelmann and P. Soldatos (eds.), *Federalism and International Relations: The Role of Subnational Units*. Oxford: Clarendon.

Stevenson, G. (1982). *Unfulfilled Union: Canadian Federalism and National Unity*, revised ed. Toronto: Gage.

UN (2004). *A More Secure World: Our Shared Responsibility*. Report of the Secretary-General's High-Level Panel on Threats, Challenges, and Change

Whinham, G. R. (1978–1979). "Bureaucratic Politics and Canadian Trade Negotiation." *International Journal*, vol. 34, no. 4: 64–89.

Wilson, K. (2006). "Pandemic Prescription." *Diplomat and International Canada*, vol. 17, no. 2: 14–16.

12. GAME THEORY AND INTERGOVERNMENTAL NEGOTIATIONS
The Case of the 2006 Quebec–Ontario Trade and Cooperation Agreement

ALEXANDRE BRASSARD[1]

It has often been said that unlike other federations in the world, Canada does not grant its regions a voice in its central institutions. Canadian senators do not represent their home provinces, and although members of the House of Commons do represent their constituencies, they are muzzled by party discipline. Cabinet ministers are bound by ministerial solidarity, and first ministers' conferences are too sporadic and too much under Ottawa's control to serve the interests of the provinces. In other words, Canada suffers from a lack of "intrastate federalism" (Caron, Laforest, and Vallières-Roland 2009; McRoberts 1997; Simeon 2006; Smiley and Watts 1986).

E pur si muove! Federal bodies are not adept at serving local interests, but the federation itself works because demands are aggregated and overall coordination is managed at another level, that of intergovernmental negotiations. The country's eleven governments are in constant communication, formulating public policy and organizing its implementation. These discussions can be formal or informal and take place at various levels, be they committees of public servants, interministerial meetings, or first ministers' conferences. They can be bilateral or multilateral, vertical or horizontal.

1. The author wishes to thank his translators and James McLennan for revising the English text.

Canada is perpetually under negotiation and Canadian federalism cannot be understood without taking into account the scope and scale of intergovernmental diplomacy.

Political scientists recognize this reality. They have shown particular interest in *vertical* (federal–provincial) relations on constitutional issues (Banting and Simeon 1983; Cameron 2001; Gagnon 2009; Rocher 2009; Seymour 2009; Simeon and Nugent 2008), public policy (Brock 2008; Broschek 2004, Cameron and Simeon 2002; Fortin 2009; Graefe 2006; Leo 2006; McIntosh 2004; Vaillancourt and Thériault 2009), and tax policy (Bird and Tarasov 2004; Courchene and Telmer 1998; Gibbins 2007; Lachapelle and Bernier 1998; Noël 2009; Théret 1999; Watts 2005). On the other hand, we know far less about *horizontal* relations. This is an important gap, because interprovincialism has grown significantly since the beginning of the new millennium.

The Council of Atlantic Premiers was created in 2000 as a coordinating forum. Similarly, Alberta and British Columbia organized their first joint cabinet meeting in 2003, a mechanism that was subsequently adopted by the other western provinces, and then by central Canada. Summit meetings have generated a myriad of interprovincial cooperation agreements in a variety of sectors, from education to labour mobility to infrastructure. In 2003 the provinces also created the Council of the Federation, tasked with promoting interprovincial cooperation (Pelletier 2006).

What theoretical frameworks allow us to study this type of interaction? How can we explain this apparent intensification of interprovincial relations? What are its consequences? We will explore these issues by examining the specific case of Quebec–Ontario negotiations and cooperation between 2003 and 2006.

I. A HISTORICAL OVERVIEW OF QUEBEC–ONTARIO RELATIONS

The recent rapprochement between Quebec and Ontario is in keeping with the expanding interprovincial agenda throughout the country, but it also marks the re-establishment of a long-standing partnership between the two provinces. The handful of historical studies that do deal directly with this topic remind us that Quebec and Ontario have a close and deeply rooted relationship (Armstrong 1982, 1986; Cook 1969; Creighton 1956; Durocher 1970; Morrison 1961; Romney 1992).

For some, these ties can be traced back to the shared experience of the War of 1812. However, this episode was more significant for Ontario than for Quebec, and it is probably more accurate to use the rebellions of 1837 as a starting point, when democratic movements in Upper and Lower Canada joined forces against the colonial government. The rebellions failed, but their leaders continued to cooperate. They reformulated their demands, insisting on responsible government, and their struggle enabled them to forge political alliances in United Canada (1840). This period culminated in the coalition government of Lafontaine and Baldwin and the achievements of the "great ministry." The friendship between the two leaders became legendary, and is sometimes evoked to symbolize cooperation between the two provinces (Ralston Saul 2010).

Relations between Canada East and Canada West deteriorated, however, with the rise of religious and linguistic tensions between reformers, Orangemen, and ultramontanes. The resulting political deadlock led the two regions to support Confederation. Together they defined and defended the federal model that underpinned the *British North America Act*. From this point of view, Ontario and Quebec can be considered as the two founding pillars of the country. Their political ties were mirrored in their complementary geography and economy, what Creighton (1956) later called the *Commercial Empire of the St. Lawrence*.

After 1867, Quebec and Ontario continued to assume joint leadership. The two provinces were the main beneficiaries of Macdonald's National Policy (1878) and its impact on transportation, manufacturing, and the banks. They also united to defend provincial rights against Ottawa's centralist tendencies. While Macdonald saw the provinces as junior partners of the federal government, premiers Honoré Mercier and Oliver Mowat interpreted the Constitution as a founding pact between the provinces. They convened the first interprovincial conference in 1887. The agenda included increases in federal transfers to the provinces and the abolition of federal spending power, right of disallowance, and declaratory power. This was the start of modern, horizontal intergovernmental relations (Morrison 1961).

During the Great Depression, Ottawa took on a more interventionist role and established the first assistance programs for the poorer provinces. Mitchell Hepburn and his Quebec allies (Alexandre Taschereau and, later, Maurice Duplessis) fought together against these measures, which penalized their provinces. They unanimously rejected the authority of the Rowell–Sirois Commission and its recommendations (Durocher 1970). This common front resurfaced when Ottawa adopted broad, postwar Keynesian policies.

With the Quiet Revolution and the rise of Quebec nationalism in the 1970s, relations between the two central provinces underwent a realignment. Ontario began playing the role of mediator between Quebec and the rest of the country. Later, during the Meech Lake negotiations, the Ontario of David Peterson and Bob Rae supported demands for a renewed federalism.

Although relations between the two provinces cooled during the Péquiste period between 1994 and 2003, the arrival of Jean Charest's Liberals paved the way for normalization and the reaffirmation of what Dalton McGuinty called their "shared destiny."

2. THEORETICAL FRAMEWORKS

We now move from a historical, descriptive survey to a contemporary theoretical discussion. For this, the work of Richard Simeon is key. The author of *Federal–Provincial Diplomacy* proposes a detailed analytical framework for understanding intergovernmental relations in Canada. His approach has influenced most subsequent research in this field. It can be summarized as follows:

> There is a set of interdependent *actors*, or partisans; they operate within a certain *social and institutional environment*; they share some *goals* but differ on others . . .; they have an *issue* or set of issues on which they must negotiate; none has hierarchical control over the others; they have varying *political resources*; they use the resources in certain *strategies and tactics*; they arrive at certain *outcomes*; and these outcomes have *consequences* for themselves, for other groups in the society, and for the system itself *(Simeon 2006: 11–12)*.

Simeon lists several different variables that can affect intergovernmental relations in Canada. His analysis, which focuses on three negotiations and draws on 129 interviews with negotiators, enables him to identify the strongest trends in intergovernmental diplomacy. He observes that Canadian society is comprised of economically, linguistically, and electorally diverse regions. Canadian identity is too fragile to counter these centrifugal forces, and federal institutions are poorly designed to accommodate local interests. Moreover, the Westminster system promotes the concentration of power in the country's eleven cabinets. Together, these factors encourage collective decision making by separate governments that maintain few organic ties and that are chiefly in contact through their political leaders. In this social and institutional context, intergovernmental negotiations are inevitable.

More than three decades after its publication, this book still has much to teach us. Practitioners of federalism will find it useful, even though few of them can use Simeon's methodology, which requires direct access to decision makers, numerous interviews, and extensive data analysis. This type of macroscopic and retrospective analysis also poses certain problems when used as a guideline for action.

This is where the model developed by Bueno de Mesquita could well be useful. Based on game theory, the *expected utility model* is designed to apply to all negotiating situations, whether they involve international, national, corporate, or individual actors (Bueno de Mesquita 1994, 2002a, 2002b, 2003, 2009; Bueno de Mesquita and Organski 1994; Bueno de Mesquita and Stokman 1994). It has been applied to intergovernmental issues in Canada a number of times (Imbeau 1990, 1991, 1993; James 1998; James and Lusztig 1996, 1997a, 1997b).

The expected utility model (EUM) facilitates analysis. It does not question the social and institutional context underpinning interprovincial negotiations, which Simeon describes in detail. The EUM provides a schematic view based on the principle that negotiating strategies and tactics depend solely on actors' instrumental rationality and relative strength rather than on their values. The EUM does not try to assess the social and systemic consequences of the negotiations. The model is streamlined and focuses on only a few attributes of the actors involved: their interest in the issue being negotiated (*position*), their relative influence (*capacity*), and their level of commitment to the issue (*salience*). The model operationalizes the concepts of "issues," "goals and object-ives," and "political resources" that Simeon also uses.

Whereas Simeon studied Canada's eleven governments, Bueno de Mesquita used a more microscopic scale. He leaves room for infra-governmental actors who are important to a specific round of nego-tiations: certain key individuals (first ministers, ministers, chiefs of staff, etc.), administrative units (first ministers' offices, Privy Council, cabinet, departments, committees, etc.), and even public opinion in the various provinces.

Instead of examining federal phenomena retrospectively, the EUM seeks to define a current strategic situation and forecast how it will evolve. It looks to the future and offers a predictive tool for practition-ers, negotiators, and decision makers.

In this chapter we use Bueno de Mesquita's conceptual categories to paint a broad portrait of recent negotiations between Quebec and Ontario. In addition to providing a description, we hope that the exercise will enable us to test the retrodictions generated by the model. Would the EUM have predicted the 2006 Quebec–Ontario Trade and Cooperation Agreement? If so, we would be encouraged to continue exploring the model. It could be used to speculate on future intergovernmental negotiations.

3.   MODELING INTERGOVERNMENTAL DIPLOMACY

We used game theory to model the dynamics of Quebec–Ontario negotiations. Following Bueno de Mesquita's approach, two negotiators (*A* and *B*) act in turn. Each player possesses a series of strategic alternatives. A player can either wait or make a proposal, which the other player can accept or refuse. In the case of a refusal, Player *B* can either offer a concession or make a threat. The other player can then either give in to or resist the threat.

These decisions are based on the players' utility calculation (i.e., their position), their level of influence and involvement, and their probabilistic assessment of the opponent's psychology. Is the other player a "hawk" prepared to threaten, or a "dove" who prefers to compromise? Is the adversary a "retaliator" who strikes back when threatened or a "peacemaker" who gives in? Depending on the circumstances, these dyadic interactions will lead to the status quo, an agreement, more negotiations, resigned acceptance by one of the players, or a crisis situation. This game can be represented by a tree diagram (Figure 1).

Of course the 2004–2006 Quebec–Ontario negotiations involved more than two actors. In addition to the two provincial premiers, the roles played by their cabinets and intergovernmental affairs ministers, the opposition parties, lobbies, and public opinion must be considered. To take into account all of these actors, the dyadic process must be repeated for all possible pairs. The game is repeated a number of times, equal to the factorial of the number of players. For example, three players require six games: $A \to B$, $A \to C$, $B \to A$, $B \to C$, $C \to A$, and $C \to B$. In the present case, the negotiations involved 16 players, which gives the astronomical number of 2,012 dyadic games.

Figure I
Negotiation Dynamics

A submits a proposal
    B accepts → **Agreement**
    B refuses
        A (dove) offers a concession
            B (dove) offers a concession → **The negotiations continue**
            B (hawk) threatens
                A (peacemaker) gives in → **A acquiesces**
                A (retaliator) resists → **Crisis**
        A (hawk) threatens
            B (peacemaker) gives in → **B acquiesces**
            B (retaliator) resists → **Crisis**
A waits
    B waits → **Status quo**
    B submits a proposal
        A accepts → **Agreement**
        A refuses
            B (dove) offers a concession
                A (dove) offers a concession → **The negotiations continue**
                A (hawk) threatens
                    B (peacemaker) gives in → **B acquiesces**
                    B (retaliator) resists → **Crisis**
            B (hawk) threatens
                A (peacemaker) gives in → **A acquiesces**
                A (retaliator) resists → **Crisis**

Source: Negotiation dynamics adapted from Bueno de Mesquita 2009a: 25.

All these games are simultaneous in the sense that they do not take into consideration the results of other games. However, the effects of these interactions are compiled at the end of each round. This modifies the players' positions, expectations, and beliefs for the next round, thus changing the negotiations as a whole. From one round to another, their positions converge or diverge, and eventually become fixed. The analyst then has a prediction for the outcome of the negotiations.

When a strategic situation reaches this level of complexity, computers are indispensable. We used the software application developed by Bueno de Mesquita to process the data and generate the interaction tables.

The data consists of a list of the actors involved and their characteristics. In the case under study, the key players were the first ministers, the ministers of intergovernmental affairs, the opposition parties, and public opinion in Quebec, Ontario, and Canada. Also included were the cities of Ottawa and Gatineau, the private sector in the two provinces, as well as the Council of the Federation.

Five attributes were defined for each actor: 1) position on the issue, 2) degree of influence, 3) level of salience, 4) flexibility or rigidity with respect to their own negotiating position, and 5) power (or lack thereof) to veto the signing of an agreement. These values were estimated based on a variety of qualitative sources. They took into consideration the throne speeches of the two provincial governments, speeches by the ministers involved, press releases issued by both governments, news articles published at the time, the texts of the agreements, and confidential interviews with three people actively involved in Quebec–Ontario relations.

These attributes were assigned a numerical code and processed by the program as interval variables. More specifically, the actors' positions were coded between 1 and 100, where 100 expresses unfailing support for the highest possible level of cooperation between the two provinces. Such an actor would favour major, long-term financial commitments, even on very controversial or complex issues. The aims of each actor are coded according to the scale set out in Table 1.

According to this scale, the agreement signed in 2006 would be coded 50. The resources committed by the provinces require a moderate financial and administrative contribution, but they apply to relatively complex areas such as labour mobility.

To advance their positions, actors must have a certain amount of influence. Actors are considered influential if they have significant resources for rallying the other parties to their points of view on Quebec–Ontario relations. These resources can take a number of forms: authority inherent to a position, support of public opinion, money, political experience, staff and technical expertise. From a more tactical standpoint, actors may also gain influence if they control the negotiations' decision-making process and agenda. Paradoxically, certain constraints can also reinforce an actor's power if they prevent the player from making concessions. This scale also goes from 1 to 100, where 100 represents actors with the most resources (Table 2).

Table I

Scale with Respect to Position on a Quebec–Ontario Agreement

90–100	Agreement containing mainly *major commitments*: joint management of a key program, substantial joint multiyear funding of an initiative, harmonization of laws, interprovincial dispute resolution mechanisms, etc. It resolves *very controversial or complex issues*: constitutional reform, centralization of securities regulation, etc.
70–89	Agreement containing mainly *major commitments*: joint management of a key program, substantial joint multiyear funding of an initiative, harmonization of laws, creation of a joint agency, interprovincial dispute resolution mechanisms, etc. It resolves *controversial or complex issues*: limitation of the federal spending power, high-speed rail, labour mobility, opening up government contracts to businesses in the other province, etc.
50–69	Agreement containing mainly *moderate commitments*: joint, one-time funding of an initiative, regulatory harmonization, sharing of expertise and equipment, common position with respect to Ottawa, creation of a joint agency or secretariat, etc. It resolves *controversial or complex issues*: limitation of the federal spending power, high-speed rail, labour mobility, opening up government contracts to businesses in the other province, etc.
30–49	Agreement containing mainly *moderate commitments*: joint, one-time funding of an initiative, regulatory harmonization, sharing of expertise and equipment, common position with respect to Ottawa, creation of a joint agency or secretariat, etc. It resolves *consensual or simple issues*: mutual cultural appreciation, improved services for Franco-Ontarians, tourism in border regions, interprovincial transportation, etc.
10–29	Agreement containing mainly *minor commitments*: joint, one-time funding of an initiative, regulatory harmonization, sharing of expertise and equipment, common position with respect to Ottawa, etc. It resolves *consensual or simple issues*: mutual cultural appreciation, improved services for Franco-Ontarians, tourism in border regions, interprovincial transportation, etc.
2–9	Agreement containing mainly *minor commitments*: framework for studying possibilities for cooperation, sharing of data and information, etc. It resolves *very consensual or simple issues*: public land management, forests, quality of health care, cross-border environmental impacts, emergency preparedness, etc.
1	No agreement

Table 2

Influence Scale

90–100	The most influential actor on Quebec–Ontario cooperation
70–89	Very influential actor on Quebec–Ontario cooperation
50–69	One of several actors that can influence Quebec–Ontario cooperation
30–49	Important actor but without significant influence on Quebec–Ontario cooperation
10–29	Actor with very little influence on Quebec–Ontario cooperation
< 10	Actor with no influence on Quebec–Ontario cooperation

Actors' influence remains latent if they are not concerned with an issue. To have an impact, their power must be deployed. Here we have adapted the salience scale suggested by Bueno de Mesquita (Table 3).

Table 3

Salience Scale

90–100	Quebec–Ontario cooperation is essential for these actors. They will drop all other activities and focus entirely on this issue whenever necessary.
70–89	Quebec–Ontario cooperation is very important for these actors. It is one of their priority issues. They will make a serious effort to change their schedule in order to spend more time on this issue when necessary.
50–69	Quebec–Ontario cooperation is an issue that counts, although other issues are more important. Actors would put this issue aside if others arose, but would otherwise spend time on it.
30–49	Quebec–Ontario cooperation is significant, but not a priority issue for these actors. They have a number of other issues to cover and will not drop their activities to deal with this one. These actors will generally focus on other things.
10–29	Quebec–Ontario cooperation is a minor issue for these actors. They neither pay much attention nor devote much time to it.
< 10	These actors are not really interested in Quebec–Ontario cooperation.

Source: Adapted from Bueno de Mesquita 2009b.

4. STRATEGIC SITUATION OF QUEBEC–ONTARIO NEGOTIATIONS

Now that we have defined the model's main categories, we can use them to describe the strategic situation underlying the Quebec–Ontario negotiations between 2003 and 2006.

4.1. Actors in Quebec

Developing interprovincial relationships was particularly important for the Belle Province. In 2003, The Quebec Liberal Party (QLP) returned to power. After nine years of Péquiste government and a sovereignty referendum, the QLP wanted to improve the image of Canadian federalism among Quebecers. Knowing that Ottawa was opposed to revisiting the constitutional issue, the QLP made no major promises to renew the federation. Instead, it set itself the more modest goal of protecting and strengthening the province's autonomy through other means: federal–provincial agreements, administrative reforms, development of new constitutional conventions, and so forth.

To achieve its objectives, Quebec had to reoccupy the field of intergovernmental relations. It therefore sought to forge strategic alliances, and Ontario seemed to be the ideal partner. Premiers Jean Charest and Dalton McGuinty were both Liberals, they shared a common vision of economic development, and they were both keen on protecting provincial jurisdictions from potential federal intrusions. Their interests seemed to converge.

Given this, Quebec's premier advocated major commitments on complex issues. He wanted to join forces with Ontario to push certain issues in Ottawa, such as limiting federal spending power and building a high-speed rail link in the Quebec–Windsor corridor. He favoured a series of joint initiatives that would require substantial resources over a number of years (position = 75). Yet public ratification of such an agreement was somewhat more important for Charest than the defence of a specific negotiating position (flexibility = 70). He had to demonstrate the QLP's effectiveness at the national level. Along with his Ontario counterpart, Premier Charest was undoubtedly the key actor with respect to cooperation between the two provinces (influence = 100). In theory, he could also put a halt to the negotiating process at any time and reject a final agreement (veto = 1). Charest spent considerable time in interprovincial meetings, thus signalling that this was one of his priority issues (salience = 75).

Other actors in Quebec were generally favourable to interprovincial cooperation, but to varying degrees. Benoît Pelletier, the minister of intergovernmental affairs, had the greatest ambitions in this regard (position = 80). He even hoped to obtain support from Queen's Park to limit federal spending power. Naturally, Pelletier was particularly committed to these issues because they were central to his mandate (salience = 90). Quebec entrepreneurs also supported a relatively comprehensive agreement (position = 75). They hoped to gain free access to Ontario's lucrative construction market and crown corporation service contracts. The cities of Ottawa and Gatineau are relatively well integrated, and Mayor Yves Ducharme (and subsequently Mayor Marc Bureau) seemed supportive of regulatory harmonization between the two border municipalities, although they also wished to avoid provincial interference in local affairs (position = 55).

Opinion leaders and the official opposition were less enthusiastic on the issue (position = 35). The Parti Québécois (PQ) could hardly oppose the anticipated economic spinoffs of a Quebec–Ontario agreement, yet neither did it want to see any overly positive examples of federal harmony. Moderate commitment to consensual issues was more up its alley (position = 35). In any case, the PQ was not very committed to this issue. This period coincided with a certain instability among the PQ leadership, with Bernard Landry, Louise Harel, and André Boisclair succeeding each other at the sovereignist party's helm (salience = 35).

4.2. Actors in Ontario

For Premier Dalton McGuinty, closer cooperation with Ontario's neighbour would allow him to achieve three objectives. First it would increase his stature at the national level. By cooperating more closely with Quebec's main federalist party, McGuinty hoped to strengthen national unity. This would allow him to frame himself as an important mediator between Quebec and the rest of Canada.

His second objective was to maintain and reinforce the Ontario Liberal Party's electoral base among the province's Francophones. McGuinty hoped that Ontario's French-speaking minority would develop a higher profile with Quebecers and thus benefit from an exchange of services.

The premier's third objective was to obtain Quebec's help in alleviating the impact of a sagging economy. Ontario was suffering from higher energy prices, and the core of its industrial base, the automobile sector, was in serious trouble. The Ontario–Quebec trade corridor and continental gateway projects were designed to create a new economic space in the heart of the North American continent. In short, although the stakes were not as high for McGuinty as for Charest, the former was nevertheless very committed to the negotiations (salience = 70) and favourable to a major agreement (position = 70).

Other actors in Ontario had similar positions to their Quebec counterparts, even though they seemed to support an agreement that was slightly more ambitious. Without the strong, identity-based reservations of their colleagues in Quebec, they could focus more on economic integration. They also wanted to avoid interprovincial tensions that the PQ might exploit. Their salience and influence levels are comparable to those in Quebec, although Ontario's minister of intergovernmental affairs (Marie Bountrogianni) seemed to be somewhat less committed than her colleague.

4.3. Other Actors

Most federal actors had little influence on or commitment to Quebec–Ontario negotiations. Admittedly, the prime minister and the federal intergovernmental affairs minister could have drawn on Ottawa's considerable resources had they wanted to try to influence the two provinces' behaviour, but the issue was beyond the federal government's sphere of jurisdiction and legitimacy (influence = 55). Moreover, neither was very committed to the issue. They had more to lose than to gain by getting involved in interprovincial affairs (salience = 15): Paul Martin and Lucienne Robillard supported an agreement that could potentially convince Quebecers of federalism's flexibility and promote harmony among members of the Canadian "family," but at the same time they did not want the central provinces to impose their priorities or act as a counterweight to federal government influence. The ideal result for them would have been a modest, mainly symbolic Quebec–Ontario agreement (position = 30). Canadian public opinion was in line with this position, but was even more indifferent to this issue (salience = 1), which was perceived as local and excessively complicated.

Gilles Duceppe's Bloc Québécois took a similar stance to that of the federal government on the issue, but its motivations were different. Although a moderate agreement would be of substantial economic benefit to Quebec, too much success was not desirable. The Bloc did not want an agreement that could serve as a powerful tool for promoting federalism. The PQ and the BQ were on the same wavelength on this question (position = 35).

The only central actor with a strong interest in Quebec–Ontario negotiations was the Council of the Federation. The organization monitored developments closely, since the agreement's procedures and content would influence the interprovincial agenda across the country and potentially have direct consequences for the organization itself (salience = 75). A relatively wide-ranging agreement would attest to the importance of interprovincial relations without discrediting the multilateral approach or eliminating the Council's raison d'être (position = 55). Yet the Council was a rather new institution with very little influence on actors in either of the two provinces. The executive director of the Council of the Federation Secretariat, Loretta O'Connor, had a limited staff and budget, and she played an administrative role rather than one of political leadership (influence = 15).

In all, there were sixteen Quebec, Ontario, and pan-Canadian actors who could influence the negotiations to varying degrees and in opposing directions. Table 4 summarizes the data on these actors and their attributes.

5. PREDICTIONS AND OUTCOME OF THE NEGOTIATIONS

The compiled data was entered into the computer program and processed according to the expected utility model described above. The computer generated a series of tables and graphs that provided a prediction—or in this case, a retrodiction—about the negotiating dynamics and the negotiations' outcome.

The analysis describes how the hypothetical positions of each actor changed after each round of negotiations. It can be summarized as in Table 5.

Table 4

Actors and Their Attributes

	Influence	Position	Salience	Veto	Flexibility
Actors in Quebec					
• Premier	100	75	75	1	70
• Minister of Intergovernmental Affairs	80	80	95	0	75
• Parti Québécois	35	35	35	0	10
• Public opinion	35	75	10	0	50
• Entrepreneurs	10	75	35	0	50
• City of Gatineau	15	55	45	0	50
Actors in Ontario					
• Premier	100	70	70	1	70
• Minister of Intergovernmental Affairs	70	75	90	0	75
• Conservative Party	30	40	20	0	30
• Public opinion	35	40	5	0	50
• Entrepreneurs	10	75	35	0	50
• City of Ottawa	20	60	45	0	50
Other actors					
• Federal government	55	30	15	0	50
• Bloc Québécois	15	35	35	0	50
• Public opinion	35	30	1	0	50
• Council of the Federation	15	55	75	0	50

Table 5
Predicted Position Changes

	T1	T2	T3	T4	T5	T6	T7	T8	T9	T10	T10–T1
Charest	75	65.7	58.6	56.1	56.1	55.8	55.7	55.4	54.4	53.5	–21.5
Pelletier	80	65.9	55.1	56.2	56.7	56.7	56.3	55.0	54.0	53.7	–26.3
Boisclair	35	35.5	35.8	35.9	36.0	36.0	36.1	36.1	36.1	36.1	1.1
Quebecers	35	39.1	39.2	39.3	39.3	39.4	39.5	39.5	39.6	39.6	4.6
Quebec businesses	75	70.6	61.9	55.9	53.5	54.0	54.1	53.8	53.5	53.1	–21.9
Gatineau	55	59.5	60.7	59.2	55.0	55.0	54.6	54.1	53.5	52.9	–2.1
McGuinty	70	63.7	57.9	57.7	57.6	57.1	55.3	53.6	53.6	53.5	–16.5
Bountrogianni	75	65.7	58.2	58.5	57.8	56.7	56.1	55.4	54.6	53.9	–21.1
Tories	40	43.1	43.1	42.9	42.7	42.5	42.5	42.5	42.5	42.5	2.5
Ontario residents	40	43.5	43.5	42.9	42.6	42.3	42.1	42.1	42.0	42.1	2.1
Ontario businesses	75	70.6	61.9	55.9	53.5	54.0	54.1	53.8	53.5	53.1	–21.0
Ottawa	60	61.1	61.5	59.6	58.0	55.5	53.8	53.9	53.5	53.0	–7
Martin	30	34.7	34.8	34.9	35.0	35.1	35.2	35.3	35.3	35.3	5.3
Duceppe	35	39.1	39.3	39.4	39.6	39.7	40.0	40.3	40.3	40.4	5.4
Canadians	30	34.7	34.7	34.8	34.8	34.8	34.8	34.8	34.8	34.8	4.8
O'Connor	55	59.6	60.3	59.5	57.7	54.0	54.4	54.2	53.7	53.3	2.3

The model predicted that the premiers, their intergovernmental affairs ministers, and the business lobby would compromise, while the other actors would shift their positions very little. For example, minister Benoît Pelletier would concede 26.3 position points (= T1 – T10) whereas the Parti Québécois would cede only 1.1 point during the discussions. The most ardent defenders of a strong agreement would be the most flexible. For them the intensity and scope of the final agreement would be somewhat less important than achieving progress. In this situation, the other interests would exert a force of inertia on the process and could dilute the content of a Quebec–Ontario agreement.

The program also calculated the median position of all the actors throughout the negotiations. This can be represented by a Cartesian graph illustrating the evolution of the negotiations right up to agreement ratification (Figure 2). In the case at hand, the negotiations follow a descending curve. The model predicted that initial support for a strong agreement would dissolve rapidly and the actors' median position would decline from 67 to 55 in only four rounds before gradually stabilizing at 50.

Figure 2
Predicted Course of the Negotiations

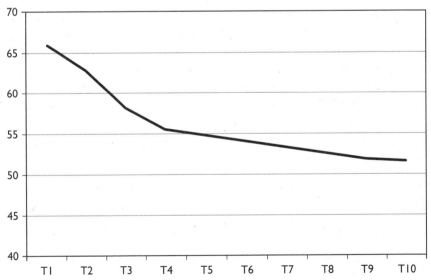

Are these predictions accurate? The three participants surveyed did not provide specific details on the confidential negotiations, so it is impossible to check whether the internal dynamics corresponded to the model's predictions. However, the informants did confirm that the objectives of the initial project were in fact revised downwards in the final agreement.

More interesting is comparing the predicted result—i.e. an agreement coded 51.6 on the position scale—with what actually happened. At the Château Laurier in Ottawa, the Quebec and Ontario governments ratified and released seven bilateral initiatives on June 2, 2006:

- Protocol for Cooperation between the Government of Ontario and the Government of Quebec
- Agreement for Cooperation and Exchanges between the Government of Ontario and the Government of Quebec with respect to Francophone Affairs—and action plan 2006–2007
- Agreement on Labour Mobility and Recognition of Qualifications, Skills and Work Experience in the Construction Industry between the Government of Ontario and the Government of Quebec
- Agreement for Cooperation on Culture between the Government of Ontario and the Government of Quebec
- Agreement for Cooperation on Emergency Management between the Government of Ontario and the Government of Quebec
- Agreement for Cooperation on Tourism between the Government of Ontario and the Government of Quebec
- Agreement Concerning Transportation between the Government of Ontario and the Government of Quebec
- Agreement Concerning Transboundary Environmental Impacts between the Government of Ontario and the Government of Quebec

The provisions of these agreements match relatively closely the results described for code 50–69 on the position scale. There was no grand Quebec–Ontario alliance on the constitutional debate, nor any agreement on the delicate issue of securities regulation. Those who defended a strong agreement did not carry the day. The results were nonetheless significant, and went well beyond the ritual handshake and traditional photo op.

The provincial governments' commitments were moderately demanding from an administrative and financial point of view. Some initiatives required joint, dedicated funding, but they were often limited to the sharing of expertise, information, or equipment. A number of issues were covered under the agreement and most were consensual and simple, although more complex and controversial issues like labour mobility were also included. In short, the predictive model was not wrong. It would have provided a good general idea of the results of Quebec–Ontario negotiations.

CONCLUSION

Interprovincial relations have gained new impetus in Canada since 2000. This is reflected in the closer relationship between Ontario and Quebec. Certain historical factors help put recent developments in context, but these developments can also be explained by the current situation, the actors involved, and their attributes.

It would be worth studying Quebec–Ontario cooperation in more depth by conducting a series of interviews using the categories developed by Richard Simeon. Without this kind of access to decision makers, however, a more schematic approach was adopted—the expected utility model derived from game theory. This type of analysis is more than just a stopgap solution. It can be applied to a wide variety of intergovernmental situations and enables practitioners to rapidly identify the main characteristics of their own strategic situation. It can also be used to formulate general predictions that help guide action.

The analysis used here focused on the general outlines of a broad interprovincial agreement touching on a number of areas, including culture, emergency management, health, and the environment. A more in-depth analysis could examine the actors and dynamics at work for *each* of the issues covered by the agreement. It would generate more precise predictions for testing the value of the model. Our results do not go that far, but they suggest that it would be worth exploring the subject further.

By consulting a series of primary sources and thoroughly examining the Quebec–Ontario case through the lens of the expected utility model, we identified and described a small group of actors who directly or indirectly took part in the Quebec–Ontario negotiations. This exercise also made it possible to evaluate the initial goals of premiers Charest and McGuinty, their flexibility, and the types of compromises that led to the 2006 agreement.

This study ends in 2006, but cordial relations between Quebec and Ontario have continued. The two governments held three joint cabinet meetings between 2008 and 2010, and another trade and cooperation agreement was signed in 2009. A change in government in Toronto or Quebec City could stifle the amicable relationship, but the historical, geographical, and economic ties between the two provinces will continue. Quebec and Ontario cannot escape their "shared destiny."

BIBLIOGRAPHY

Armstrong, C. (1982). *The Politics of Federalism: Ontario's Relations with the Federal Government, 1867–1942.* Toronto: University of Toronto Press.

Armstrong, C. (1986). "Ceremonial Politics: Federal–Provincial Meetings before the Second World War." In K. Carty and P. Ward (eds.), *National Politics and Community in Canada.* Vancouver: University of British Columbia Press: 112–150.

Banting, K. and R. Simeon (1983). *And No One Cheered: Federalism, Democracy, and the Constitution Act.* Toronto: Methuen.

Bickerton, J. (2010). "Deconstructing the New Federalism." *Canadian Journal of Political Science,* vol. 4, no. 23: 56–72.

Bird, R. and A. Tarasov (2004). "Closing the Gap: Fiscal Imbalances and Intergovernmental Transfers in Developed Federations." *Government and Policy,* vol. 22: 77–102.

Bolleyer, N. (2006). "Federal Dynamics in Canada, the United States, and Switzerland: How Substates' Internal Organization Affects Intergovernmental Relations." *Publius,* vol. 36: 471–502.

Booth, W. J., P. James, and H. Meadwell (eds.) (1993). *Politics and Rationality.* Cambridge: Cambridge University Press.

Brock, K. (2008). "The Politics of Asymmetrical Federalism: Reconsidering the Role and Responsibilities of Ottawa." *Canadian Public Policy,* no. 34: 143–161.

Broschek, J. (2004). "'Collaborative Federalism' in Canada: A New Era in Intergovernmental Relations?" *Zeitschrift für Parlamentsfragen,* vol. 35: 428–448.

Brown, D. and J. Hiebert (eds.) (1994). *Canada: The State of the Federation 1994.* Kingston: Institute of Intergovernmental Relations.

Bueno de Mesquita, B. (1994). "Political Forecasting: An Expected Utility Method." In B. Bueno de Mesquita and F. Stokman (eds.), *European Community Decision Making: Models, Applications, and Comparisons.* New Haven: Yale University Press: 71–104.

Bueno de Mesquita, B. (2002a). "Accomplishments and Limitations of a Game-Theoretic Approach to International Relations." In F. Harvey and M. Brecher (eds.), *Evaluating Methodology in International Studies.* Ann Arbor: University of Michigan Press: 59–80.

Bueno de Mesquita, B. (2002b). *Predicting Politics.* Columbus: Ohio State University Press.

Bueno de Mesquita, B. (2003). "Ruminations on Challenges to Prediction with Rational Choice Models." *Rationality and Society,* vol. 15, no. 1: 136–147.

Bueno de Mesquita, B. (2009a). "A New Model for Predicting Policy Choice: Preliminary Tests." Paper prepared for the 50th Meeting of the International Studies Association. New York. Online: <http://www.allacademic.com/meta/p312200_index.html>, retrieved in November 2009.

Bueno de Mesquita, B. (2009b). *The Predictioneer's Game.* New York: Random House. Online: <http://www.predictioneersgame.com/game>, retrieved on January 20, 2011.

Bueno de Mesquita, B. and A. Organski (1994). "Policy Outcomes and Policy Interventions: An Expected Utility Analysis." In B. Bueno de Mesquita and F. Stokman (eds.), *European Community Decision Making: Models, Applications, and Comparisons*. New Haven: Yale University Press: 131–160.

Bueno de Mesquita, B. and F. Stokman (1994). "Models of Exchange and of Expected Utility Maximization: A Comparison of Accuracy." In B. Bueno de Mesquita and F. Stokman (eds.), *European Community Decision Making: Models, Applications, and Comparisons*. New Haven: Yale University Press: 214–228.

Cameron, D. (2001). "Les structures des relations intergouvernementales dans les systèmes fédéraux." *Revue internationale des sciences sociales*, no. 167: 131–138.

Cameron, D. (2002). *Intergovernmental Relations in Canada*. Ottawa: Forum of Federations. Online: <http://www.forumfed.org>.

Cameron, D. and R. Simeon (1997). "Ontario in Confederation: The Not-So-Friendly Giant." In G. White (ed.), *The Government and Politics of Ontario*. Toronto: University of Toronto Press: 158–185.

Cameron, D. and R. Simeon (2002). "Intergovernmental Relations in Canada: The Emergence of Collaborative Federalism." *Publius*, vol. 32, no. 2: 49–72.

Caron, J.-F., G. Laforest, and C. Vallières-Roland (2009). "Canada's Federative Deficit." In A.-G. Gagnon (ed.), *Contemporary Canadian Federalism: Foundations, Traditions, Institutions*. Toronto: University of Toronto Press: 132–162.

Charland, G. (2007). *Comparaison des relations intergouvernementales au sein de quelques fédérations*. Quebec: Observatoire de l'administration publique de l'ÉNAP. Online: <http://www.etatquebecois.enap.ca/docs/pp/intergouvernemental/a-pp-intergouv.pdf>.

Conlan, T. (2006). "From Cooperative to Opportunistic Federalism: Reflections on the Half-Century Anniversary of the Commission on Intergovernmental Relations." *Public Administration Review*, no. 66: 663–676.

Cook, R. (1969). *Provincial Autonomy, Minority Rights, and the Compact Theory, 1867–1921*. Ottawa: Queen's Printer.

Côté, L. (ed.) (2005). *L'État du Quebec*. Quebec City: École nationale d'administration publique.

Courchene, T. and C. Telmer (1998). *From Heartland to North American Region State: The Social, Fiscal, and Federal Evolution of Ontario*. Toronto: University of Toronto Press.

Creighton, D. (1956). *The Empire of the St. Lawrence*. Toronto: University of Toronto Press.

Dufour, C. (1997). "Les relations intergouvernementales du Quebec." In J. Bourgault, M. Demers, and C. Williams (eds.), *Administration publique et management public. Expériences canadiennes*. Quebec City: Les Publications du Québec.

Durocher, R. (1970). "Taschereau, Hepburn et les relations Québec-Ontario, 1934–1936." *Revue d'histoire de l'Amérique française*, no. 24: 341–355.

Dyck, R. (1991). *Provincial Politics in Canada*, 3rd ed. Toronto: Macmillan.

Flanagan, T. (1998). *Game Theory and Canadian Politics*. Toronto: University of Toronto Press.

Fortin, S. (2009). "From the Canadian Social Union to the Federal Social Union of Canada." In A.-G. Gagnon (ed.), *Contemporary Canadian Federalism: Foundations, Traditions, Institutions*. Toronto: University of Toronto Press: 303–329.

Gagnon, A.-G. (2009). "Taking Stock of Asymmetrical Federalism in an Era of Exacerbated Centralization." In A.-G. Gagnon (ed.), *Contemporary Canadian Federalism: Foundations, Traditions, Institutions*. Toronto: University of Toronto Press: 255–272.

Gibbins, R. (2007). "Federalism in the 21st Century: Defining the Common Economic Space." *Policy Options*, no. 28: 11–21.

Graefe, P. (2006). "State Restructuring, Social Assistance, and Canadian Intergovernmental Relations: Same Scales, New Tune." *Studies in Political Economy*, no. 78: 93–117.

Gross Stein, J. (2006). "Canada by Mondrian: Networked Federalism in an Era of Globalization." In R. Gibbins, A. Maionis, and J. Gross Stein (eds.), *Canada by Picasso: The Faces of Federalism*. Ottawa: Conference Board of Canada: 15–58.

Heinmiller, T. (2002). "Finding a Way Forward in the Study of Intergovernmental Policy-Making." *Canadian Public Administration*, no. 45: 427–433.

Horgan, G. (2003). "Devolution and Intergovernmental Relations: The Emergence of Intergovernmental Affairs Agencies." *Public Policy Administration*, vol. 18, no. 3: 12–24.

Hueglin, T. and A. Fenna (2006). *Comparative Federalism: A Systematic Inquiry*. Toronto: Broadview.

Imbeau, L. M. (1990). "Voting Games and Constitutional Design: The 1981 Constitutional Negotiation in Canada." *The Journal of Commonwealth and Comparative Politics*, no. 28: 90–105.

Imbeau, L. M. (1991). "Le compromis est-il encore possible? La négociation constitutionelle de l'après-Meech à la lumière de la théorie des jeux." In L. Balthazar, G. Laforest, and V. Lemieux (eds.), *Le Québec et la restructuration du Canada, 1980–1992*. Quebec City: Septentrion: 281–309.

Imbeau, L. M. (1993). "Procedural Constraints and Conflictual Preferences in Collective Decision-Making: An Analysis Based on the Constitutional Decision of November 1981 in Canada." *International Journal of Conflict Management*, vol. 3, no. 3: 181–206.

James, P. (1998). "Rational Choice?: Crisis Bargaining over the Meech Lake Accord." *Conflict Management and Peace Science*, no. 16: 51–86.

James, P. and M. Lusztig (1996). "Beyond the Crystal Ball: Modeling Predictions about Quebec and Canada." *American Review of Canadian Studies*, no. 26: 559–575.

James, P. and M. Lusztig (1997a). "Assessing the Reliability of Prediction on the Future of Quebec." *Quebec Studies*, no. 24: 197–210.

James, P. and M. Lusztig (1997b). "Quebec's Economic and Political Future with North America." *International Interactions*, no. 23: 283–298.

Johns, C., P. O'Reilley, and G. Inwood (2006). "Intergovernmental Innovation and the Administrative State in Canada." *Governance*, no. 19: 627–649.

Johns, C., P. O'Reilley, and G. Inwood (2007). "Formal and Informal Dimensions of Intergovernmental Administrative Relations in Canada." *Canadian Public Administration*, no. 50: 21–41.

Lachapelle, G. and L. Bernier (1998). "Le fédéralisme fiscal: le Canada peut-il devenir une démocratie d'accommodation?" In M. Tremblay (ed.), *Les politiques publiques canadiennes*. Quebec City: Les Presses de l'Université Laval.

Leach, R. (1959). "Interprovincial Co-operation: Neglected Aspects of Canadian Federalism." *Canadian Public Administration*, no. 2: 83–99.

Leo, C. (2006). "Deep Federalism: Respecting Community Difference in National Policy." *Revue canadienne de science politique*, vol. 39, no. 3: 481–506.

Leslie, P. (2006). "Two Faces of Open Federalism." In K. Banting, R. Gibbins, P. Leslie, A. Noël, R. Simeon, and R. Young (eds.), *Open Federalism: Interpretations, Significance*. Kingston: Institute of Intergovernmental Relations.

Mahler, G. (1993). "American Approaches to Canadian Domestic Politics: A Distinction without Difference." In K. Gould, J. Jockel, and W. Metcalfe (eds.), *Northern Exposures: Scholarship on Canada in the United States*. Washington: The Association for Canadian Studies in the United States.

McIntosh, T. (2004). "Intergovernmental Relations, Social Policy, and Federal Transfers after Romanow." *Canadian Public Administration*, vol. 47, no. 1: 25–52.

Meekison, P., H. Telford, and H. Lazar (2003). "The institution of executive federalism: Myths and realities." In P. Meekison, H. Telford, and H. Lazar (eds.), *Canada: The State of the Federation. Reconsidering the Institutions of Canadian Federalism*. Montreal and Kingston: McGill-Queen's University Press.

Morrison, J. C. (1961). *Sir Oliver Mowat and the Development of Provincial Rights in Ontario: A Study in Dominion–Provincial Relations, 1867–1896*. Toronto: University of Toronto Press.

Morrow, J. D. (1994). *Game Theory for Political Scientists*. Princeton: Princeton University Press.

Noël, A. (2006). "Il suffisait de presque rien: Promises and Pitfalls of Open Federalism." In K. Banting, R. Gibbins, P. Leslie, A. Noël, R. Simeon, and R. Young (eds.), *Open Federalism: Interpretations, Significance*. Kingston: Institute of Intergovernmental Relations.

Noël, A. (2009). "Balance and Imbalance in the Division of Financial Resources." In A.-G. Gagnon (ed.), *Contemporary Canadian Federalism: Foundations, Traditions, Institutions*. Toronto: University of Toronto Press: 273–302.

Opeskin, B. (2001). "Mechanisms for Intergovernmental Relations in Federations." *International Social Sciences Journal*, vol. 53, no. 167: 129–138.

Painter, M. (1991). "Intergovernmental Relations: An Institutional Analysis." *Revue canadienne de science politique*, vol. 24, no. 2: 269–288.

Pelletier, R. (2002). *Les mécanismes de coopération intergouvernementale: facteurs de changement?* Commission sur l'avenir des soins de santé au Canada, étude no. 29.

Pelletier, R. (2006). "Le Conseil de la fédération: un premier bilan." In F. Petry, É. Bélanger, and L. M. Imbeau (eds.), *Le Parti libéral: enquête sur les réalisations du gouvernement Charest*. Quebec City: Les Presses de l'Université Laval: 361–278.

Raiffa, H. (1982). *The Art and Science of Negotiation*. Harvard: The Belknap Press of Harvard University Press.

Ralston Saul, J. (2010). *Louis-Hippolyte Lafontaine and Robert Baldwin*. Toronto: Penguin.

Riker, W. and P. Ordeshook (1973). *An Introduction to Positive Political Theory*. Englewood Cliffs: Prentice-Hall.

Rocher, F. (2009). "The Quebec–Canada Dynamic or the Negation of the Ideal of Federalism." In A.-G. Gagnon (ed.), *Contemporary Canadian Federalism: Foundations, Traditions, Institutions*. Toronto: University of Toronto Press: 81–131.

Romney, P. (1992). "The Nature and Scope of Provincial Autonomy: Oliver Mowat, the Quebec Resolutions, and the Construction of the *British North America Act*." *Canadian Journal of Political Science*, vol. 25, no. 1: 3–28.

Saxena, R. (2007). *Situating Federalism: Mechanisms of Intergovernmental Relations in Canada and India*. New Delhi: Manohar.

Schelling, T. (1960). *The Strategy of Conflict*. Cambridge: Harvard University Press.

Seymour, M. (2009). "On Not Finding Our Way: The Illusory Reform of the Canadian Federation." In A.-G. Gagnon (ed.), *Contemporary Canadian Federalism: Foundations, Traditions, Institutions*. Toronto: University of Toronto Press: 187–212.

Simeon, R. (2000). "Recent Trends in Federalism and Intergovernmental Relations in Canada: Lessons for the UK?" *Round Table*, no. 354: 231–354.

Simeon, R. (2002). "Conclusion." In P. Meekison (ed.), *Intergovernmental Relations in Federal Countries: A Series of Essays on the Practice of Federal Governance*. Ottawa: Forum of Federations. Online: <http://www.forumfed.org>.

Simeon, R. (2006a). "Making Federalism Work." In K. Banting, R. Gibbins, P. Leslie, A. Noël, R. Simeon, and R. Young (eds.). *Open Federalism: Interpretations, Significance*. Kingston: Institute of Intergovernmental Relations.

Simeon, R. (2006b). *Federal–Provincial Diplomacy: The Making of Recent Policy in Canada*, 2nd ed. Toronto: University of Toronto Press.

Simeon, R. and A. Nugent (2008). "Parliamentary Canada and Intergovernmental Canada: Exploring the Tensions." In H. Bakvis and G. Skogstad (eds.), *Canadian Federalism: Performance, Effectiveness, and Legitimacy*. Toronto: Oxford University Press.

Simeon, R. and I. Robinson (2009). "The Dynamics of Canadian Federalism." In J. Bickerton and A.-G. Gagnon (eds.), *Canadian Politics*, 5th ed. Toronto: University of Toronto Press: 239–262.

Smiley, D. (1987). *The Federal Condition in Canada*. Toronto: McGraw-Hill Ryerson.

Smiley, D. and R. Watts (1986). *Intrastate Federalism in Canada*. Ottawa: Supply and Services Canada.

Théret, B. (1999). "Regionalism and Federalism: A Comparative Analysis of the Regulation of Economic Tensions between Regions by Canadian and American Federal Intergovernmental Transfer Programmes." *International Journal of Urban and Regional Research*, vol. 23, no. 3: 479–512.

Vaillancourt, Y. and L. Thériault (2009). "Social Economy, Social Policy, and Federalism in Canada." In A.-G. Gagnon (ed.), *Contemporary Canadian Federalism: Foundations, Traditions, Institutions*. Toronto: University of Toronto Press: 330–357.

Watts, R. (1999). *Comparing Federal Systems*, 2nd ed. Kingston: Queen's Institute of Intergovernmental Relations.

Watts, R. (2005). *Autonomy of Dependence: Intergovernmental Financial Relations in Eleven Countries*. Kingston: Institute for Intergovernmental Affairs.

Wheare, K. C. (1963). *Federal Government*, 4th ed. London: Oxford University Press.

Young, R. and C. Leuprecht (eds.) (2006). *Canada: The State of the Federation 2004*. Montreal and Kingston: McGill-Queen's University Press.

CONTRIBUTORS

Michel Bock is associate professor at the University of Ottawa and chair-holder of the Chaire de recherche sur l'histoire de la francophonie du Québec. His work examines the factors behind the rise and fall of French Canada as both an identity marker and an institutional reality, as well as the origin and scope of subsequent movements in French-speaking Canada. He has won the Governor General's Award, the Prix Michel-Brunet (from Institut d'histoire de l'Amérique française), the Prix Champlain (from Conseil de la vie française en Amérique), and a medal from Quebec's National Assembly.

Alexandre Brassard is director of research at Glendon, the bilingual campus of York University in Toronto. He is also coordinator of the Center for Global Challenges, a bilingual public policy forum associated with the Glendon School of Public and International Affairs. He teaches courses in Quebec and Canadian politics, research methodology, and international studies.

Linda Cardinal is professor at the School of Political Studies and chair-holder of the Chaire de recherche sur la francophonie et les politiques publiques at the University of Ottawa. Her research has focused on the connection between politics and language, public policy and minority languages, the debate surrounding citizenship in Canada and Quebec, and Quebec and French Canadian intellectual history. She has published many articles and edited a number of works on these themes, including a recent special issue of *Politique et sociétés*, "Minorités, langue et politique" (2010), and a book, *Le fédéralisme asymétrique et les minorités linguistiques et nationales* (2008).

Guy Chiasson is professor of political science and regional development at Université du Québec en Outaouais. His chief research interest is territorial governance, including both rural areas and mid-sized cities. Recent work has focused primarily on changes in natural resource governance at both the local and public policy level. He is director of the Centre de recherche sur la gouvernance des ressources naturelles et du territoire and editor in chief of the journal *Économie et solidarités*.

Louis Côté is full professor at École nationale d'administration publique (ENAP) where he directs the Observatoire de l'administration publique research centre and edits *Télescope* magazine. For over twenty years he has worked as a consultant and trainer helping civil servants carry out administrative reform in Quebec and abroad. His two most recent works, *L'État démocratique : fondements et défis* (2008) and *État stratège et participation citoyenne* (coedited with Benoît Lévesque, 2009) were both published by Presses de l'Université du Québec.

Alain-G. Gagnon is a professor at Université du Québec à Montréal's Political Science Department and holds the Canada Research Chair in Quebec and Canadian Studies. He heads up Centre de recherche interdisciplinaire sur la diversité au Québec (CRIDAQ) as well as Groupe de recherche sur les sociétés plurinationales (GRSP). Among his writings are *La raison du plus fort: plaidoyer pour le fédéralisme multinational* (2008) and *L'âge des incertitudes: essais sur le fédéralisme et la diversité nationale* (2011). In 2008 he received the award of excellence from Société québécoise de science politique. In 2009, he was awarded a Universidad Carlos III de Madrid–Santander Bank Chair of Excellence, and in 2010 a Trudeau Foundation fellowship

Marie-Christine Gilbert is a Ph.D. candidate in political studies at the University of Ottawa, where she is a member of the Institute of Canadian Studies and coordinator of the Chaire de recherche sur la francophonie et les politiques publiques. Her work has focused on Canadian federalism, specifically antifederalist thought in a historical perspective. In 2010 she published "(Re)Federalizing Canada: Refocusing the Debate on Decentralization" with F. Rocher in R. Hubbard and G. Paquet (eds.), *The Case for Decentralized Federalism*.

Catalina Gonzalez Hilarion is a Ph.D. student in political science at the University of Ottawa. She has taken part in a number of research projects on current trends in natural resource governance and other areas. Her own research examines the governmentalization of forestry policy from a comparative perspective.

Peter Graefe is associate professor of political science at McMaster University, teaching in Canadian politics and public policy. He holds a Ph.D. from Université de Montreal. His research interests include economic and social development policies in Ontario and Quebec and intergovernmental relations in the field of social policy.

Louis M. Imbeau is full professor of political science at Université Laval and member of Centre d'analyse des politiques publiques (CAPP). He has been visiting professor at Institut des Études Politiques (IEP) in Lille, Université d'Auvergne, Université de Paris I-Sorbonne, and Université La Sapienza in Rome. His *Donor Aid: The Determinants of Development Allocations to Third World Countries* (1989) received the Stein Rokkan Award. He has edited *Politiques publiques comparées dans les États fédérés* (2005) and *Do They Walk Like They Talk: Speech and Action in Policy Processes* (2009) and coedited a number of other works including *Comparing Government Activity* (1996).

Moktar Lamari, Ph.D., is professor of policy evaluation and director of the Centre de recherche et expertise en évaluation (CREXE) at École nationale d'administration publique. He has authored a number of articles and book chapters on public sector management and public policy evaluation. In 2003, he received the American Society for Public Administration (ASPA)'s Louis Brownlow Award for the best article published in the *Public Administration Review*. He also received the 2002 Elsevier Award for the best article appearing in *Technological Forecasting and Social Change*. His research focuses on counter-cyclical policy evaluation.

Édith Leclerc is a Ph.D. candidate in applied social sciences at Université du Québec en Outaouais (UQO), with a focus on governance and forestry land development. Her dissertation examines the place of regional governance in forestry management in Quebec. She is a member of UQO's research group on natural resource governance.

François Laplante-Lévesque is the scientific activities coordinator at Centre de recherche interdisciplinaire sur la diversité au Québec (CRIDAQ). He completed a Master's thesis on Canadian executive federalism at Université du Québec à Montréal (UQAM)'s Political Science Department.

Martin Normand is a Ph.D. candidate at Université de Montréal. His M.A. thesis won the Prix René-Lupien for an outstanding French-language thesis that contributes to the Canadian Francophonie. He is part of the Community–University Research Alliance (CURA) on linguistic minorities' understanding of community governance and member of the University of Ottawa's Chaire de recherche sur la francophonie et les politiques publiques and Université de Montréal's Centre de recherche sur les politiques et le développement social. His publications include articles, book reviews, and notes in a number of journals and other forums.

Angela Orasch is currently completing her Master's in Political Science at York University. Her research interests include Canadian social policy, intergovernmental relations, and the urban policy landscape of the Greater Toronto Region.

Stéphane Paquin is associate professor at École nationale d'administration publique. He has also taught at Université de Sherbrooke's École de politique appliquée and Chicago's Northwestern University, and has been senior lecturer at Institut d'études politiques (Paris). He has edited and coedited several books including *International Policy and Politics in Canada* (with Kim Richard Nossal and Stéphane Roussel, 2010), *L'analyse des politiques publiques* (with Luc Bernier and Guy Lachapelle, 2010) and published widely in international journals including *The Hague Journal of Diplomacy*.

Ian Roberge, Ph.D., is chair of the Political Science Department and associate professor at Glendon College, York University. He obtained his Ph.D. in comparative public policy from McMaster University. His research focuses on politics of financial services sector regulation and reform, counter organized crime policy, and policies combating money laundering and terrorism financing.

François Rocher is full professor at the University of Ottawa's School of Political Studies. He has also been a professor at Carleton University where he directed the School of Canadian Studies. His work has focused on the major underlying issues of Canadian politics including the constitution, federalism, cultural diversity management policy, and the sociopolitical manifestations of Quebec nationalism. He recently published *Guy Rocher. Entretiens* (2010) and co-authored *Immigration, diversité et sécurité: les associations arabo-musulmanes face à l'État au Québec et au Canada* (with M. Labelle and R. Antonius, 2009).

Jean-François Savard is associate professor at École nationale d'administration publique. His work has focused chiefly on public policy development in federal regimes and aboriginal issues. Specifically, he is interested in public policy coherence in federal and confederal regimes. He has authored several articles on aboriginal self-government and contributed to a number of recent works on the public policy analysis and aboriginal issues. He also coedited *Le dictionnaire terminologique de l'administration publique* with Louis Côté.

MARQUIS

Québec, Canada

RECYCLED
Paper made from
recycled material
FSC® C103567

Printed on Enviro 100% post-consumer EcoLogo certified paper, processed chlorine free and manufactured using biogas energy.